Best Dog Hikes North Carolina

Best Dog Hikes
North Carolina

Melissa Watson

FALCONGUIDES

GUILFORD, CONNECTICUT
HELENA, MONTANA

For my boys, Mikey and Bandit
You kept me warm at night in the tent and safe on the road. You
brought pure joy to my heart as I watched you run, play, and enjoy the
journey as much as I did. Along the way you made lots of new friends,
and I made many wonderful memories. I'll treasure you boys forever!
Mikey, you are the love of my life and the best hiking partner I've ever had.
Bandit, you're learning from the BEST and growing up to be a fantastic little man.
Thank you both!

FALCONGUIDES®

An imprint of Rowman & Littlefield
Falcon, FalconGuides, and Make Adventure Your Story are registered trademarks of Rowman & Littlefield.

Distributed by NATIONAL BOOK NETWORK

Copyright © 2016 by Rowman & Littlefield

All interior photographs by Melissa Watson.

Maps: Alena Pearce © Rowman & Littlefield.

British Library Cataloguing-in-Publication Information available

Library of Congress Cataloging in Publication Data available

ISBN 978-1-4930-1855-0
ISBN 978-1-4930-1856-7

∞™ The paper used in this publication meets the minimum requirements of American National Standard for Information Sciences—Permanence of Paper for Printed Library Materials, ANSI/NISO Z39.48-1992.

Contents

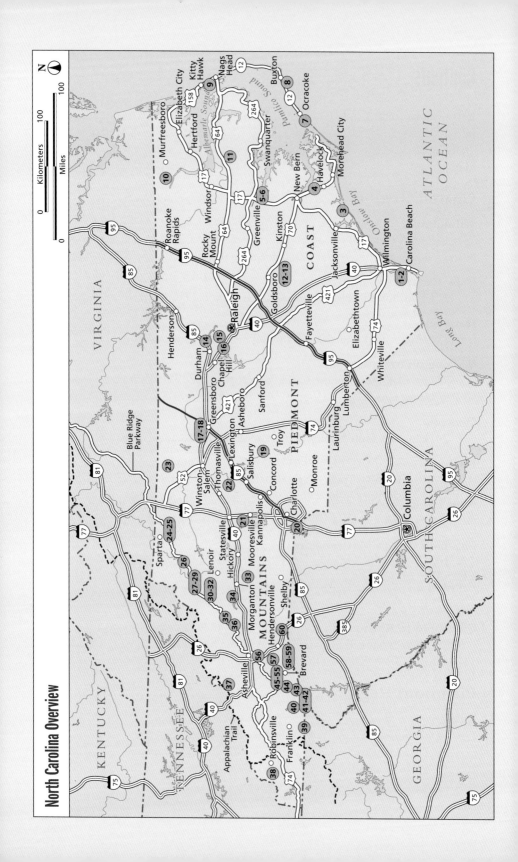

North Carolina Overview

Acknowledgments

I must send a special THANK YOU out to my mother, Terri Sansonetti; my niece, Christina Payton; and my friend, Cheryl Arcand. These very special people put hours of work into this book, helping me research the hotels and restaurants and choose photos for the final cut. They tirelessly made phone calls, visited websites, and put in the footwork so I could concentrate on the more technical and creative aspects. I can't begin to tell you how helpful you ALL *were* and *are* in my daily life. THANK YOU!!!

To my entire family, for always being there unconditionally. I LOVE YOU!

Terri Sansonetti, Maria, Frazier, Christina, Cory and Parker Peyton, Sue, Tom, Frank, Amy, Thomas, Luana, Joe, Dena, Grace, Kristen, Rebecca, Nathaniel, Katilee, Mark, Jonathon and Joshua, Silas Strazza, Michelle, Roland, Lucas and Zackary Arisolo, Doug and Claire Watson. I LOVE YOU ALL!

To my friends, Dawn McKinney, Shari Santos, Irene Freer, Liz Martinez, Cheryl Giavagnorio, and Jenn Getter, thank YOU for your patience. I love you all!

To my crew Craig Hatton, Chris Uzzo, Robert Burns, Chris Harris, and Mike Osuna at Fire House 51, thanks guys!

To Amber Miranda and Dr. Lucy Cruickshank for taking good care of my canine kids all these years!

To Troutman Animal Hospital, you were kind, caring, and HELPFUL when my little man Bandit had a battle with a "tick bomb." Thank YOU!!

To all the people I met along the trail, who allowed me take photos of them and their puppies: Jean Tate; Maris Herold; Jennifer Chilton; Hanes Hoffman; Ann and Don Toupin; Christie Jones; Alex Dornburg; Rachel Etter; Rachel Stepp; Carlos Vargas; Zachary Anderson; David and Michael Dyer; Hannah Chason; Jon Hogan; Jake and Alisha Edmiston; Linda Konrad; Doug Bickerstaff; Kate, David, Eric, Megan, Morgan, and Asher Pugh; Kang Yoon Bae; Felicia Busk; Geoff Kenlan; Jeanne and Martin Toder; Claire Daughtry; Jamie Gray; Sarah Rhoades; Jane and Kemp Dauster; Kyle Nelson; Jan O'Hara; Bill Allen; Anne Lanzi; Dana and Johanne Tuttle; Arielle Abel; Janelle, Amber, Corinna, and Charles Siebsen; Kevin Perez; Marci Ingram; Elaine Bailey; and Greg Stevenson.

To those at the state parks, national forests, and park service for once again ensuring accuracy. Thank You!!

And to those at Rowman & Littlefield Publishing Company who worked tirelessly on this book. Editing text, photos, and maps; diligently working to get every detail correct. Dave Legere, Ellen Urban, Katie Benoit, Melissa Evarts, Katie Sharp, and the entire staff, thank you ALL!

The boys enjoy a break on the soft grass along the paved Woodland Trail (hike 17).

Introduction

Whether you have one dog, or ten, whether they are inseparable or independent, they will love getting outdoors and exploring the trails of North Carolina. And within these pages I've compiled a collection of sixty of the best dog hikes in the state. Lakes, rivers, creeks, and waterfalls, from mountain views to the coveted coastline—I've covered it all. Whether your dogs are experienced hikers or new to the trail, whether you're looking for an easy stroll or a strenuous trek, there's a trail for you. And what better way to enjoy the great outdoors than with your best friends, your pampered pups, your canine companions at your side? Spending quality time on the trail together will bring pure joy to you both; it's a win-win. While you enjoy the scenery, dramatic views, flowing waterfalls, and pristine lakes, they get to explore, taking in the fresh new sights, scents, and sounds of the forest, dipping their paws in a clear mountain creek, or running free on a long sandy beach, happily wagging their tail every step of the way. And even more important . . . they get to be with you. I haven't met a dog yet that wasn't in heaven while hiking. Romping around, sniffing new smells, splashing in the creeks, and making new friends are all part of the journey, and any dog can do it, from toy poodles to Saint Bernards and every breed in between. The key is knowing your dogs, and what they are capable of. It's up to you to know their limitations. Just like people, you simply need to find the right trail for your dogs.

If your dogs aren't in fantastic shape, you can still take them on a short hike. To work up to longer hikes, begin by taking brisk walks together every day. Week by week you can increase the length of your walks, and eventually you can build up to longer hikes on the trail. Just as you would for yourself, if your pooches have any medical conditions, check with your vet before taking them out on the trail. It's important to use common sense with your babies. No matter how trail hardy your dogs are, it's up to you to know what they can, and cannot, handle. Dogs will go, go, go to a fault to spend the day with their best friend. But you need to know their limitations, and your own, so you can enjoy hike after hike for years to come, with your trusty pups at your side.

How to Use This Guide

Before you begin your endeavor, here's some important information on how to use this guide.

As you become familiar with it, you'll see the hikes have been divided into geographic area. This way, when you plan to visit a certain area, you can easily see what hikes are nearby. Each hike has its own coinciding trail map. Every hike in this book follows the same format, which begins with a brief description of the hike. Next you'll see what's known as the hike "specs." This section provides you with important information about the trail such as where the trail starts, the distance you'll hike

1

(round-trip), the blaze color, the trail's difficulty, the trailhead's elevation, the trail's highest point, the seasons you can visit, the trail's surface, other trail users you might encounter, whether or not a leash is required for your companion, and the trail's land status. Along with this vital information, also listed are any required fees or permits. Here is a key to the fees:

$ = $0-$10
$$ = $11-$19
$$$ = $20 or more

Recommended maps, trail contacts, and nearest towns are also listed. As you will notice, *DeLorme North Carolina Atlas & Gazetteer* map page and coordinates are provided to supplement the maps already found in this book. The *DeLorme Atlas & Gazetteer* is highly recommended for any state you plan to hike. You'll also find the National Geographic Trails Illustrated topographic map information, if applicable. These maps, too, are an invaluable resource when navigating through the mountain region. Lastly, you'll find "trail tips." Here you'll find pertinent information such as if there are water fountains or trash cans near the trailhead, or whether you should bring a hiking stick or extra drinking water. Following the hike specs, you will see "Finding the trailhead." Plain and simple, you can't enjoy the hike if you can't find the trailhead. This includes explicit driving directions from two different points of reference, either using a main intersection or a state line as your starting point. Many of the trailheads are located on forest service roads (FR), most of which are unmarked dirt roads, and there may be several of these in any given area. For this reason the driving distances are given in mileage rounded to the nearest tenth of a mile, with accuracy as the goal. Also, whenever parking near a forest service gate, do not block the gate. While I prefer a good old-fashioned map and compass, GPS systems are getting better and better and proving to be another useful tool in the navigational toolbox. For this reason, GPS coordinates for the trailhead are included, along with those for any highlights along the way. Next, you will find "The Hike." This is where you'll get a general description of the hike, what to expect along the trail, and some entertaining facts about the trail, area, history, and folklore, if applicable.

Now on to the meat and potatoes, the "Miles and Directions." This is the heart of the matter, the trails themselves, step by step. In this section you'll find thorough directions, where every fork and every T has been documented. You'll see the distance from the trailhead at which you reach them, and then left/right directions with corresponding compass directions.

I have made every effort to keep you and your happy hounds from getting lost, but please remember that trails do change over time and with each passing season. This is why I return time and time again to these trails and am always greeted with a new fabulous experience.

After the Miles and Directions, you'll find a listing of hotels, campgrounds, and restaurants where you and your dogs will be welcomed with open arms.

Last but not least, you'll see "Puppy paws and golden years." It's understandable that not all dogs can hike some of the longer trails in this book, especially the very young and very old. But this doesn't mean that you have to leave them at home. You can still get these furry friends out to explore. That's why in this section I've provided alternate options. So no matter what age your puppies or senior dogs may be, they will enjoy getting outdoors, breathing in the fresh air, and spending some quality time with their best friend—you.

For You and Your Dog's Safety

Preparation is the best way to keep you and your four-legged friends safe. Here are a few friendly reminders to help you both enjoy your time on the trail to the fullest.

Weather

The weather in North Carolina can range from hot, hot, hot on the coast in summer to snow on the mountaintops in winter. Do your homework before you head out. Dress in layers; this way you can be prepared for any fluctuations that Mother Nature may throw at you. And always carry rain gear, just in case. Zip-off pants and wool socks are ideal. The pants are great because they're thin but still keep you warm, and they double as shorts by zipping off the legs. Wool socks retain heat when needed, and dry quickly. Cotton is the worst material you can wear in the woods. Once cotton gets wet, it stays wet, keeping your body temperature dangerously low in cold weather. I recommend wearing quick-dry materials. They're fantastic for their moisture-wicking ability, keeping you dry so you can comfortably enjoy the hike. While most of the trails are shaded, when necessary, sunscreen is recommended.

Water and Hydration

It's essential that you bring enough drinking water for both you and your canine compadres. And of course bring a bowl for them to drink from, too. It's easy to forget you're actually exercising while taking in such beautiful scenery, but it's essential to stay hydrated. A good rule of thumb is to drink every fifteen minutes. And, of course, if you drink, have the dogs drink too. I recommend wearing a hydration pack on your back. You can fill it with water, put ice in it to make the water more quenching, and hike hands free. It's natural for your pups to sip from the cool mountain creeks, but do your best to not let them gulp it down. Keep in mind that even the clearest creek or river still carries tiny bacteria and parasites. Prevention is the best medicine.

It's important to bring lots of water and a bowl for your dog.

If you notice your dog is vomiting or has diarrhea after a hike, he or she may have drank from a bad source. If it continues, call your veterinarian. Also, do not let your dogs drink salt water. It *will* make them sick, and can cause dehydration, which can be a serious condition.

Leashes, Collars, and Harnesses

Even if a trail is leash free, it's important to carry a leash along in your pack. It's also a great idea to keep an extra leash in the car at all times in case the first one snaps, or a frustrated puppy chews through it. There are disputes over whether or not you should use a retractable leash. Personally, that's all I use. I like to give the boys a little extra freedom on the trail. If you know how to use it properly, you can reel them in quickly when other hikers approach. Also, you can shorten it to the required six feet as needed. If a trailhead is near a roadway, or the hike is heavily populated, keep the dogs on a leash even if it's not required—at least until you move away from the road or crowd. Also, despite their innate survival instincts, puppies may not always have common sense. It's up to you to keep them away from steep drop-offs and to be cautious of swift currents. Leash them as needed, for their own safety.

Collars with tags are essential! God forbid your dogs get lost, but if they do, at least they have a chance of being returned with an up-to-date tag. If your dogs have a microchip, fantastic, but that's not a substitute for a dog tag. Harnesses are especially good if your dogs are pullers. Clip the harness in the front, and it will help alleviate pulling. But harnesses, as well as dog collars, can get caught up on tree branches and bushes if the dogs wander off the path. Always keep a close eye on your pooches as you would your children. And bring along a copy of their current vaccines, just in case.

Dog Packs

I personally don't mind extra weight in my pack, but I have had my dogs carry a pack on occasion. If you do put a pack on your pooch, it's essential that it fits properly. An ill-fitted pack can cause chafing on the armpits and belly. Also, start with an empty pack so the dog can adjust to this strange coat on his or her back. As your dogs adapt, you can add weight, up to 25 percent of their body weight, but no more or they will be prone to injury. Then you'll be carrying the extra weight—and your poor injured puppy—out of the forest.

Body Language

Knowing your dogs' body language is key. Are they panting excessively? Limping? Slowing down? Just not acting like themselves? It's up to you, as a responsible puppy parent, to notice these signals when you take your furry friends on the trail. Remember: Dogs can't sweat like we do. Their natural way to eliminate excessive heat is to pant. If you're tired, panting, and working up a sweat, they feel the same way. Overheating is a serious condition for dogs. If you notice your dogs are panting excessively, cool them down immediately. Give them water, cool them down in a creek, pour water over their heads, keep them in the shade, and wait until they cool off before you continue hiking.

If you have the dogs off-leash, make sure they are under voice control at all times.

Stance

Pay attention to your dogs' stance, ears, and tail. These are tell-tale signs of what they see, hear, and smell. They may alert you that there's a beautiful doe up ahead, or a barred owl on a branch up above. Their keen senses can help you spot wildlife and will give you a chance to see it before they spook it off.

Booties

When people hike, foot care is essential. This is just as important to your four-legged friends. Your pups are out to please you, at all costs, so they may push beyond their limits. It's up to you, as a good dog owner and parent, to know your dogs' limits. If you see them limping, check their pads and joints. Buffered aspirin may help with pain, but you need to get to the root of the problem. But never give them Advil or Tylenol. If they've strained something, call it a day, and apply ice when you're settled in. Bring a first aid kit for you both. If they've injured a pad, you can bandage it up and use booties to keep the bandage in place. Better yet, have them wear booties to prevent problems in the first place, especially on rough or gravel terrain or if your pups are tenderfooted. Booties also protect pooches in winter time, allowing you to take them with you year-round. For trail surfaces where booties are recommended, you will see a Paw Alert! 🐾

Poison Ivy, Oak, and Sumac

All three of these plant irritants are found in the forests of North Carolina. If you do your homework and know how to identify them, you may save yourself some unpleasant itching. A nice little rule of thumb is "leaves of three, let it be," since poison ivy and oak both typically have three leaflets to a leaf.

Bugs, Bees, and Ticks

Depending on when and where you hike, you may encounter mosquitoes, horseflies, ticks, or chiggers. Insect repellant with DEET helps keep mosquitoes and horseflies at bay. If you get chiggers, you'll know it! It's an experience you'll *never* forget. If you think poison ivy itches, multiply that tenfold and you're still not at the level of chiggers. The solution is clear nail polish and lots of it. Cover the red bumps completely, and reapply often. As for ticks, I *highly* recommend that before you even hit the trail you give your dog a preventive medicine such as NexGuard. This prevents the problem all together. If you know you're hiking in an area with ticks, such as the coastal region in summertime, protect yourself as well. Insect repellant may help, but also wear light colors so the ticks are easy to spot. Tuck your shirt in, and tuck your pants into your socks. Most important: Do a thorough tick check on you and your dogs at the end of each hike, especially in summertime.

In late summer bees can inhabit underground nests alongside creeks in the mountain region. These bees can be vicious when provoked. Whether you have an allergy or not, carrying an antihistamine such as Benedryl in your pack is essential. If you have a known allergy, always carry an EpiPen.

Snakes

North Carolina is home to four species of venomous snakes. Treat all snakes, venomous or not, with respect. Again, prevention is the best medicine. Before letting the dogs explore on their own, do a quick snake check on sunny rocks near creeks. If you or your dog get bitten, stay calm and seek medical attention immediately. If you can identify the snake, fantastic, but don't delay care to try to figure it out. If your dog is romping around in the brush and you hear a yelp, check him or her for fang marks and wounds. It's quite unlikely, but if you think your dog was bitten by a snake, clean the wound immediately and mark the margins of the bite. If at all possible carry your dog out of the forest. Antivenin is the *only* treatment for a venomous snake bite, so don't bother trying to suck the venom out or use a snake bite kit. Do not elevate the limb, and do not apply ice. Call 911.

Keep the dogs clear of all snakes, even the nonvenomous ones.

Poison

The damp cool creek side is the perfect environment for a variety of mushrooms and fungi to grow. While some are edible, many are poisonous. If your dogs are prone to putting everything and anything in their mouth, keep a close eye on them. This includes choosing the right stick to toss out in the creek for them to fetch. Mountain laurel, rhododendron, and azalea are all common in the mountain region and can be toxic if ingested, so think before you throw. Keep this number in your phone, they're available 24/7: Poison Control (800) 222-1212.

Blaze Orange

If you're hiking in areas where hunting is allowed, such as national forests, always wear blaze orange during the season. And of course put some on your dogs to keep them safe, too.

Courtesy

Not everyone loves your cute and cuddly canines as much as you do. Keep this in mind when you encounter others along the trail. If the hike is leash free, this doesn't mean you let your dogs run amok. You still must keep them close by and under voice control. It's fun for them to have freedom, but it's up to you to keep them safe and to be a responsible, courteous dog owner. Just as with children, you are responsible for their behavior. Always yield to other hikers and those on horseback. And always pick up after your dogs, carrying extra waste bags with you just in case. No one wants to step in or smell dog poop while enjoying a pleasant hike in the forest, not even a dog lover.

Always pick up after your pup.

For Mother Nature's Safety

Wildlife

When you're out in the forest, you're a guest. Many animals make their home here. Some are cute and furry, like otters and beavers, others you may not like so much, such as snakes and spiders. No matter what you encounter, whether it's a white squirrel, a duck, or a chipmunk, please **do not feed the wildlife.** Often these cuddly critters cannot digest people food. If you feed them, you may be doing them more harm than good. These wild animals will also begin to associate people with food, and someone may inadvertently get bitten as a result. Please help keep wildlife wild.

Please do not feed any wildlife.

Leave NO Trace

The last thing I'd like to share with you is the concept known as No Trace hiking. Simply put . . . when you leave the forest, it should be just as you arrived. "Take nothing but pictures, leave nothing but footprints." Every stone in the creek and every wildflower along the path has a purpose within the ecosystem it lives. Please do not remove these or any items, except litter, from the forest. Instead, bring a camera, and you can preserve the memory on film while allowing others to appreciate their beauty as well. Another idea is "pack it in, pack it out." This means everything you bring into the forest, you should also bring out. Leave no trace and no signs that you were ever there. This puts less impact on the environment and allows other hikers to appreciate the natural beauty as well.

Features of a Good Dog Hike

So what is it that makes a great dog hike? Water for one thing. Almost every trail in this book has some sort of natural water source—whether it's a clear mountain stream, a crisp clean lake, or waves lapping on the sand near the sound. Just about every dog enjoys splashing around, or cooling off, in the water, and there's plenty to go around. Shade is another key component so your dogs don't overheat while they hike. Trails that are less populated, or open to foot traffic only, are also more ideal for dog hikes. Encountering fewer people takes the worry off of you, so you and your trusty companion can both enjoy the journey . . . every step of the way! Fill your pack with water, grab the leash, and load 'em up. It's time to begin a new adventure, with your four-legged friends at your side.

Other books by Melissa Watson are fantastic companion books, including *Hiking Waterfalls in North Carolina* and *Camping North Carolina*. They'll give you specific details on campgrounds across the state and offer even more hiking opportunities for you and your dogs to explore. And of course Mikey went along every step of the way.

Exploring the shores of Lake Norman, the dogs enjoy beach after beach (hike 21).

Trail Finder

Author's Favorites

4. Neusiok
5. Live Oak
7. Hammock Hills
18. Bog Garden
19. Badin Lake
21. Lake Shore
24. Stone Mountain Loop
30. Hunt Fish Falls
34. Paddy's Creek
37. Max Patch
39. Big Laurel Falls
44. Schoolhouse Falls and
    Panthertown Valley
45. Courthouse Falls
49. Skinny Dip Hole
55. Andy Cove Nature
57. South Mills River
60. Little Bradley Falls

Lakeside Hikes

11. Boardwalk
15. Lake Lynn
19. Badin Lake
20. Cove
21. Lake Shore
28. Bass Lake Loop
34. Paddy's Creek
40. Cliffside Lake Loop

Waterfall Hikes

18. Bog Garden
23. Lower Cascades
24. Stone Mountian Loop
25. Widow's Creek Falls
26. Cascade
27. Glen Burney
29. Boone Fork
30. Hunt Fish Falls
31. Harper Creek Falls

32. Lower Falls of Upper Creek
33. High Shoals Falls Loop
35. Crabtree Falls Loop
36. Roaring Fork Falls
39. Big Laurel Falls
41. Secret Falls
43. Silver Run Falls
44. Schoolhouse Falls and
    Panthertown Valley
45. Courthouse Falls
46. Dill Falls

Leash Free (Voice Control)

4. Neusiok
19. Badin Lake
30. Hunt Fish Falls
31. Harper Creek Falls
32. Lower Falls of Upper Creek
35. Crabtree Falls Loop
36. Roaring Fork Falls
37. Max Patch
39. Big Laurel Falls
41. Secret Falls
42. Chattooga River
43. Silver Run Falls
44. Schoolhouse Falls and
    Panthertown Valley
45. Courthouse Falls
46. Dill Falls
47. Flat Laurel Creek
48. Graveyard Fields Loop
49. Skinny Dip Hole
50. Pink Beds Loop
51. Moore Cove Falls
52. Cat Gap Loop
53. Cove Creek Falls
54. Sunwall
57. South Mills River
60. Little Bradley Falls

Easy Hikes

1. Snow's Cut
2. Sugarloaf Dune
3. Cedar Point Tideland
4. Neusiok
5. Live Oak
6. Goose Creek
7. Hammock Hills
8. Buxton Woods
9. Soundside Nature
11. Boardwalk
14. Woodland Nature—Falls Lake Recreation Area
17. Woodland—Greensboro Arboretum
18. Bog Garden
19. Badin Lake
25. Widow's Creek
28. Bass Lake Loop
34. Paddy's Creek
36. Roaring Fork Falls
40. Cliffside Lake Loop
42. Chattooga River
43. Silver Run Falls
50. Pink Beds Loop
58. Hooker Falls

Strenuous and Moderate-to-Strenuous Hikes

12. Spanish Moss
24. Stone Mountain Loop
27. Glen Burney
29. Boone Fork
30. Hunt Fish Falls
32. Lower Falls of Upper Creek
33. High Shoals Falls Loop
35. Crabtree Falls Loop

Moss-covered rocks line the banks en route to Big Laurel Falls (hike 39).

Map Legend

═══⟨40⟩═══	Interstate Highway	▪	Building/Point of Interest
──⟨70⟩──	US Highway	▲	Campground
──⟨49⟩──	State Highway	▲	Campsite
═⟨1114⟩#⟨FR477⟩═	County/Forest Road	⊛	Capital
────	Local Road	†	Cemetery
══════	Unpaved Road	▬	Dam
▬▬▬▬▬▬	Featured Trail	⦗	Gate
-----------	Trail	⊕	Hospital
....	Off-Trail Hike	⌁	Lighthouse
— — — — —	Ferry	🅿	Parking
—·—··—···	State Line	▲	Peak/Summit
⌒⌒⌒	Small River/Creek	⛩	Picnic Area
⬭	Body of Water	🛈	Ranger Station
Marsh	Marsh	⍟	Restaurant
Sand	Sand	⍟	Restrooms
National Forest	National Forest	⧏	Scenic View/Viewpoint
State/County Park	State/County Park	⚬⎯	Spring
Other Park	Other Park	○	Town/City
National Seashore	National Seashore	①	Trailhead
✈	Airport	❓	Visitor/Information Center
⛴	Boat Launch	🚰	Water
⌣	Bridge	⋰	Waterfall

Coastal Region

Over a dozen fabulous trails are found within the coastal region of the state, from Wilmington to Winton and everywhere in between. Hike along the expansive Neuse River as you delve into the Croatan National Forest. Let the dogs run free on sandy beach after sandy beach near Snow's Cut. Climb the largest sand dune on the Eastern seaboard at Jockey's Ridge, or visit the tallest brick lighthouse in the US near Buxton Woods. Take a dip in Phelps Lake, where thousands of white tundra swans gather each winter, or view the Cliffs of the Neuse from the crackled banks of the river. Whether you explore the shores of Pamlico Sound, or those along the Merchants Millpond, you'll be dazzled and amazed at the diversity this region has to offer. Stand in awe as you watch the wild mustangs of Corolla pass you by, or stop in to see the Wright Brothers monument, paying tribute to Wilbur and Orville, who gave the state bragging rights for "first in flight." Four-wheel drive on the beach, pitch a tent on the sands of the Atlantic, and enjoy stunning sunrises like no other. Whatever you choose, the opportunities are endless right here on the captivating coast of North Carolina.

Mikey is ready to explore the coast.

WILMINGTON

1 Snow's Cut Trail

Within the wonderful confines of Carolina Beach State Park, this easy-to-follow flat mulch path is suitable for dogs of all ages. The trail parallels the waterway for which it's named and leads out to a small sandy beach alongside Snow's Cut. Tall sandy banks lined with downed trees add to the scenery. The trail also leads to the park's campground, but unless you're staying here, I recommend hiking to the "beach" and back, which shortens the hike to a half-mile round-trip.

Start: Snow's Cut trailhead at the northeast end of the picnic area behind the restrooms
Distance: 0.6-mile out and back
Hiking time: 20 minutes
Blaze color: Red
Difficulty: Easy
Trailhead elevation: Sea level
Highest point: Sea level
Seasons: Year-round. December–February, 7:00 a.m.–7:00 p.m.; March, April, and October, 7:00 a.m.–9:00 p.m.; May–September, 7:00 a.m.–10:00 p.m.; November, 7:00 a.m.–8:00 p.m. Closed Christmas Day.
Trail surface: Flat mulch path, sandy beach
Other trail users: None

Canine compatibility: Leash required
Land status: North Carolina Department of Natural Resources
Fees and permits: None
Map: *DeLorme: North Carolina Atlas & Gazetteer*, page 85, F6
Trail contact: Carolina Beach State Park, 1010 State Park Rd., Carolina Beach; (910) 458-8206; www.ncparks.gov/Visit/parks/cabe/main.php
Nearest town: Carolina Beach
Trail tips: Mosquitoes tend to be out in summertime, so bring bug spray. Restrooms and a large picnic area are located near the trailhead. Trail maps available at the visitor's center.

Finding the trailhead: *From the junction of US 421 and NC 132 near Wilmington*, drive south on US 421 for 6.6 miles and turn right onto Dow Road. Travel for 0.2 mile to a right onto State Park Road. Travel for 0.8 mile to the picnic area and parking lot on your right.

From Southport, take the Southport Ferry to Fort Fisher (approximately 35 minutes). From Fort Fisher, drive north on US 421 for approximately 7.4 miles and turn left onto Dow Road and follow directions above. GPS: N34 03.050'/W77 54.809'

The Hike

Suitable for dogs and people of all ages, this hike is short, flat, and easy to follow. The trail begins within a large picnic area and heads due east into the woods. You immediately pass an outdoor seating area with a lectern, where the park hosts educational programs. Beyond the seating area, the trail parallels Snow's Cut, the waterway for which it's named. A small patch of forest separates you from the water, and the sound of boats echoes through the trees while birds tweet and crickets chirp. When you

The dogs will love playing on the sand near Snow's Cut.

come to a T, the left is a spur trail that leads you north to a delightful little sandy beach along the water's edge. Tall banks, with downed trees lining the edge, add to the scenery. The dogs enjoy romping about and digging in the sand, or wading out into the water to cool off while you appreciate the stellar views. The T also leads south to the campground where the trail ends. If you're camping here, you can access your campsite from here, or hike the trail backward from the campground to the sandy beach and picnic area. If you're not staying here, skip the leg to the campground. This shortens the hike to a half mile. If you're looking for a longer trail, head over to the Sugarloaf Dune Trail (hike 2). This trail leads you to the top of Sugarloaf Dune, where you'll enjoy stunning views of the Cape Fear River from the tallest point in the park. Carolina Beach State Park also has a marina, boat ramp, and fishing deck, but there's no swimming allowed anywhere in the park. Not to fret; The town of Carolina Beach is home to Freeman Park, a public beach where dogs are allowed. They can even be off leash from October 1 to March 31. If you do take the dogs to the beach, bring an umbrella to keep them cool, lots of drinking water, and booties for their pads if the sand is hot. A good rule of thumb: If you need sandals, then they need shoes too. To access Freeman Park, you have two options. You can park and walk to the beach for free, or if you have four-wheel drive you can drive on the beach for a fee. This park even allows tent camping on the beach in designated areas. For more information call (910) 458-2977 or visit www.carolinabeach.org/site_new/pages/freeman_park.html.

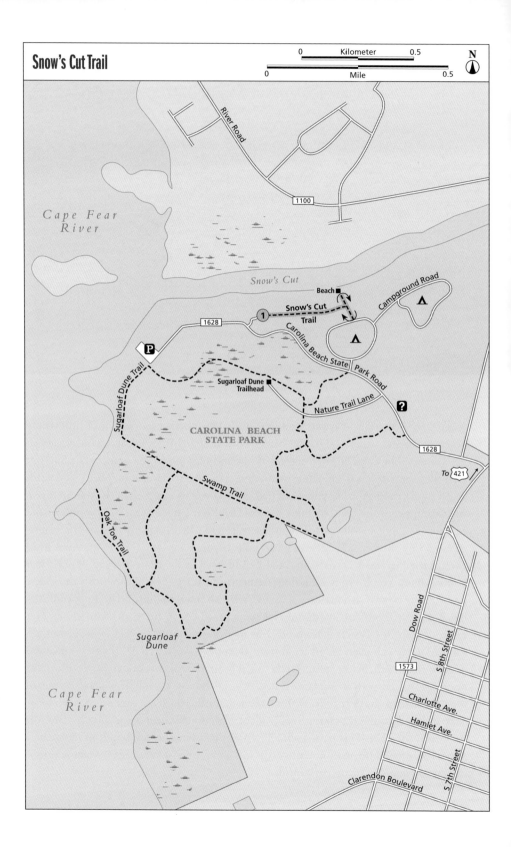

Snow's Cut Trail

Cape Fear River

River Road

1100

Snow's Cut

Beach ■

Campground Road

1 Snow's Cut Trail

1628

Carolina Beach State Park Road

🅿

Sugarloaf Dune Trailhead ■

Sugarloaf Dune Trail

Nature Trail Lane

❓

CAROLINA BEACH STATE PARK

1628

To 421

Swamp Trail

Oak Toe Trail

Sugarloaf Dune

Cape Fear River

Dow Road

S. 8th Street

1573

Charlotte Ave.

Hamlet Ave.

S. 7th Street

Clarendon Boulevard

0   Kilometer   0.5

0   Mile   0.5

N

Miles and Directions

0.0 Hike due east on the flat mulch path and immediately pass a seating area with benches lined up to form an outdoor lectern area.

0.2 Arrive at a T. Go left (north) toward the water.

0.23 Arrive at a perfect sandy beach with long-range views of Snow's Cut. Here the dogs can run and play near and in the water (N34 03.098'/W77-54.594'). Return to the T.

0.26 Arrive back at the T, head the opposite direction (south).

0.3 The trail ends at the campground (N34-03.051'/W77-54.565'). Backtrack to the trailhead.

0.6 Arrive back at the trailhead.

Option: Skip the leg to the campground and return to the trailhead after the dogs play by the water.

Resting up: Beacon House Inn Bed and Breakfast, 715 N. Carolina Beach Ave., Carolina Beach; (910) 458-6244.

Drifters Reef Motel, 701 N. Lake Park Blvd., Carolina Beach; (910) 458-5414; www .driftersreef.com; two dogs any size, pet fee per dog per night.

Camping: Onsite.

Fueling up: Gibbys Dock & Dine, 315 Canal Dr., Carolina Beach; (910) 458-3625.

Island Hots, 103A Cape Fear Blvd., Carolina Beach; (910) 274-5875.

Lazy Pirate, 701 N. Lake Park Blvd., Carolina Beach; (910) 458-5299.

A sandpiper takes flight.

2 Sugarloaf Dune Trail

Carolina Beach State Park has several hiking trails, and the Sugarloaf Trail is the longest of them all. It leads through the center of the park, past the marina, and out to the banks of the Cape Fear River. Here the dogs can get some energy out running and playing in and out of the water on a long sandy beach. Beyond the beach, the trail continues for another three quarters of a mile to the top of the Sugarloaf Dune.

Start: From the Flytrap Trail parking area, begin hiking northwest on the orange-blazed Sugarloaf Dune Trail.
Distance: 2.5-miles out and back
Hiking time: 1 hour, 15 minutes
Blaze color: Orange
Difficulty: Easy
Trailhead elevation: 8 feet
Highest point: 27 feet
Seasons: Year-round. December–February, 7:00 a.m.–7:00 p.m.; March, April, and October, 7:00 a.m.–9:00 p.m.; May–September, 7:00 a.m.–10:00 p.m.; November, 7:00 a.m.–8:00 p.m. Closed Christmas Day.
Trail surface: Hard-packed dirt, sand, mulch

Other trail users: None
Canine compatibility: Leash required
Land status: North Carolina Department of Natural Resources
Fees and permits: None
Map: *DeLorme: North Carolina Atlas & Gazetteer*, page 85, F6
Trail contact: Carolina Beach State Park, 1010 State Park Rd., Carolina Beach; (910) 458-8206; www.ncparks.gov/Visit/parks/cabe/main.php
Nearest town: Carolina Beach
Trail tips: Restrooms are located at the marina, which you'll hike past at 0.35 mile. Trail maps are available at the visitor's center.

Finding the trailhead: *From the junction of US 421 and NC 132 near Wilmington*, drive south on US 421 for 6.6 miles and turn right onto Dow Road. Travel for 0.2 mile to a right onto State Park Road. Travel for 0.4 mile to a left onto Nature Trail Lane. Follow the road for 0.3 mile to the end.
From Southport, take the Southport Ferry to Fort Fisher (approximately 35 minutes). From Fort Fisher, drive north on US 421 for approximately 7.4 miles and turn left onto Dow Road and follow directions above. GPS: N34 02.908'/W77 54.824'

The Hike

The trail begins under the shady cover of a diverse area of forest. Bamboo, oak, and pine trees sit side by side, and birdlife is plentiful. You'll hear the occasional woodpecker pecking away at the trees, while the rest of the birds peacefully chirp and sing as you hike by. As you pass the marina you could fill your water if need be, and there's a concession here too. The trail soon becomes sugar sand, and the ground gives way beneath your feet. You'll catch glimpses of the river between the trees and notice the terrain is quite diverse with marshland to the right and mixed forest to the left. The soft sand makes the trail a bit more challenging, but a gentle steady breeze balances it out. You soon reach a pristine, long, hard-packed sandy beach, which is a highlight for

The view from atop Sugarloaf Dune is pristine.

the dogs. Here they can run and play in and out of the water. It's a perfect opportunity for them to get some energy out, while you enjoy watching them play. Beyond the beach the Sugarloaf Dune Trail merges with the Swamp Trail, and the mulch path gives you a reprieve from the soft sand. You'll pass through a marshy wetland, but trees offer shade for you and your canine companions. Soon the orange-blazed Sugarloaf Dune Trail forks off to the right and enters a forest of long-leaf pines. The pine trees stand tall, straight, and proud, but they don't offer much shade, so bring lots of drinking water for you and the pups. You'll come to another fork, where the blue-blazed Oak Toe Trail leads right to a marsh overlook next to the river. This is a nice side trip, but to reach the dune, go left. The trail meanders through the forest for the remainder of the way, until you come to a fence line at the foot of the dune. Climb the pathway to the left of the fence, and you'll reach a fork at the top of the hill. Go right and you quickly find yourself standing at the top of Sugarloaf Dune. Stunning views of the Cape Fear River form a backdrop to the dune-scape. At 55 feet this is the highest point in the park. The dune is protected, so please enjoy the view, but don't let the dogs roam out onto the dune. From the fork at the top of the hill, the Sugarloaf Dune Trail continues for another 1.75 miles. I recommend that you backtrack to the trailhead, rather than hike the entire loop. The remainder of this trail is very hot and doesn't offer much shade. Plus there's no water for the dogs either, since the ponds you see on the map are not suitable for dogs to drink. Another perk to backtracking is that the dogs get a second chance to play on the beach. If you want to add mileage, hike the park's Snow's Cut Trail (hike 1). It's an easy stroll that leads to another small sandy beach alongside Snow's Cut.

▶ **PUPPY PAWS AND GOLDEN YEARS:** The Snow's Cut Trail (hike 1) is found within the same state park. It's short and easy and leads from the picnic area to a fantastic sandy beach along Snow's Cut.

Miles and Directions

- **0.0** Hike northwest on the orange-blazed Sugarloaf Dune Trail.
- **0.3** Pass the marina, go left (southwest), and the trail quickly becomes sugar sand.
- **0.5** Arrive at a pristine sandy beach. After letting your dog frolic in the water, continue hiking southeast into the forest.
- **0.55** The Sugarloaf Dune Trail merges with the Swamp Trail and follows almost a perfectly straight line east-southeast.
- **0.65** Cross a footbridge, continue hiking southeast.
- **0.75** Arrive at a fork where the red-blazed Swamp Trail continues straight ahead (southeast), and the orange-blazed Sugarloaf Dune Trail leads right (southwest). Go right on the Sugarloaf Trail.
- **1.0** Arrive at a second fork, the right leads west on the blue-blazed Oak Toe Trail. Go left (southeast) on the Sugarloaf Dune Trail.

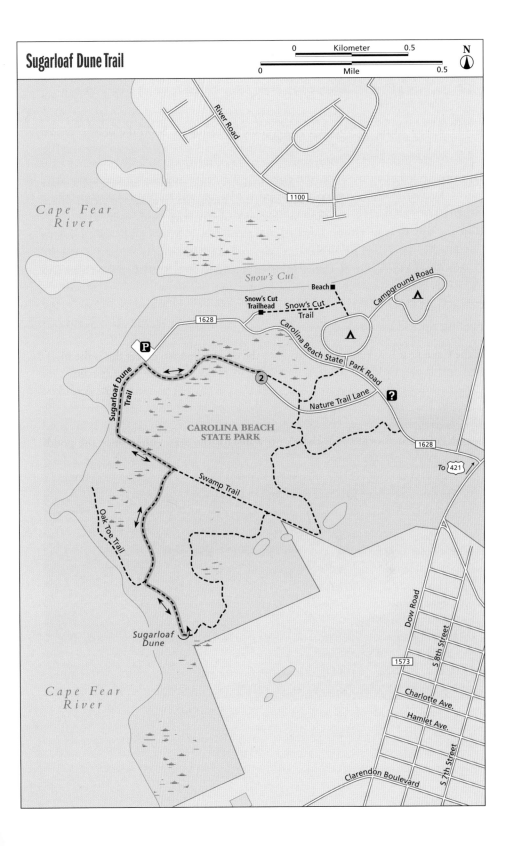

Sugarloaf Dune Trail

0   Kilometer   0.5

0   Mile   0.5

N

Cape Fear River

River Road

1100

Snow's Cut

Beach

Snow's Cut Trailhead

Campground Road

Snow's Cut Trail

Carolina Beach State Park Road

1628

P

Sugarloaf Dune Trail

2

Nature Trail Lane

?

1628

To 421

CAROLINA BEACH STATE PARK

Swamp Trail

Oak Toe Trail

Sugarloaf Dune

Cape Fear River

Dow Road

S 8th Street

1573

Charlotte Ave.

Hamlet Ave.

S 7th Street

Clarendon Boulevard

1.15 Come to an open sandy five-way intersection. Hike straight across and to the right, following the orange blazes almost due south.

1.2 You'll see a fence line directly in front of you. Follow the path to the left of the fence as it climbs the dune.

1.25 At the top of the hill, go right and arrive at the Sugarloaf Dune Overlook (N34 02.278'/ W77 55.072'). Backtrack to the trailhead.

2.5 Arrive back at the trailhead.

Option: To lengthen the hike, you could do the entire Sugarloaf Dune Loop Trail, but be forewarned: There is no water and hardly any shade. If you take this route, bring lots of water!

Resting up: Beacon House Inn Bed and Breakfast, 715 N. Carolina Beach Ave., Carolina Beach; (910) 458-6244.

Drifters Reef Motel, 701 N. Lake Park Blvd., Carolina Beach; (910) 458-5414; www .driftersreef.com; two dogs any size, pet fee per dog, per night.

Camping: Onsite.

Fueling up: Gibbys Dock & Dine, 315 Canal Dr., Carolina Beach; (910) 458-3625.

Island Hots, 103A Cape Fear Blvd., Carolina Beach; (910) 274-5875.

Lazy Pirate, 701 N. Lake Park Blvd., Carolina Beach; (910) 458-5299.

The dogs have a blast playing on the beach along the Sugarloaf Dune Trail.

CAPE CARTERET

3 Cedar Point Tideland Trail

At the southern tip of Croatan National Forest, near the mouth of the White Oak River, is the Cedar Point Recreation Area, and the Cedar Point Tideland Trail is certainly a highlight. The trail is comprised of two adjoining loops—a 0.6-mile short loop and a 1.3-miles long loop. The long loop gives you outstanding views of the tideland where the coastal forest meets the salt marsh. The recreation area also offers paddle trails, a fishing pier, a small-craft boat launch, a picnic area, and a campground.

Start: The Cedar Point Tideland trailhead in the parking lot at the end of the road
Distance: 1.4-mile loop (for both loops), 0.6-mile loop (short loop only)
Hiking time: 1 hour
Blaze color: None
Difficulty: Easy
Trailhead elevation: Sea level
Highest point: 13 feet
Seasons: Year-round
Trail surface: Smooth, wide gravel path; boardwalks
Other trail users: None
Canine compatibility: Leash required
Land status: Croatan National Forest–Croatan Ranger District
Fees and permits: None
Map: DeLorme: North Carolina Atlas & Gazetteer, page 79, E5

Trail contacts: Croatan National Forest; (252) 638-5628; www.fs.usda.gov/recarea/nfsnc/recarea/?recid=48494
Nearest towns: Swansboro and Cape Carteret
Trail tips: If possible, hike both loops. The scenery is pristine, and there's a great watering hole along the long loop. A steady breeze keeps you cool, but the sun still beats down on you, so bring plenty of drinking water and apply sunscreen before heading out. You may also want to bring bug repellent, especially in the warmer months. A wide variety of bird species reside here; bring binoculars so you can catch a peek before the dogs spook them off. Restrooms and trash cans are near the trailhead.
Special considerations: The area is a protected wildland, with a variety of bird and wildlife habitat. To protect these creatures, and for optimal viewing, keep dogs on a leash at all times.

Finding the trailhead: From the junction of NC 58 and NC 24 in Cape Carteret, drive north on NC 58 for 0.7 mile. Turn left onto VFW Road and travel 0.5 mile to a left into the Cedar Point Recreation Area. Follow the road for 0.8 mile to the end of the road. GPS: N34 41.521'/W77 05.189'

The Hike

As you drive through the town of Cedar Point, the blue-green hues of the White Oak River shimmer in the sun, and you know you're in for a treat. The trail is comprised of two adjoining loops. I recommend hiking both, especially since the long loop is where you'll find two areas for the dogs to dip their paws in Dubling Creek. But don't let them drink it. The water is brackish, so make sure you bring plenty

The scenery along the Cedar Point Tideland Trail is unmatched.

of drinking water with you. The trail begins as a gravel path with interpretive signs along the way and quickly leads to a fork where the short loop begins. Hike the loop either way, but counterclockwise is recommended, because then you finish alongside the creek, rather than inland. Along the way benches are placed here and there, and a steady breeze keeps you cool, while nature provides patches of shade to assist. You'll find yourself catching subtle glimpses of the marsh and open waterway, but the best views are yet to come. You'll reach a fork where you could circle back around on the short loop, or continue onto the long loop. The latter is recommended. As you follow the long loop, the scenery unfolds before your eyes. The marshland, waterways, and boardwalks in the distance all come into view. Enjoy the shade while you can, since you'll lose it on the second half of the loop, where the trail follows the water's edge. Footbridge crossings mix up the terrain; you'll cross a few long, vented metal board-walks when the loop begins to circle back. This stretch of trail offers stunning views of the water all around you, and the breeze is even stronger. Between the first two boardwalks, a short spur trail leads out to the water, where the dogs can cool off a bit. As they do, you'll notice dozens of tiny crabs scurrying back into their homes. Squir-rels, raccoons, deer, and a variety of birdlife also live here. Please remember you're a guest in their home. You'll pass a second spur trail that gives the dogs an even better opportunity to take a dip. From here, the trail leads to a fork. The left is the stretch of trail that divides the short and long loops in two. This is where you would come out if you just hiked the short loop. Go right (east) and you'll cross one last boardwalk

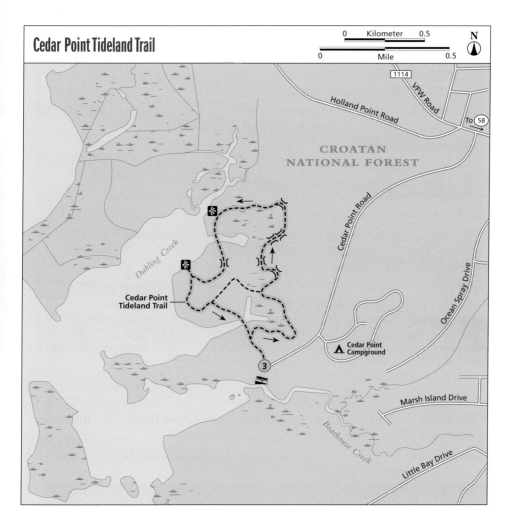

Cedar Point Tideland Trail

0   Kilometer   0.5

0   Mile   0.5

N

1114

VFW Road

Holland Point Road

To 58

CROATAN
NATIONAL FOREST

Cedar Point Road

Dubling Creek

Ocean Spray Drive

Cedar Point
Tideland Trail

Cedar Point
Campground

3

Marsh Island Drive

Boathouse Creek

Little Bay Drive

before the gravel path leads back to the trailhead. This tideland trail is proudly part of the National Recreation Trail System, and the recreation area that houses it is a nice little retreat that you can enjoy by land or by sea. A side trip to the neighboring town of Emerald Isle is also enjoyable. Dogs are allowed on the beaches there year-round, but they must remain on a leash at all times.

Miles and Directions

0.0 Hike due north on the gravel path.

0.05 Arrive at a fork where the short loop begins. You can go either way, but the trail is described in a counterclockwise fashion, so go right (northeast), continuing on the gravel path.

0.35 Arrive at a second fork. To hike the short loop only, go left (northwest) onto the boardwalk. To hike the long loop, go right (east) on the gravel path.

0.4 Cross a footbridge and hike generally west.

0.45 Cross a footbridge, and the beautiful scenery unfolds before your eyes. Continue hiking north.

0.5 Cross a footbridge, continue hiking north.

0.55 Cross a footbridge, continue hiking generally north.

0.6 Cross over a small culvert, continue hiking north.

0.65 Cross another footbridge, and the trail bends left (southwest).

0.75 Begin hiking generally west on a boardwalk.

0.8 Follow the spur trail that heads right (northwest) to the water (N34 41.823'/W77 05.323'). Return to the main path and hike southwest on another boardwalk.

0.95 Cross a footbridge and hike south on the gravel path.

1.05 Take a second spur trail right (north) to another overlook alongside Dubling Creek (N34 41.711'/W77 05.387'). The dogs can take a dip here, and then return to the main trail.

1.1 Arrive back at the main trail. Continue hiking south on the long loop.

1.25 Come to a fork. The left (northeast) is where you'd come out if you just hiked the short loop. Go right (southeast) here to hike the remaining portion of the short loop.

1.35 Arrive at the first fork, where the short loop began. Go right (south) toward the trailhead.

1.4 Arrive back at the trailhead.

Resting up: Parkerton Inn, 1184 NC 58, Cape Carteret; (252) 393-9000; www .parkertoninn.com; two dogs, pet fee per dog, per night.

Camping: Onsite.

Fueling up: Bake, Bottle, and Brew, 147 Front St., Swansboro; (910) 325-7550.

Icehouse Waterfront, 103 Moore St., Swansboro; (910) 325-0501.

Santorini's Mediterranean Grille, 114 E. Corsett Ave., Swansboro; (910) 708-1213.

An ibis waits patiently in the marshland.

HAVELOCK

4 Neusiok Trail (Northern Terminus)

Running all the way down the eastern side of Croatan National Forest, is the 20-plus-mile Neusiok Trail. Although it's more popular with backpackers, day hikers also enjoy the northern and southern reaches. The northern end is fantastic for hiking with your four-legged friends. This section of trail closely follows the Neuse River for nearly 1.5 miles before it moves away from the water. Long stretches of sandy beach give you splendid views, while the dogs enjoy some off-leash play time along the wide waterway.

Start: The Neusiok trailhead at the northwest end of the parking lot. You can either take the sidewalk down to the edge of the water, and follow the shoreline northwest. Or you can hike west through the picnic area past the bathrooms and pick the trail up at the far end. I prefer the beach route. It gives the dogs an opportunity to run and play by the water before heading into the woods.
Distance: 2.8-miles out and back
Hiking time: 1 hour and 45 minutes
Blaze Color: Silver metal tabs
Difficulty: Easy
Trailhead elevation: 42 feet
Highest point: 87 feet
Seasons: Open year-round, but optimal to hike in December or March when it's a bit cooler and there's less rain.

Trail surface: Sandy beaches, and hard packed dirt
Other trail users: None
Canine compatibility: Voice control
Land status: Croatan National Forest–Croatan Ranger District
Fees and permits: None
Map: *DeLorme: North Carolina Atlas & Gazetteer.* Page 79 B8
Trail contact: Croatan National Forest; (252) 638-5628; www.fs.usda.gov/recarea/nfsnc/recreation/hiking/recarea/?recid=48486&actid=51
Nearest town: Havelock
Trail tips: Restrooms, trash cans, and a large picnic area are located near the trailhead.

Finding the trailhead: *From the junction of NC 101 and US 70 in Havelock,* drive east on NC 101 for 5.3 miles to a left onto NC 306 (Ferry Road). Travel for 3.2 miles to a left onto Pine Cliff Road (FR 132). Travel for 1.5 miles to the end of the road.
From the town of Minnesott Beach, on the north side of the Neuse River, you can take a 20-minute ferry ride south across the river. From the ferry terminal, drive south on NC 306 (Ferry Road) for 1.2 miles to a right onto Pine Cliff Road (FR 132) and follow directions above. GPS: N34 56.358'/W76 49.375'

The Hike

While the full length of the Neusiok Trail stretches over 20 miles, the best part of the trail for dogs is the far northern reaches. This portion begins in the Pine Cliff

Picnic Area, and from the trailhead you have two options. You can hike through the picnic area and head straight to the official trailhead, but this route skips a nice long stretch of sandy beach along the banks of the Neuse River. I recommend beginning the hike by following the sidewalk directly down to the water's edge. From here hike west alongside the river, and the beach leads you past a field of boulders. Large pieces of driftwood add to the scenery, and you'll find this portion of the "trail" extremely peaceful. After following the coastline for nearly 0.25 mile, it leads around a bend and to an area where people camp on the sandy beach. You may see a hammock strung up or a tent tucked away as you pass by. From this camping area hike south into the woods, and you'll find the Neusiok Trail running behind it.

Driftwood adds to the scenery along the Neusiok Trail.

Follow the trail west, and it leads across Gum Branch. Despite the fact that the river is right there, the trail is fairly wooded and shady. Silver metal fireproof tabs act as blazes, and you may have to scurry around the occasional downed tree. The terrain is surprisingly hilly for the coastal region, with sinkholes here and there adding to the topography. You can smell the dampness in the air, as the trail continues to follow the edge of water. You'll hike through a forest of mixed hardwoods, with maples, oaks, and poplar blending nicely with the pine trees. Along the way you'll come to three forks. Stay right at them all, and as a general rule the well-blazed trail follows the river west. At 1.4 miles the trail leads you up to a small bluff overlooking the Neuse River. Near the overlook you'll see what looks like a horse tie-off, although no horses are allowed on the Neusiok Trail. A picnic table gives you a perfect perch to enjoy the spectacular view of the wide waterway. Although the Neusiok Trail

▶ **PUPPY PAWS AND GOLDEN YEARS:** The first 0.3 mile of this hike follows a narrow sandy beach. Even if you don't continue the hike, the dogs can enjoy romping around on the sand and in the Neuse River.

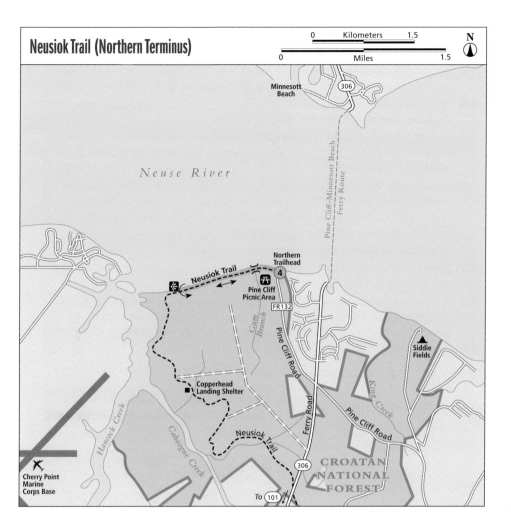

Neusiok Trail (Northern Terminus)

continues southwest and back into the forest from here, I recommend returning to the trailhead. Beyond this point the trail moves away from the water, becomes hot and overgrown, and offers no water breaks for the babies. The Croatan National Forest is a wonderful place to explore, but not necessarily with the dogs. Wildlife includes deer, black bears, raccoons, opossums, and even alligators. A variety of birdlife, from osprey to owls, turkeys to terns, and woodpeckers to wading birds all reside here. Snakes and other reptiles also make their home here, so use caution if you do delve deeper into the forest.

The Neusiok Trail is proudly part of the famous Mountains-to-Sea Trail, which literally runs the entire width of the state, from the mountains all the way to the sea. The trail covers an impressive 900-plus miles, many of which coincide with shorter trails such as the Neusiok. It begins in the Great Smoky Mountains National Park and ends at the Atlantic Ocean in Jockey's Ridge State Park.

0.0 Hike down the sidewalk northwest to the water's edge. Follow the shoreline around a bend, and you'll hike across a perfect sandy beach where people camp.

0.3 Head south back into the woods from the sandy beach, and immediately cross a foot-bridge over Gum Branch. Hike west along the coastline.

0.5 Arrive at a fork, where the narrower Neusiok Trail continues straight ahead (generally west), and a wide side trail goes left (south). Continue west on the Neusiok Trail, following the shore of the Neuse River.

0.95 The trail brings you out to a sandy beach; follow the blazes across the beachy area, while the dogs run and play in the water and you enjoy amazing views. An obscure blazed trail leads you back into the woods, where the trail follows the river from high on a bluff.

1.0 Come to a fork where a side trail heads south into the forest, bypass this and continue west on the Neusiok Trail, still following the water from above.

1.1 Come to another fork, a blue-blazed trail with pink surveyor tape heads left (west). Go right, following the silver blazes north.

1.4 Arrive at a picnic table sitting high on a bluff overlooking the Neuse River, near what looks like a horse tie-off. The Neusiok Trail continues southwest and back into the forest, but I recommend returning to the trailhead from here (N34 56.171'/W76 50.595').

2.8 Arrive back at the trailhead.

Resting up: Days Inn, 1220 E. Main St., Havelock; (252) 447-1122.

Holiday Inn Express, 103 Branchside Dr., Havelock; (252) 447-9000.

Quality Inn, 400 US 70 W., Havelock; (252) 444-1111.

Camping: Neuse River Campground (Flanners Beach); from Havelock, drive north on US 70 to a right onto Flanners Beach Road (SR 1170 and then follow signs to the campground; (252) 638-5628; for reservations visit www.recreation.gov or call (877) 444-6777.

Fueling up: Sonic Drive-in, 1301 E. Main St.; (252) 444-2553.

Ospreys nest along the banks of the Neuse River.

WASHINGTON TO BATH

5 Live Oak Trail

Deep within Goose Creek State Park, the Live Oak Trail passes through a large picnic area. The trail forms a loop, with a shortcut to the restrooms that divides the loop in two. Massive old oak trees cover the entire area with shade, as you make your way out to the grandiose Pamlico River. Here, the dogs can play in the water while you enjoy long-range views from the shoreline, making this is one of my favorites, and the dog's too!

Start: Follow the paved path southeast into the picnic area
Distance: 0.75-mile loop
Hiking time: 20 minutes
Blaze Color: Red
Difficulty: Easy
Trailhead elevation: Sea level
Highest point: 7 feet
Seasons: Year-round. November–February, 8 a.m.–6 p.m.; March–May, September, and October, 8:00 a.m.–8:00 p.m., June–August, 8:00 a.m–9:00 p.m. Closed Christmas Day
Trail surface: Paved path, hard packed gravel
Other trail users: None
Canine compatibility: Leash required

Land status: North Carolina Department of Natural Resources
Fees and permits: None
Map: *DeLorme: North Carolina Atlas & Gazetteer*, page 66, B3
Trail contact: Goose Creek State Park, 2190 Camp Leach Rd., Washington; (252) 923-2191; www.ncparks.gov/Visit/parks/gocr/main.php
Nearest towns: Washington and Bath
Trail tips: Bring a beach chair and a picnic to spend some time while the dogs enjoy playing near the water. Restrooms, trash cans, water fountain, picnic area are all found near the trailhead. Trail maps available at the Visitor's Center.

Finding the trailhead: *From the junction of US 264 and NC 32 at Douglas Crossroads*, drive east on US 264 for 2.7 miles and turn right onto Camp Leach Road (SR 1334). Travel for 2.2 miles to the entrance to the park on your right. Follow State Park Drive for 2.0 miles to the parking lot on the right.
From the junction of US 264 and NC 92 in Jessama, drive west on US 264 for less than 0.25 mile to a left onto Camp Leach Road (SR 1334) and follow directions above. GPS: N35-27.833'/ W76-54.011'

The Hike

Although the loop is short, you'll reap several benefits from this one. The paved path begins by leading you to a crossroads where the loop begins. Standing here, you can see clear across the picnic area to the expansive Pamlico River. If you head right it takes you south past a picnic shelter and to the designated swimming area. If you go left it leads southeast toward the restrooms and then out to the water. This route gets the dogs to the water a little quicker. So head left, and on the way to the river, you'll

The Live Oak Trail leads past a cemetery that dates back to the 1800s.

pass a small cemetery that's been there since the late 1800s. After paying your respects, continue hiking south on the obvious, wide path and it leads you out to the water's edge. A narrow path follows the river in both directions, although the left is not officially part of the Live Oak Trail. This area is ideal to let the dogs frolic, play, swim, and cool off in the fabulous Pamlico River. Once they've had their playtime, head right (west) and follow the sandy trail alongside the river.

As waves lap upon the sand you enjoy fantastic views and a nice breeze before passing the designated swim beach. This area is roped off, and open from Memorial Day to Labor Day, but no dogs are allowed. They are allowed on the outskirts of the area though. As the trail begins to loop back toward the trailhead it leads to a shed-like structure full of life jackets. The park hosts a fantastic life jacket loaner program and they have a variety of life vests in all sizes. If you're not a strong swimmer, or if you have small children and want to take extra precautions, you can sign a vest out for free. Please still watch your children closely. This is an unprotected beach, so there are *no lifeguards* on duty. Beyond the loaner kiosk, you'll pass a trail to the right (northeast) that splits the loop in two. And to the left (west) you'll see the blue blazed Goose Creek Trail (hike 6). If you wanted to extend the hike, this is a great option. It leads 2.5 miles to the park's campground near the mouth of Goose Creek. Other activities within the park include camping, fishing, and boating. They have paddle trails, and you can launch your own canoe or kayak in the main body of the park. To launch small motor craft, you'll have to head to Dinah's Landing on the west side of Goose Creek. The landing is in a remote section of the state park and there's no fee to launch.

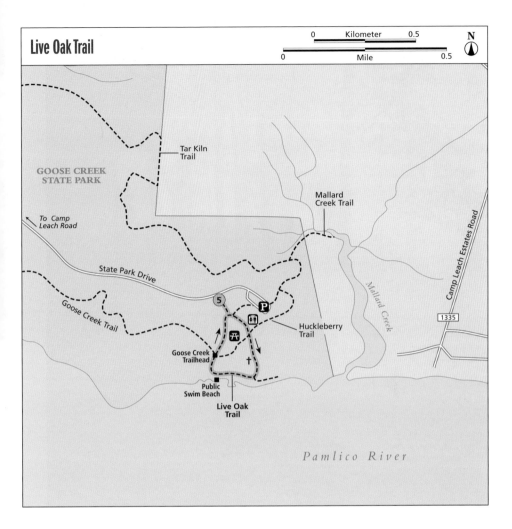

Miles and Directions

0.0 Follow the paved path southeast toward the picnic area.

200' Come to a crossroads. Hike straight across (southeast) toward the restrooms.

0.15 Hike around the restrooms and arrive at an intersection with the Huckleberry Trail to the left (east), and a shortcut through the middle of the loop to the right (west). Go straight across (south) toward the river.

0.2 Pass a cemetery, hike south toward the water.

0.3 Arrive at the Pamlico River. A narrow trail goes left (east) toward a large oak tree. This area is an ideal spot to let the dogs play in the water. The Live Oak Trail heads right (west) and follows the Pamlico River toward the public swimming area.

0.44 Pass by the designated swimming area, no dogs allowed on the official swim beach.

0.5 Pass the Goose Creek Trail on your left (west), and the shortcut to the restrooms on your right (northeast). Bypass them both, and hike north toward the picnic shelter.

Massive oak trees offer shade on the Live Oak Trail.

0.6 Pass the picnic shelter, hike north toward the trailhead.

0.74 Arrive back at the crossroads near the trailhead. Backtrack to the trailhead.

0.75 Arrive at the trailhead.

Resting up: Days Inn, 916 Carolina Ave., Washington; (252) 946-6141; two dogs any size, pet fee per pet, per night.

Tranters Creek Resort and Campground, 6573 Clarks Neck Road, Washington; (252) 948-0850; www.tranterscreekresort.com; cabin rentals–pet fee per night.

Camping: Primitive camping onsite.

Fueling up: Washington Crab and Seafood Shack, 1212 John Small Ave.; (252) 974-2722.

6 Goose Creek Trail

At 2.5 miles, the Goose Creek Trail runs nearly the entire width of the state park. Although there are no creeks or tributaries to cross, the dogs have fantastic places to swim and play in the water at both ends of the trail. Near the trailhead they can play in the Pamlico River, which is reached via the Live Oak Trail (hike 5). And at the trail's end, you'll find another great swimming hole near a pair of benches overlooking Goose Creek.

Start: At the Live Oak trailhead
Distance: 5.2 miles out and back
Hiking time: 2 hours and 40 minutes
Blaze color: Blue
Difficulty: Easy
Trailhead elevation: Sea Level
Highest point: 4 feet
Seasons: Year-round; November–February, 8:00 a.m.–6:00 p.m.; March–May, September, and October, 8:00 a.m.–8:00 p.m.; June–August, 8:00 a.m.–9:00 p.m. Closed Christmas Day
Trail surface: Hard-packed dirt
Other trail users: None
Canine compatibility: Leash required
Land status: North Carolina Department of Natural Resources

Fees and permits: None
Map: *DeLorme: North Carolina Atlas & Gazetteer*, page 66, B3
Trail contact: Goose Creek State Park, 2190 Camp Leach Rd., Washington; (252) 923-2191; www.ncparks.gov/Visit/parks/gocr/main.php
Nearest towns: Washington and Bath
Trail tips: Restrooms, trash cans, picnic area, and a water fountain are all located near the trailhead. Bring lots of water along with you. If you need a refill, you can use the water fountain in the picnic area or water spigots in the campground near the trail's end. Trail maps available at the visitor's center.

Finding the trailhead: *From the junction of US 264 and NC 32 at Douglas Crossroads*, drive east on US 264 for 2.7 miles and turn right onto Camp Leach Road (SR 1334). Travel for 2.2 miles to the entrance to the park on your right. Follow State Park Drive for 2.0 miles to the parking lot on the right.
From the junction of US 264 and NC 92 in Jessama, drive west on US 264 for less than 0.25 mile to a left turn onto Camp Leach Road (SR 1334) and follow directions above. GPS: N35 27.833'/W76 54.011'

The Hike

Nearly surrounded by water, Goose Creek State Park not only borders the Pamlico River to the south, it has a few creeks that dip into it, including the park's namesake—Goose Creek. The trail runs from one side of the park to the other, but to access it, you need to begin by hiking on the Live Oak Trail (hike 5). I recommend following this red-blazed path all the way to the river, where the dogs can play in the water before starting the longer hike. After playing in the water, backtrack to the Goose

Intricate root systems are exposed along Goose Creek.

Creek trailhead. The blue-blazed trail heads generally west and meanders through the forest along gentle curves. The underbrush is an interesting combination of wildflowers, ferns, and unexpected bamboo plants mixed in with oak tree saplings. Shaded most of the way, this is a great route for running with your dog as well. It's easy to follow, and if you went out and back, you'd get a nice 5.0-mile run in.

But hiking here is just as enjoyable. Birdlife is abundant, which enhances the pleasant sound of nature in the background. Although you can't see the water from the trail, it parallels the river, so you get a nice breeze. At 1.1 miles, bypass the bailout trail to the right that leads to the main park road, and continue following the blue blazes northwest. Several boardwalk planks help keep your feet dry through a swampy area, while tall cypress trees add to the diversity. Frogs leap from the cypress knees, and you'll notice a portion of the "swamp" is covered with duckweed, making it look like

Goose Creek Trail

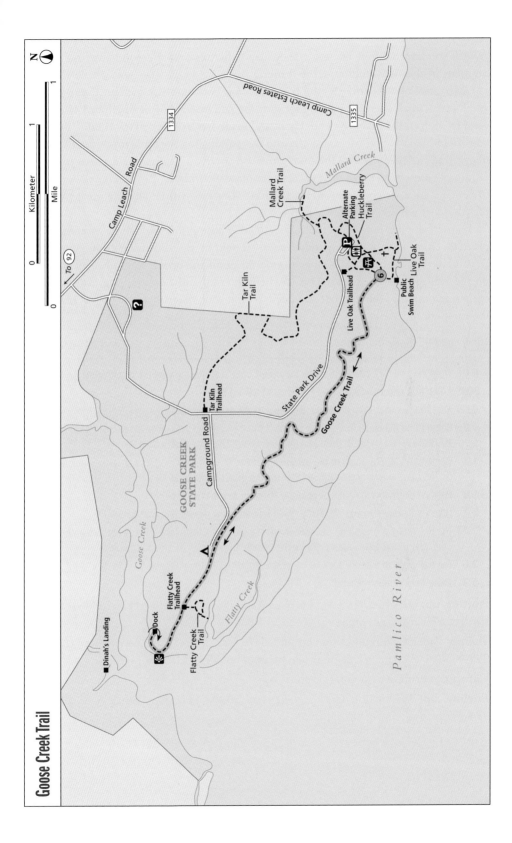

grass. If you have a puppy like mine, they may think this is solid ground. Keep an eye on them, or they may end up in the drink.

After crossing a boardwalk, the trail takes you back into the fragrant forest and you'll pass a small alternate parking lot near the entrance to the campground. If you want to shorten the hike, you could park and begin here. Or, if you're camping here, you could hike the trail backward. Beyond this parking lot, the trail crosses the Flatty Creek Trail and then parallels the campground. At nearly 2.5 miles, you'll arrive at the mouth of Goose Creek, where it makes its confluence with the Pamlico River. A pair of benches are a welcome reward for reaching your destination. This is a great place for you to sit while the dogs play in the water.

Those camping here have the luxury of this little point 24/7. It's a wonderful place to enjoy your morning coffee, read a book, or treasure the evening sunset. Beyond the benches, the trail swings around the point and brings you to a small dock on the banks of Goose Creek. This is where the trail ends, and the dogs can once again wade out into the water. If you need to refill your water, there are spigots inside the campground.

Miles and Directions

0.0   From the Live Oak trailhead, follow the paved path southeast toward the picnic area.

200'   Come to a crossroads. Go right (southwest) toward the picnic area.

0.15   Pass the picnic shelter, continue hiking south toward the water.

0.25   Come to an intersection. The right (west) is the trailhead for the Goose Creek Trail (N35 27.686'/W76 54.032'). Hike west into the woods following blue blazes.

1.1   Come to a T, where a trail to the right heads east toward a park road and acts as a bailout. Go left (northwest), and continue following the blue-blazed trail.

1.9   Pass an alternative parking lot near the entrance to the campground.

2.2   Hike west straight across the Flatty Creek Trail and now parallel the campground.

2.45   The trail leads you to some benches overlooking Goose Creek. Take a break here while the dogs play in the water. After enjoying the respite, hike northeast around the point.

2.6   The trail ends at a small dock by the creek. Backtrack to the trailhead.

5.2   Arrive back at the trailhead.

Resting up: Days Inn, 916 Carolina Ave., Washington; (252)946-6141; two dogs any size, pet fee per pet per night.

Tranters Creek Resort and Campground, 6573 Clarks Neck Rd., Washington; (252) 948-0850; www.tranterscreekresort.com; cabin rentals; pet fee per night.

Camping: Primitive camping onsite.

Fueling up: Washington Crab and Seafood Shack, 1212 John Small Ave.; (252) 974-2722.

OCRACOKE

7 Hammock Hills Nature Trail

Rolling-hill topography, stunted trees, and stunning views of the marshland are all found along this delightful loop trail. Interpretive signs offer insight into the flora and fauna of this maritime forest as you hike over a diverse range of terrain. The trail itself, and its close proximity to the charming village of Ocracoke, lands this one on the Author's Favorites List.

Start: Hammock Hills Nature Trail trailhead at the north end of the parking area
Distance: 0.8-mile loop
Hiking time: 30 minutes
Blaze color: None
Difficulty: Easy
Trailhead elevation: 51 feet
Highest point: 59 feet
Seasons: Year-round
Trail surface: Grass, sand, hard-packed dirt; boardwalks

Other trail users: None
Canine compatibility: Leash required
Land status: Cape Hatteras National Seashore
Fees and permits: None
Map: *DeLorme: North Carolina Atlas & Gazetteer*, page 68, F4
Trail contact: (252) 473-2111; www.nps.gov/caha/planyourvisit/hiking.htm
Nearest towns: Ocracoke and Hatteras
Trail tips: The trail can be buggy in the summertime.

Finding the trailhead: *From Swan Quarter*, take the Swan Quarter–Ocracoke Ferry to the village of Ocracoke (2.5-hour ferry ride). Once you exit the ferry, drive east on NC 12 (Irvin Garrish Highway) for 3.0 miles to the parking area on the left (just south of the campground).

From Hatteras Island, take the Hatteras–Ocracoke ferry (35 minutes ferry ride). Once you exit the ferry, drive west on NC 12 for 9.8 miles to the parking area on your right (just south of the campground). **Note:** During the summer months cars may be lined up for nearly a mile waiting to get onto the Hatteras Ferry to exit Ocracoke Island. GPS: N35 07.531'/W75 55.423'

The Hike

Reached only by ferry, Ocracoke Island sits well out in the middle of the Atlantic Ocean at the southern end of the Cape Hatteras National Seashore. The island packs a punch, and the charming village of Ocracoke has a Key West feel to it. The village is home to a British cemetery, the Ocracoke Lighthouse, and Springer's Point Preserve, where the pirate Blackbeard met his demise.

As you travel up the island, you'll notice "ramps" where you can access the beach to drive on if you have four-wheel drive. Permits are required and can be obtained at the National Park Service visitor's center near the village ferry port. This long, narrow barrier island also houses a campground, and wild pony pens, where you can view the

Visitors enjoy expansive views along the Hammock Hills Nature Trail.

magnificent mustangs of Ocracoke. This herd of horses has inhabited the island since the 1500s. Today the "wild" ponies are kept in captivity within a 180-acre enclosure to protect the species. If you're lucky, you'll catch a glimpse of them feeding near the fence line that keeps them in.

▶ **PUPPY PAWS AND GOLDEN YEARS:** Take a trip to Springers Point, a lovely little nature preserve at the western end of Ocracoke Village, near the lighthouse. A short and easy trail leads through this maritime forest to a sandy beach where the water is surprisingly shallow. It's perfect for the dogs to wade out in the ocean and enjoy the refreshing blue water.

As you drive farther up the island, sand dunes line the roadway. This hike gives insight into what lies beyond the dunes on the sound side of the island. The trailhead sits across from the Ocracoke Campground, and the interpretive trail begins by following a wide grassy path into a maritime forest. You can't help but notice the trees are short and stunted from the ocean breeze and salt water in the air, nearly forming a canopy-type tunnel for the first 0.1 mile. The loop begins at a T on a boardwalk. You can hike either way, but it's described counterclockwise. As you get deeper into the forest, the pine trees seem to get taller, and a thick understory makes the path easy to follow. Signs along the way educate you on the flora, fauna, and natural phenomena of the area. The terrain is surprising, as rolling hills seem to flow with ease. Along this peaceful hike you'll hear the ocean in the distance, the

Ocracoke's Silver Lake is stunning at sunset.

birds chirping, and your dog's tags jingling. The best time to visit is early morning or late afternoon, when it's not so hot out. But you'll still need to bring drinking water along for you and the dogs.

When you reach a T, take the spur trail to an overlook with stunning views of the marsh. After enjoying the serenity of the sedge-covered land, the loop trail leads back toward the trailhead. You'll hike over boardwalks, grass, sand, and hard-packed dirt as you continue south to the T where the loop began. The diversity of the terrain and trail, education you receive along the way, and the fact that Ocracoke has so much more to offer, make this one of my favorite trails in the coastal region. If you have time, take the dogs down to Springer's Point in the village of Ocracoke, and they can play in the water along the National Seashore. Dogs also are allowed anywhere on the beach that people can go, but they must remain on a leash at all times.

Miles and Directions

- **0.0** Follow the wide grassy path northeast.
- **0.1** Arrive at a boardwalk T where the loop begins. You can go either way, but the trail is described counterclockwise. Go right (east).
- **0.2** Cross a footbridge, and the trail begins to climb north on soft sugar sand.
- **0.4** Come to a T. Go right (north), and the path leads 50 feet to an overlook (N35 07.793'/ W75 55.333'). Enjoy the stunning views of the marsh and then return to the T. Head the other way (west), as you begin to loop back toward the trailhead.

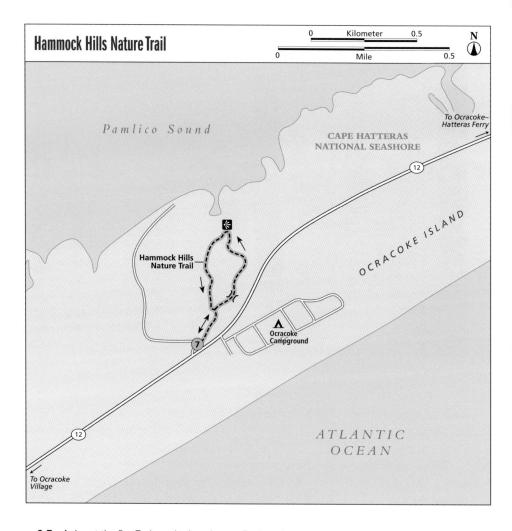

0   Kilometer   0.5

N

0   Mile   0.5

Pamlico Sound

CAPE HATTERAS
NATIONAL SEASHORE

To Ocracoke–
Hatteras Ferry

12

OCRACOKE ISLAND

Hammock Hills
Nature Trail

Ocracoke
Campground

7

12

To Ocracoke
Village

ATLANTIC
OCEAN

0.7 Arrive at the first T where the loop began. Backtrack to the trailhead.

0.8 Arrive back at the trailhead.

Resting up: The Island Inn, 25 Lighthouse Rd., Ocracoke; (252) 928-4351. Black-beard's Lodge, 111 Back Rd., Ocracoke; (252) 928-3421.

Silver Lake Motel and Inn, 395 Irvin Garrish Hwy., Ocracoke; (252) 928-5721.

Camping: Ocracoke Campground, 4352 Irvin Garrish Hwy., Ocracoke; (252) 473-2111; www.nps.gov/caha/planyourvisit/campgrounds.htm; April–October; for reservations visit www.recreation.gov or call (877) 444-6777.

Fueling up: Dajio, 305 Irvin Garrish Hwy., Ocracoke; (252) 928-7119; www.dajio restaurant.com.

Jolly Roger Pub & Marina, 396 Irvin Garrish Hwy., Ocracoke; (252) 928-3703.

BUXTON

8 Buxton Woods Trail

Within view of the Cape Hatteras Lighthouse, you'll find a lovely little rustic picnic area along the edge of Buxton Woods. Tables, trash cans, and a pair of vault toilets near the trailhead give you a place to grab a snack before heading into the forest. Interpretive signs along this loop trail educate you on the flora and fauna found here. This hike makes a nice pit stop as you make your way up or down the Outer Banks. Be sure to visit the lighthouse while you're here.

Start: The Buxton Woods trailhead is in the middle of the parking lot for the picnic area, on the north side of the road
Distance: 0.75-mile loop
Hiking time: 25 minutes
Blaze color: None
Difficulty: Easy
Trailhead elevation: 3 feet
Highest point: 21 feet
Seasons: Year-round
Trail surface: Hard-packed sand
Other trail users: None
Canine compatibility: Leash required

Land status: Cape Hatteras National Seashore
Fees and permits: None; a fee is required to climb the Cape Hatteras Lighthouse; pets are not allowed inside the lighthouse
Map: *DeLorme: North Carolina Atlas & Gazetteer*, page 69, D8
Trail contact: (252) 473-2111; www.nps.gov/caha/planyourvisit/hiking.htm
Nearest town: Buxton
Trail tips: The trail can be buggy in summertime. Picnic tables, trash cans, and a pair of vault toilets are located near the trailhead.

Finding the trailhead: *From NC 12 in Buxton*, drive south onto Lighthouse Road and travel 1.1 miles to the parking and picnic area on the right. **Note:** The parking area is just past the turn off to the lighthouse.

From Ocracoke Island, take the Ocracoke-Hatteras Ferry (35 minutes). Once you exit the ferry, drive east on NC 12 for 11.9 miles to a right turn onto Lighthouse Road and follow directions above. GPS: N35 15.172'/W75 31.724'

The Hike

The Cape Hatteras National Seashore spans more than 70 miles of coastline along the largest migratory barrier island chain in the country. Sand dunes line the roadway that cuts through these narrow islands, and as you explore the Outer Banks, quaint little towns add character to your visit. Among those towns, Buxton is home to the famed Cape Hatteras Lighthouse. The lighthouse is the second-tallest brick lighthouse in the world and was actually picked up and moved to the current position back in 1999. It was quite a feat, and left unharmed. Today visitors to the cape can climb the

A trip to see the wild Corolla mustangs is a must when visiting the Outer Banks.

lighthouse for a fee, but no dogs are allowed inside the structure. The lighthouse is one of many along the coast and is used to help seafarers navigate around the "Diamond Shoals" of the cape. Throughout the years many ships have wrecked off the coast of the Outer Banks, giving this area the moniker "Graveyard of the Atlantic." Now those shipwrecks are used for underwater exploration, as SCUBA divers delve into the depths of the deep blue sea.

▶ **PUPPY PAWS AND GOLDEN YEARS: Dogs are allowed on the beach anywhere along the Cape Hatteras National Seashore that people are allowed. Bring an umbrella, a bowl, and lots of water to help keep your furry friends cool. And of course, pick up after them and keep them on a leash at all times.**

Fishers, shell collectors, off-road drivers, surfers, and beachgoers alike enjoy the coast of Hatteras. And the best part about it: You can bring dogs on the beach anywhere that people are allowed year-round. Just make sure you clean up after them and that they're on a leash at all times. Right around the corner from the lighthouse is a patch of forest known as Buxton Woods. This also has boasting rights, as it's the largest maritime forest on the National Seashore. The Buxton Woods Trail is a nice 0.75-mile loop. It's a self-guided tour that leads through the forest and marshland. Signs along the path educate you on the nature of the wooded landscape. Bayberry, dogwood, loblolly, and pines keep you shaded most of the way, but there's not much of a breeze, which is surprising, given your location. A variety of birds inhabit the area and serenade you as

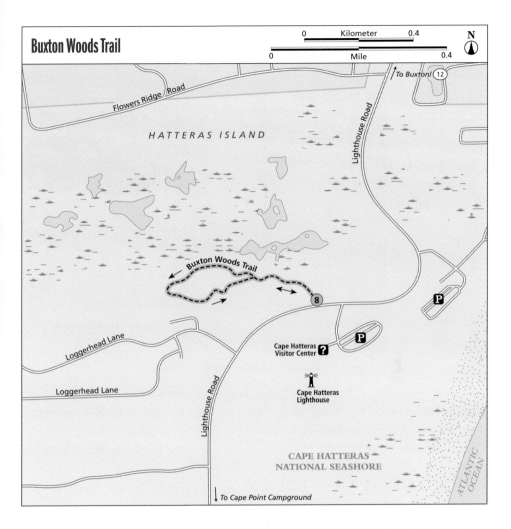

Buxton Woods Trail

0   Kilometer   0.4

0   Mile   0.4

N

To Buxton/ 12

Flowers Ridge Road

HATTERAS ISLAND

Lighthouse Road

Buxton Woods Trail

8

P

Loggerhead Lane

Cape Hatteras Visitor Center ?

P

Loggerhead Lane

Lighthouse Road

Cape Hatteras Lighthouse

CAPE HATTERAS NATIONAL SEASHORE

ATLANTIC OCEAN

To Cape Point Campground

you hike on by. Deer, squirrels, and other small mammals also make this their home, as evidenced by the game trails you'll see running off the main path. Whether you're heading up to Nags Head, down to Ocracoke, or staying right here in Buxton, this hike is a nice way to stretch your legs, get the dogs out of the car, and enjoy a small slice of nature.

Miles and Directions

0.0   Hike due north into the forest.

0.15 Come to a fork where the loop begins. The left leads southwest. Go right (northwest) and downhill.

0.3   A short boardwalk heads over a sedge, continue hiking southwest.

0.6   Arrive at the fork where you began the loop. Backtrack to the trailhead.

0.75 Arrive back at the trailhead.

Driving on the beach is a highlight of the Cape Hatteras National Seashore.

Resting up: Cape Pines Motel, 47497 NC 12, Buxton; (252) 995-5666; www
.capepinesmotel.com; two dogs any size, pet fee per dog per night.

Outer Banks Motel, 46577 NC 12, Buxton; (252) 995-5601; www.outerbanksmotel
.com.

Camping: Cape Point Campground, 46700 Lighthouse Rd., Buxton; (252) 473-
2111; www.nps.gov/caha/planyourvisit/campgrounds.htm.

Frisco Campground, 53415 Billy Mitchell Rd., Frisco; (252) 473-2111; www.nps
.gov/caha/planyourvisit/campgrounds.htm; although Cape Point Campground is
closer to the trailhead, Frisco Campground offers much more space and privacy
between campsites, which is less distracting to the dogs.

Fueling up: The Wreck Tiki Bar and Food, 58848 Marina Way, Hatteras; (252)
996-0162.

NAGS HEAD

⑨ Soundside Nature Trail

A well-marked path leads through the sand dunes of Jockey's Ridge State Park. While there's no shade, you typically enjoy a nice breeze since the park is perfectly perched between the Roanoke Sound and the Atlantic Ocean. The trail forms a large loop through the dune-scape, and if you hike counterclockwise, the second half of the trail leads you along the shoreline. The entire family will enjoy wading out into the surprisingly shallow water of Roanoke Sound.

Start: The trailhead is located in the Soundside Access Area of Jockey's Ridge State Park, in an isolated part of the park, at the north end of the parking lot.
Distance: 0.8-mile loop
Hiking time: 30 minutes
Blaze color: None
Difficulty: Easy
Trailhead elevation: 25 feet
Highest point: 30 feet
Seasons: Year-round. Soundside Access Gate, where the trailhead is located: October–March, 8:00 a.m.–5:00 p.m.; April–September, 8:00 a.m.–7:00 p.m. Closed Christmas Day. Main park hours: November–February, 8:00 a.m.–6:00 p.m.; March, April, September, 8:00 a.m.–8:00 p.m.; October, 8:00 a.m.–7:00 p.m.; May–August, 8:00 a.m.–9:00 p.m. Closed Christmas Day.
Trail surface: Soft sand
Other trail users: None

Canine compatibility: Leash required
Land status: North Carolina Department of Natural Resources
Fees and permits: None
Map: *DeLorme: North Carolina Atlas & Gazetteer*, page 49, B7
Trail contact: Jockey's Ridge State Park, 300 W. Carolista Dr., Nags Head; (252) 441-7132; www.ncparks.gov/Visit/parks/jori/main.php
Nearest town: Nags Head
Trail tips: During the summer months, especially in midday, the sand surface can be hot on your dogs' paws, just as it is on our own barefeet. Booties are recommended. Vault toilets, outdoor showers, and trash cans are located near the trailhead. Wear sunscreen and bring lots of drinking water for you and the dogs. The Roanoke Sound is brackish water, so don't let the dogs drink it. Trail maps are available at the visitor's center in the main body of the park.

Finding the trailhead: *From the junction of US 158 and NC 12 in Kitty Hawk*, drive south on US 158 for 11.2 miles to a right onto West Soundside Road. Travel for 0.4 mile to the parking area on the right. **Note:** When driving south on US 158, make sure you bypass the main park entrance.
From the junction of US 158 and US 64 in Whalebone, drive north for approximately 3.9 miles and turn left onto West Soundside Road and follow directions above. GPS: N35 57.180'/W75 37.950'

The Hike

Location, location, location! Without a doubt, Jockey's Ridge State Park has a perfect one. To the south you can visit the Bodie Island Lighthouse, or head down to Pea Island where you may see deer grazing alongside the dunes or spy the remains of the *Oriental* shipwreck. To the north you'll find the Wright Brothers National Monument, which pays tribute to Orville and Wilbur Wright, who gave North Carolina the bragging rights of "first in flight." Beyond that, you'll pass through quaint towns like Duck and up to Currituck, home to the Currituck Beach Light. This marvelous lighthouse was constructed of one million bricks back in 1875 and stands 162 feet tall.

Continue farther north, and reach the grand finale of the Outer Banks—the Currituck National Wildlife Refuge. The refuge is home to the wild Corolla mustangs. This herd of horses roams freely among the sand dunes, and at times can be seen cooling off near the edge of the ocean. These endangered species are descendants of the Spanish steeds that landed here hundreds of years ago. If this isn't enough, Jockey's Ridge is home to the tallest natural sand dune system in the eastern United States. You can even learn to hang glide from the top of the dune through an onsite vendor—Kitty Hawk Kites. But save that for another day when you don't have the dogs with you.

▶ **PUPPY PAWS AND GOLDEN YEARS:** If your dogs aren't up for the full hike, enter the public beach at the south end of the parking lot. This beach area is fantastic for dogs of all ages. The water is shallow for quite a ways out, so you and the pups can wade out into the sound and enjoy splashing around. Bring a beach umbrella, since there's no shade. Also, bring enough drinking water for both you and your canine companions.

As you begin this engaging hike, you can see the gigantic dunes in the distance, but a visit to the main body of the park is a *must* to appreciate them from a closer vantage point, and even walk to the top where you'll get 360-degree views. The Soundside Nature trail forms a loop and gives insight into a diverse terrain. From open wetlands to maritime forest thickets, you'll hike through small sections of each. Counterclockwise is optimal for the dogs, because the second half of the loop follows the water's edge back to the parking lot. The Roanoke Sound is surprisingly shallow, so you and the pups can wade well out into the water. It's perfect for playing fetch, or simply letting them cool off as they splash around in the water. Because the water is brackish, don't let them drink it. Instead, bring enough drinking water for you both, and remember a bowl too.

As you follow the shoreline, you'll see people on kayaks, on kite boards, wind surfing, or balancing on stand-up paddleboards. Driftwood offers the only shade on the beach, so if you stay awhile, bring an umbrella to shield you and the dogs from the sun. The "trail" soon leads into the public beach area, which is typically very populated. Keep a tight leash through here, and a small boardwalk leads you back to the parking lot where you

Jockey's Ridge is the tallest active sand dune on the Eastern seaboard.

began. Showers and a foot rinse are useful to clean yourself and the dogs before loading up and heading off to the next adventure.

Miles and Directions

0.0 Begin at the north end of the parking lot. The trail leads north into the sand dune landscape.

0.15 Cross a few footbridges, and continue hiking northwest on the soft sand.

0.5 Hike over a boardwalk, and the trail puts you on a small ridge with views of the sound in the distance.

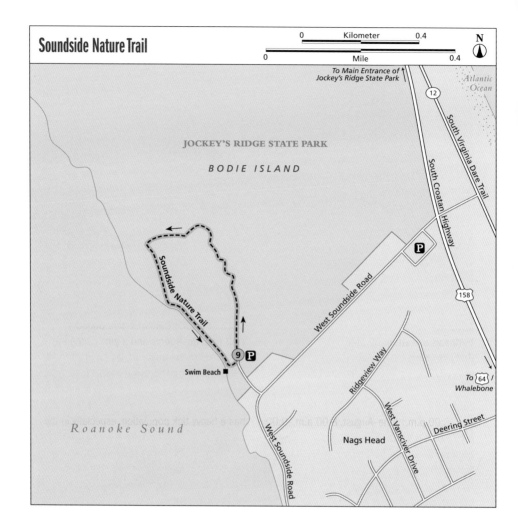

Soundside Nature Trail

0   Kilometer   0.4

0   Mile   0.4

N

To Main Entrance of
Jockey's Ridge State Park

Atlantic Ocean

12

JOCKEY'S RIDGE STATE PARK

BODIE ISLAND

South Virginia Dare Trail

South Croatan Highway

Soundside Nature Trail

West Soundside Road

P

158

9 P

Swim Beach

Ridgeview Way

To 64 / Whalebone

Roanoke Sound

West Soundside Road

West Vansciver Drive

Deering Street

Nags Head

0.75 Hike through the public swim beach.

0.8 Cross a small boardwalk leading back to the parking lot.

Resting up: Comfort Inn South Ocean Front, 8031 Old Oregon Inlet Rd., Nags Head; (252) 441-6315; two dogs any size, pet fee per night.

Sandbar Bed and Breakfast, 2508 S. Virginia Dare Trail, Nags Head; (252) 489-1868; two dogs any size, pet fee per night.

Camping: Oregon Inlet Campground, NC 12, Nags Head; (252) 473-2111; www .nps.gov/caha/planyourvisit/campgrounds.htm.

Fueling up: Mulligans Raw Bar & Grille, 4005 S. Croatan Hwy, Nags Head; (252) 480-2000.

South Beach Grille, 6806 Virginia Dare Trail, Nags Head; (252) 449-9313.

Surfin Spoon, 2408 S. Virginia Dare Trail, Nags Head; (252) 441-7873.

ELIZABETH CITY TO MURFREESBORO

10 Lassiter Trail

This long loop leads through a diverse variety of terrain. You'll pass the Merchants Millpond, Lassiter Swamp, and the rolling hills of the forest that surrounds it. Mileposts help keep track of your progress, and to hike the entire loop takes a full three hours. The park also has bike trails, a picnic area, camping, and canoe rentals, and you can fish on the park's namesake—the Merchants Millpond.

Start: At the southeast corner of the parking lot for the AB Coleman Picnic Area
Distance: 5.4-mile loop
Hiking time: 3 hours minimum
Blaze color: White
Difficulty: Moderate
Trailhead elevation: 52 feet
Highest point: 52 feet
Seasons: Year-round. November–February, 8:00 a.m.–6:00 p.m.; March and October, 8:00 a.m.–8:00 p.m.; April, May, September, 8:00 a.m.–8:00 p.m.; June–August, 8:00 a.m.–9:00 p.m. Closed Christmas Day.
Trail surface: Hard-packed dirt, many footbridge crossings
Other trail users: Mountain bikers
Canine compatibility: Leash required
Land status: North Carolina Department of Natural Resources
Fees and permits: None

Map: *DeLorme: North Carolina Atlas & Gazetteer,* page 25, C5
Trail contact: Merchants Millpond State Park, 176 Millpond Rd., Gatesville; (252) 357-1191; www.ncparks.gov/Visit/parks/memi/main.php
Nearest towns: Gatesville and Sunbury
Trail tips: Restrooms and a picnic area are located near the trailhead. If you forgot to fill up your drinking water, you could do so here. This is a long trail. You'll need lots of water to stay hydrated while you hike. The state park has a heavy tick population, especially in the warmer months. Give your dogs tick preventive medicine before you hike. As for your own protection, tuck your shirt into your pants and your pants into your socks. Wear light colors so you can spot ticks easily. Use bug repellant, and do a thorough tick check of you and the dogs when you get off the trail. Trail maps are available at the visitor's center.

Finding the trailhead: *From the junction of US 158 and NC 32 in Sunbury,* drive west on US 158 for 5.1 miles and turn left onto Millpond Road (SR 1403). Follow Millpond Road for 0.8 mile to the main entrance to the park on your left. Travel for 0.4 mile to the parking area for the AB Coleman Picnic Area.

From the junction of US 158 and NC 37 at Eleanors Crossroads, drive east on US 158 for 3.7 miles and turn right onto Millpond Road (SR 1403) and follow directions above. GPS: N36 26.259'/W76 41.652'

The Hike

As you follow the Lassiter Trail through Merchants Millpond State Park, you're in for a real treat. The trail leads through a diverse variety of terrain. It begins by passing through a picnic area, and at 0.1 mile you get your first glance of the millpond from the peak of a hill. You soon find yourself crossing over the duckweed-covered millpond. The floating flora shifts hourly with the wind and current, forming an ever-changing work of art. Giant cypress trees eerily stand out while waterfowl wander across the pond. The croaking of frogs echoes across the water, but as soon as you reenter the forest, songbirds drown them out. Over 200 species of birds reside here. Deer are abundant, and other mammals such as mink, raccoons, otters, and bobcats also inhabit the park.

At 0.3 mile you reach the beginning of the loop. You can go either way, but the trail is described and designed as a counterclockwise hike. This is optimal for the dogs, since the second half of the loop crosses several tributaries. This trail leads you over *many* footbridges; they're not all over clear running water, so take advantage of the creeks and tributaries as they arise. As the trail moves away from the millpond, it leads you through the Lassiter Swamp, which is small potatoes compared to the

Deer are abundant in Merchants Millpond State Park.

neighboring Great Dismal Swamp. It still offers insight into this type of ecosystem, and elevated boardwalks lead over wet portions of the path. Along with swampland, the trail leads you through a forest of oak, maple, pine, and poplar, along with many other species of trees, and mile markers along the way help you keep track of your progress. You'll come to a fire road beyond the 1.0-mark, where the right leads to some backcountry camping. The trail now follows the fire road east for 0.4 mile before veering off into the woods on a narrow footpath.

Over the next mile the path skirts the edge of the swamp and crosses several footbridges. The first one has a small tributary just big enough for the dogs to enjoy. At the north end of the loop, you'll reach another fork with a trail that leads to back-country camping. Go left, and the loop leads west. The occasional bench gives you a place to rest. Between milepost 3.0 and 4.0, the trail alternates between wet and dry sections, and the last mile of the loop is over drier terrain. It does cross over tributaries though, so the dogs enjoy some water breaks. This part of the park butts up against private property where hunting is allowed. Wear blaze orange during hunting season, and put some color on the dogs as well. Also, keep them on a leash. When the loop ends, backtrack to the trailhead.

Miles and Directions

0.0 Immediately arrive at a fork. The left leads straight ahead (south), go right (southwest) into a picnic area and pass the bathrooms.

0.1 Come to a T, the right quickly dead-ends. Go left (northeast), and the trail heads downhill.

0.15 Cross a footbridge, and the trail splits. The left leads north back to the parking lot. Go right (east) and follow the Lassiter Trail.

0.17 Cross a footbridge.

0.18 Cross a footbridge over the duckweed-covered Merchants Millpond, continue hiking southeast.

0.3 Arrive at a fork where the loop begins. Go right (southeast).

0.5 Cross a footbridge over a creek; the dogs enjoy cooling down in the water. Continue hiking west alongside the millpond.

0.7 Arrive at a fork. The right leads southeast to some backcountry camping. Go left and continue hiking northeast.

0.9 A pair of boardwalks leads over wet portions of the trail.

1.3 Arrive at an intersection with the orange-blazed bike trail. Hike straight across (southeast).

1.4 Come to a T at a fire road. Go left (east) and follow the fire road for the next 0.4 mile.

1.55 Cross a culvert.

1.8 The white-blazed Lassiter Trail veers off the fire road to the right (east). Follow the trail into the forest.

1.9 Cross a footbridge over a tiny tributary.

1.95 Cross a footbridge over dry land, continue hiking east.

2.0 Cross a footbridge, begin climbing east.

2.45 Cross a footbridge, and the trail climbs north.

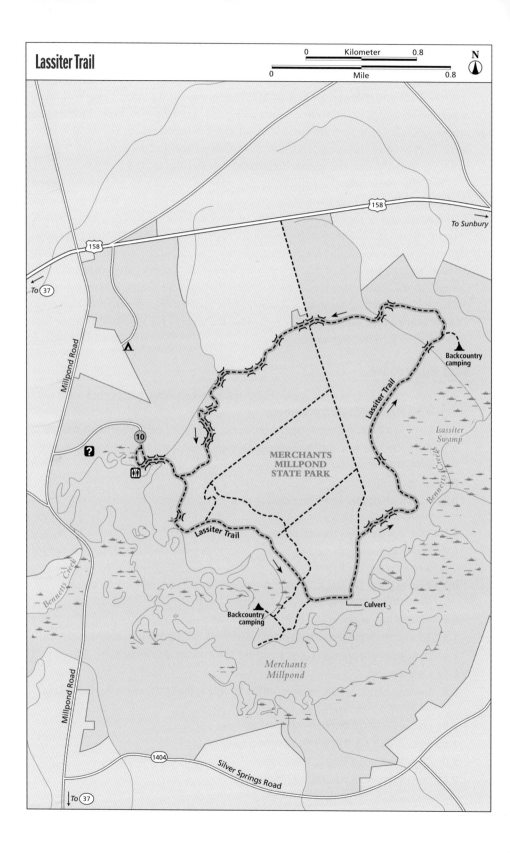

Lassiter Trail

0   Kilometer   0.8

0   Mile   0.8

N

To Sunbury

To 37

Millpond Road

Backcountry camping

Lassiter Trail

Lassiter Swamp

10

Bennetts Creek

MERCHANTS MILLPOND STATE PARK

Lassiter Trail

Culvert

Backcountry camping

Bennetts Creek

Merchants Millpond

1404

Silver Springs Road

To 37

2.85 Cross a footbridge over a copper-color creek with deep banks, continue hiking northeast.

2.95 Come to a fork; the right is a blue-blazed trail that leads east toward a backcountry camping area. Go left at the fork, as you continue to hike north northeast on the Lassiter Trail.

3.5 Cross a footbridge, continue hiking west.

3.55 Cross a footbridge, continue hiking southwest.

3.8 Cross a footbridge, continue hiking northwest.

3.85 Cross a footbridge, and it leads you directly to a service road. Cross the road and you'll immediately come to another footbridge. Cross this one as well, and continue hiking west back into the woods.

4.1 Cross a footbridge, continue hiking southwest.

4.2 Cross a footbridge, continue hiking southwest.

4.25 Cross a footbridge over a tiny creek, and the trail bends west.

4.4 Cross a footbridge, and the trail bends left (south).

4.45 Cross a footbridge, and the trail climbs steeply, leading you west-southwest across a ridge.

4.6 Cross a footbridge over a tiny creek, continue hiking south.

4.8 Cross a footbridge, continue hiking south.

4.83 Cross a footbridge, continue hiking south.

4.85 Cross a footbridge, continue hiking south.

4.9 Cross a footbridge.

5.1 Arrive at the fork where the loop began. Backtrack toward the trailhead.

5.3 Arrive at the T in the picnic area. Either way leads to the trailhead.

5.4 Arrive back at the trailhead.

Camping: Onsite.

Frogs enjoy lounging in the Lassiter Swamp.

CRESWELL

11 Boardwalk Trail

Resting on the northern banks of Lake Phelps, Pettigrew State Park is full of activities both on and off the water. The Boardwalk Trail begins near the picnic area and leads to the swimming pier. The water is shallow enough for you and the dogs to take a dip. Past the pier, the path continues on to Somerset Place. Although dogs aren't allowed inside the buildings of this historic homestead, you'll still enjoy a visit as you step back in time.

Start: Just past the picnic area on the left (east)

Distance: 0.8-mile out and back

Hiking time: 20 minutes

Blaze color: None

Difficulty: Easy

Trailhead elevation: 68 feet

Highest point: 68 feet

Seasons: Year-round. November–February, 8:00 a.m.–6:00 p.m.; March–May, September and October, 8:00 a.m.–8:00 p.m.; June–August, 8:00 a.m.–9:00 p.m. Closed Christmas Day.

Trail surface: Wooden boardwalk, grass

Other trail users: None

Canine compatibility: Leash required

Land status: North Carolina Department of Natural Resources

Fees and permits: None

Map: DeLorme: *North Carolina Atlas & Gazetteer*, page 47, D8

Trail contact: Pettigrew State Park, 2252 Lake Shore Rd., Creswell; (252) 797-4475; www.ncparks.gov/Visit/parks/pett/main.php

Nearest town: Creswell

Trail tips: Bring a towel so you and the dogs can swim at the swimming pier. Bring plenty of drinking water for you and the pups. If you think your dogs will need to use the bathroom, take them for a quick walk before hitting the boardwalk trail. A trash can is located near the trailhead. Trail maps are available at the office.

Finding the trailhead: *From Columbia,* drive west on US 64 for approximately 7.0 miles to exit 558 and head toward Creswell. Follow 6th Street for 0.5 mile and turn left onto Main Street (SR 1142). Travel for 1.8 miles and turn right onto Thirty Foot Canal Road (SR 1160). Travel for 3.9 miles to a stop sign at Cherry Road (SR 1165). Continue straight across and travel for another 0.6 mile to a left onto Lake Shore Road. The entrance to Pettigrew State Park is immediately on your right. Drive past the office and stay right. **Note:** Main Street becomes Spruill Bridge Road.

From Plymouth, drive east on US 64 to exit 558 and then follow directions above. GPS: N35 47.462'/W76 24.618'

The Hike

Bordered by a national wildlife refuge to the south, and the state park to the north, Phelps Lake is a natural treasure. During the winter months thousands of great white tundra swans flock to this 16,000-acre lake, where they stay for the season. That alone

The dogs enjoy the swimming pier at Pettigrew State Park as much as you do.

is worth a visit to Pettigrew State Park, but this petite park packs a punch. There's a picnic area, a campground, and several massive state champion trees. They showcase Native American dug-out canoes, including the longest one in the southeast, which was found below the surface of Phelps Lake. The lake is easily the highlight. A fishing pier, canoe rentals, a boat ramp, and a swimming pier give visitors plenty to do on

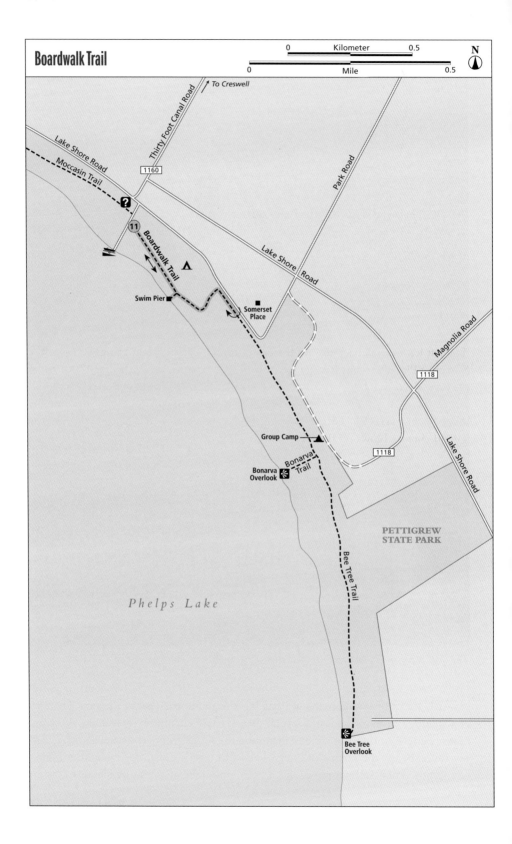

Boardwalk Trail

0   Kilometer   0.5

0   Mile   0.5

N

To Creswell

Thirty Foot Canal Road

Lake Shore Road

Moccasin Trail

1160

Park Road

Lake Shore Road

Boardwalk Trail

Swim Pier

Somerset Place

Magnolia Road

1118

Group Camp

Bonarva Trail

Bonarva Overlook

1118

Lake Shore Road

PETTIGREW STATE PARK

Phelps Lake

Bee Tree Trail

Bee Tree Overlook

the water. While hiking and biking trails and the historic Somerset Place keep you entertained on land. The Boardwalk Trail offers a combination of both.

The trail begins near the picnic area and follows an elevated boardwalk through a wet area where woodland ducks swim in the swamp alongside the path. As you follow the wooden walkway, you'll notice a variety of birdlife. Hawks, osprey, cardinals, bluebirds, chickadees, and woodpeckers all make their home here. Bring binoculars so you can spy them all. In less than a quarter mile, you'll arrive at the long swimming pier that juts out into the lake. There are no lifeguards on duty, so swim at your own risk. The pier offers amazing views of the water, and a strong breeze blows off the lake. Spectacular sunsets greet you each evening, and in the mornings color from the sky dances on the water. Although there's a drop off from the pier, ladders help you get back onto the decking, and the water is very shallow. It typically sits about 2 feet deep near the first ladder, and 4 feet at the end, so you and the pups can both enjoy the water.

After passing the pier, the trail loses the shade of the forest and opens up into the bright sun. Although this hike is short, it still gets hot in the warmer months, so bring plenty of water for you and your happy hounds. The footpath soon leads to a T. The left leads north back toward the campground, and the right brings you south to Somerset Place. This historic site was a slaver's plantation back in the late 1700s. Today the park offers tours, and although the dogs aren't allowed inside any of the buildings, you'll still enjoy taking an abridged version of the tour as you let your imagination step back in time. Near the plantation, giant sycamore trees offer plenty of shade, and a gentle breeze blows off the lake.

Miles and Directions

0.0 Hike southeast on the boardwalk.

0.2 Arrive at the swimming pier (N35 47.331'/W76 24.506'). You and the pups can take a refreshing dip in Phelps Lake. After enjoying the water and cool breeze, continue hiking southeast on the boardwalk.

0.35 Come to a T at a wide, grassy, roadlike trail. The left leads west to the campground. Go right (east).

0.4 Arrive at Somerset Place (N35 47.314'/W76 24.361'). After exploring this wonderful historic site, backtrack to the trailhead.

0.8 Arrive back at the trailhead.

Resting up: Holiday Inn Express, 840 US Hwy. 64 W, Plymouth; (252) 793-4700; dogs must be in kennels, pet fee per stay.

Port-O Plymouth Inn, 510 Hwy. 64 E, Plymouth; (877) 411-3436; three dogs less than 25 pounds, pet fee per dog per night.

Camping: Onsite.

GOLDSBORO TO KINSTON

12 Spanish Moss Trail

This short loop trail is found within Cliffs of the Neuse State Park. The park has wooded campsites, a large lake with a swimming area, and canoe rentals. The cliff overlook gives you a bird's-eye view, and the trail itself brings you right down to the river's edge.

Start: The Spanish Moss trailhead is near the restrooms, at the northeast end of the parking lot for the Cliff Overlook.
Distance: 0.6-mile loop
Hiking time: 20 minutes
Blaze color: Orange
Difficulty: Moderate to strenuous
Trailhead elevation: 91 feet
Highest point: 114 feet
Seasons: Year-round. December-February, 7:00 a.m.-7:00 p.m.; March and April, 7:00 a.m.-9:00 p.m.; May-September, 7:00 a.m.-10:00 p.m.; October and November, 7:00 a.m.-8:00 p.m. Closed Christmas Day.
Trail surface: Hard-packed dirt and man-made steps

Other trail users: None
Canine compatibility: Leash required
Land status: North Carolina Department of Natural Resources
Fees and permits: None
Map: DeLorme: North Carolina Atlas & Gazetteer, page 64, D2-E2
Trail contact: Cliffs of the Neuse State Park, 240 Park Entrance Rd., Seven Springs; (919) 778-6234; www.ncparks.gov/Visit/parks/clne/main.php
Nearest towns: Seven Springs, Goldsboro, and Kinston
Trail tips: There's running water in the restrooms, if you need to top off your water. Trail maps are available at the visitor's center.

Finding the trailhead: From the junction of NC 111 and NC 55 near Seven Springs, drive north on NC 111 for 2.3 miles and turn right onto Park Entrance Road (SR 1743). Follow Park Entrance Road for 0.5 mile to the entrance to the park. Once you enter the park, follow the road all the way to the end.

From the junction of NC 111 and US 70 near Goldsboro, drive south on NC 111 for 8.3 miles and turn left onto Park Entrance Road (SR 1743); follow the directions above. GPS: N35 14.430'/W77 53.073'

The Hike

This pleasant state park borders the shoreline of the Neuse River. The river was named for the Neusiok Tribe of Native Americans who once lived along the banks. At an impressive 275 miles, the Neuse is the longest river contained completely within North Carolina. The Spanish Moss Trail gives you an up-close and personal view from the water's edge.

A steep stairway leads down to the Neuse River on the Spanish Moss Trail.

The trail begins near the cliff overlook, where you can view the water from high above, and then leads steeply down a set of steps. When you reach the bottom of the hill, you come to a three-way fork. To the left the loop continues north, the middle is a set of steps that leads down toward the river, and the right crosses a footbridge and climbs a separate set of stairs back up to the trailhead. To hike the whole loop, go left, and the trail rises and falls over natural terrain and man-made steps. Bypass a trail to the left that leads to the group camp, and follow the orange-blazed loop through a mixed forest as it begins to flatten out. You'll come to another fork. The left leads

At times, the ground below the cliffs of the Neuse River resembles a cobblestone road.

to the river, and the right leads back to the three-way fork you encountered at the beginning of the hike. Take the side trip to the river, and you almost immediately feel a soft breeze in the air. There's no swimming allowed, but you can let the dogs play near the water. But keep them on a leash. Depending on water levels, they may end up with some seriously muddy paws.

From the river's edge, you'll get a great view of the "cliffs" of the Neuse looming high above. If you're lucky, you may see some birds of prey soaring overhead, crying out with each pass. When water levels are low, the ground near the shoreline hardens and cracks, resembling a cobblestone road. You can clearly see where the water had risen, and retreated, leaving the ground tarnished. After enjoying the waterfront, head up the steps to the three-way fork. Go left (south), cross the footbridge, and make one final climb back to the trailhead. If you're looking for a longer hike, stay in the park, and explore the Lake Trail (hike 13). The trailhead is near the lake access area.

Miles and Directions

0.0 Hike north and steeply down the steps.

0.1 Arrive at a three-way fork. The left is north and begins the loop. The middle heads down steps toward the water (this is where the loop returns), and right leads south across a footbridge and back to the trailhead. Go left, and follow the Spanish Moss Trail north.

0.2 The trail bends right and begins to loop back south.

0.3 Arrive at a T. The left leads northeast to the group camp. Go right, continue hiking south.

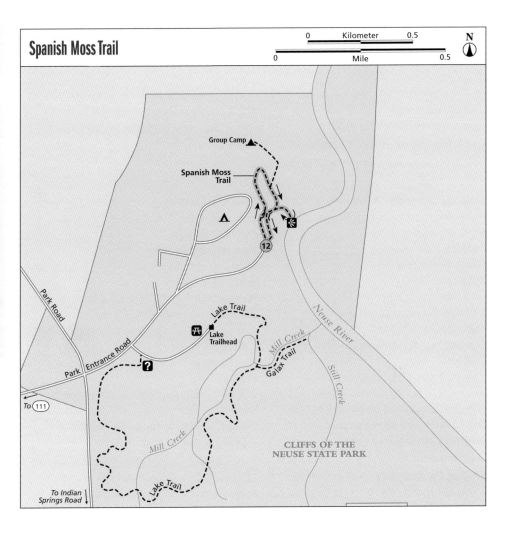

0   Kilometer   0.5

0   Mile   0.5

N

0.35 Come to a fork. The left leads east down to the Neuse River. The right heads west up some steps for about 100 feet to the three-way fork where the loop began. Go left toward the river.

0.4 Arrive at the river. Enjoy the views, and then return to the fork.

0.45 Arrive at the fork, head west up the steps. At the top of the steps, go left (west).

0.5 Cross a footbridge, and climb more steps west toward the trailhead.

0.6 Arrive back at the trailhead.

Resting up: Best Western, 909 N. Spence Ave., Goldsboro; (919) 751–1999; two dogs up to 80 pounds each, pet fee per pet per night.

Econo Lodge, E. New Bern Rd., Kinston; (252) 527–4155; two dogs up to 50 pounds each, pet fee per pet per night.

Hampton Inn, 905 N. Spence Ave., Goldsboro; (919) 778–1800; two dogs any size, no fee.

Camping: Onsite.

13 Lake Trail

As the name suggests, the Lake Trail circles the park's 11-acre lake. The dogs can play near the shore early on, but beyond 0.3 mile this becomes a wooded forest hike rather than a waterfront walk. While you're here, take advantage of the campground, where you'll find wooded and well-spaced sites. The park also has a fabulous swimming beach and boat rentals open seasonally.

Start: The Lake trailhead is at the east end of the parking lot for the swimming area, marked with a sign reading "Trails."
Distance: 1.95-mile loop
Hiking time: 1 hour
Blaze color: None
Difficulty: Easy to moderate
Trailhead elevation: 93 feet
Highest point: 105 feet
Seasons: Year-round. December–February, 7:00 a.m.–7:00 p.m.; March and April, 7:00 a.m.–9:00 p.m.; May–September, 7:00 a.m.–10:00 p.m.; October and November, 7:00 a.m.–8:00 p.m. Closed Christmas Day.
Trail surface: Hard-packed sand
Other trail users: None

Canine compatibility: Leash required
Land status: North Carolina Department of Natural Resources
Fees and permits: None
Map: *DeLorme: North Carolina Atlas & Gazetteer*, page 64, D2-E2
Trail contact: Cliffs of the Neuse State Park, 240 Park Entrance Rd, Seven Springs; (919) 778-6234; www.ncparks.gov/Visit/parks/clne/main.php
Nearest towns: Seven Springs, Goldsboro, and Kinston
Trail tips: Bring lots of drinking water; there are only two natural water stops along the way, at 0.3 and 0.7 mile. Trail maps are available at the visitor's center.

Finding the trailhead: *From the junction of NC 111 and NC 55 near Seven Springs*, drive north on NC 111 for 2.3 miles to a right turn onto Park Entrance Road (SR 1743). Follow Park Entrance Road for 0.5 mile to the entrance to the park. Enter the park, and drive 0.1 mile to a right turn toward the "Lake Area" (just past the visitor's center). Travel for 0.2 mile to the end of the road.
From the junction of NC 111 and US 70 near Goldsboro, drive south on NC 111 for 8.3 miles to a left turn onto Park Entrance Road (SR 1743) and follow the directions above. GPS: N35 14.243'/W77 53.220'

The Hike

Cliffs of the Neuse State Park is not only popular for its namesake, the Neuse River, but also for the large lake that offers a multitude of recreational activities. A sandy beach and diving platform enhance the swimming area, and there's a boathouse where you can rent canoes, kayaks, stand-up paddleboards (SUP), and pedal boats. Private boats are not permitted. Open Memorial Day through Labor Day, a fee is required to enter this area. The large waterfront picnic area and Lake Trail are open year-round and free of charge. Fishing is limited to the river.

Keep your eyes peeled for colorful creatures like this blue-tailed skink.

The Lake Trail was newly cut in 2014 and is the park's longest. It begins as a wide roadlike path and follows a slow descent down to the water. During summertime you'll see people paddling around in kayaks, or keeping their balance on a SUP. The swim area is within view, but dogs aren't allowed. They can enjoy the lakeshore, though, as you follow it south toward Mill Creek. The creek forms a small spillway. Stepping stones keep your feet dry, while the puppies traipse right across. Let them play around here, because the next tributary is at 0.7 mile.

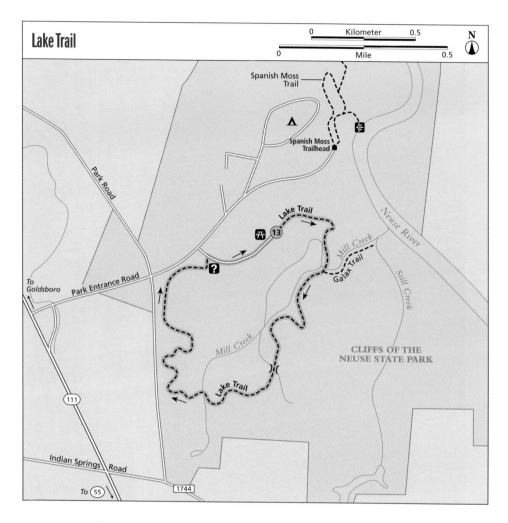

0   Kilometer   0.5

0   Mile   0.5

N

Spanish Moss Trail

Spanish Moss Trailhead

Park Road

Lake Trail

13

?

Lake Trail

To Goldsboro

Park Entrance Road

Neuse River

Mill Creek

Galax Trail

Still Creek

Mill Creek

CLIFFS OF THE NEUSE STATE PARK

Lake Trail

111

Indian Springs Road

To 55

1744

Immediately after crossing the creek, hike straight across the Galax Trail too. The Lake Trail begins to loosely circle the lake, and you can hear families frolicking near the lake. A gentle breeze urges you on a long climb, and when you reach the top of the hill, the trail stands high above the lake. You'll catch glimpses of the water here and there, but a forest of trees separates you from it. There are no blazes, but the path is easy to follow. At 0.7 mile you'll cross a footbridge over a tiny tributary. Take advantage of this watering hole for the dogs. This is the only water for the remainder of the hike. That being said, bring lots of drinking water for you and the dogs.

The trail moves away from the lake and skirts the park's southern boundary before it swings back toward the park's visitor's center (VC). Virginia pine trees stand tall and straight amid a forest of holly, oak, maple, and poplar. The trail leads you across a service road and ends at the VC. This fantastic facility doubles as a museum and educational center, but only service dogs are allowed inside. Restrooms on the outside of the building are useful to top off your water. From the VC you could return the way you came, or finish by walking past it and down the park road to the trailhead. You'll also enjoy hiking the Spanish Moss Trail. It's more strenuous, but shorter, and leads to the river where you can view the cliffs of the Neuse River from below.

Miles and Directions

0.0 Follow the wide roadlike path north into the woods. It begins a long, slow descent and bends east.

0.25 Arrive alongside the lake, hike south along the shoreline.

0.3 Cross Mill Creek over stepping stones. Let the dogs play in the water before you cross the creek and come to a fork. The Galax Trail heads left (east). Stay right (south) on the Lake Trail.

0.7 Cross a footbridge over a tiny tributary. Continue hiking west and uphill.

1.25 Cross a park service road. Continue hiking north.

1.65 Arrive at the sidewalk in front of the visitor's center. Hike down the road to the lake area parking lot.

1.95 Arrive back at the trailhead.

Options: To shorten the hike, head down to Mill Creek, let the dogs play in the water, and then return to the trailhead. To lengthen the hike, when you reach the visitor's center backtrack to the trailhead.

Resting up: Best Western, 909 N. Spence Ave., Goldsboro; (919) 751–1999; two dogs up to 80 pounds each, pet fee per pet per night.

Econo Lodge, E. New Bern Rd., Kinston; (252) 527–4155; two dogs up to 50 pounds each, pet fee per pet per night.

Hampton Inn, 905 N. Spence Ave., Goldsboro; (919) 778–1800; two dogs any size, no fee.

Camping: Onsite.

Take advantage of the water breaks along the Lake Trail; they're infrequent.

Your canine companions will enjoy the sunset as much as you do.

Piedmont Region

As the mountains fade into foothills, and the coast blends into the center of the state, you'll find rolling-hill topography and sprawling farmland. From the capital city of Raleigh to the queen city of Charlotte, you can easily access the spectacular trails of the Piedmont. Explore the forested pinelands of Uwharrie National Forest or stroll through the structured gardens of the Greensboro Arboretum. Discover an astonishing variety of wildlife at the Bog Garden, or take a dip in Falls Lake. Whether you circle around Lake Lynn, or hike the banks of Badin Lake. An array of geese and ducks will greet you at one, while osprey nest and circle overhead at the other. Enjoy stunning sunsets and breathtaking views as you and your canine companions get out and delve into the delightful depths of North Carolina's Piedmont.

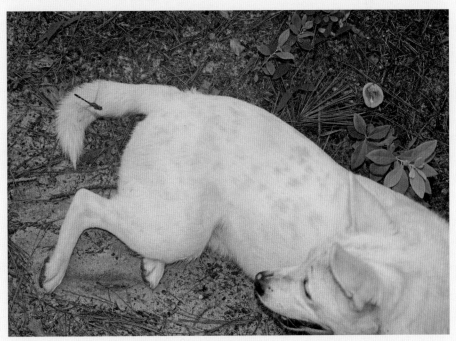

Bandit made a new friend with this curious dragonfly.

RALEIGH

14 Woodland Nature Trail

This fabulous forest stroll leads you on a self-guided hike around the loop. Brochures near the trailhead are filled with educational information that coincides with the numbered posts along the path. You'll learn about a variety of species within the woods, while this diverse forest keeps you shaded the entire way.

Start: Within the Sandling Beach section of Falls Lake State Recreation Area. The Woodland Nature Trail trailhead is on the east side of the road, across the road from the parking lot.
Distance: 0.75-mile loop
Hiking time: 30 minutes
Blaze color: None
Difficulty: Easy
Trailhead elevation: 284 feet
Highest point: 320 feet
Seasons: Open March 15 to November 1
Trail surface: Hard packed dirt
Other trail users: None
Canine compatibility: Leash required

Land status: North Carolina Department of Natural Resources
Fees and permits: None
Map: *DeLorme: North Carolina Atlas & Gazetteer*, page 40, A2
Trail contact: Falls Lake State Recreation Area; (919) 676-1027; www.ncparks.gov/Visit/parks/fala/main.php
Nearest town: Durham
Trail tips: Bring water for you and the dogs. Falls Lake is nearby, but there's no water crossings on the hike. Restrooms and a water fountain are located near the trailhead.

Finding the trailhead: *From the junction of NC 50 and NC 56 in Creedmoor,* drive south on NC 50 for 5.5 miles to a right at the sign for Sandling Beach. Travel for 0.7 mile to a left into the recreation area. Follow the road for approximately 0.3 mile to the parking lot on the right.

From the junction of NC 50 and NC 98, drive north on NC 50 for approximately 3.9 miles to a left at the sign for Sandling Beach and follow directions above. GPS: N36 02.098'/W78 42.372'

The Hike

Most people leave the hustle and bustle of the city and visit the recreation area for the sprawling 12,000-acre Falls Lake, but you'll be surprised to see how enjoyable it is to stay on dry land as well. The Woodland Nature Trail leads you through a wonderful wooded forest that's surprisingly diverse. Maple, oak, beech, hickory, poplar, and pine trees keep the trail shaded, and you can learn about them as you take the self-guided tour along this interpretive trail. Numbered posts guide you around the loop, and you can grab a brochure near the trailhead to follow along.

Benches placed here and there give you a place to enjoy this peaceful patch of forest in an area that's most widely appreciated by water. Although there are no watering

Sunsets are stunning on Falls Lake.

holes on this trail, Falls Lake is near the trailhead, so you can take the dogs for a dip before and after you hike. The only place you cannot swim the dogs is in the designated swimming area for people. With such close proximity to the lake, you certainly get the best of both worlds. The trail is closed in winter, but during spring and summer the wildflowers blossom, and in fall leaf peepers can enjoy the changing of the leaves. The Falls Lake State Recreation Area lies just outside Durham and minutes from Raleigh. With such easy access from the state's capital, it gets busy on weekends and in the summertime, but the Woodland Nature Trail doesn't see that much traffic.

The recreation area is divided into seven separate areas, each offering its own variety of outdoor opportunities. Several swim beaches and boat ramps make access to the water easy, and fishing is popular just about anywhere on the lake. If you prefer dry land, you can head across the street to mountain bike at Beaverdam. You can camp, enjoy the picnic areas, and get out and explore many miles of hiking trails. And the good news: Dogs are allowed on every one of them. For more information call (919) 676-1027, visit www.ncparks.gov/Visit/parks/fala/main.php, or stop in the visitor's center.

Miles and Directions

0.0 Hike northeast into the forest.

0.05 Arrive at a fork where the loop begins. Go right (southeast), hiking the loop counterclockwise, in numerical order.

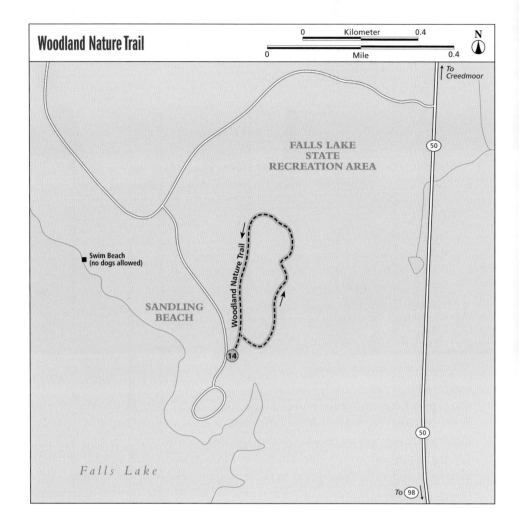

0.3 Climb up the steps, continue hiking north.

0.7 Arrive back at the fork where the loop began. Backtrack to the trailhead.

0.75 Arrive back at the trailhead.

Resting up: Comfort Inn & Suites Crabtree Valley, 6209 Glenwood Ave., Raleigh; (919) 782-1112; two dogs any size, pet fee per dog per night.

Days Inn Raleigh Crabtree, 6619 Glenwood Ave., Raleigh; (919) 782-8650; two dogs any size, pet fee per dog per night; pets cannot be left unattended in the room.

Extended Stay America Raleigh Crabtree Valley, 4810 Bluestone Dr., Raleigh; (919) 510-8551; two dogs any size, pet fee per dog per night.

Camping: Several campgrounds are located within Falls Lake State Recreation Area; (919) 676-1027; www.ncparks.gov/Visit/parks/fala/main.php.

North Carolina is home to a variety of birds of prey.

Fueling up: Boylan Bridge Brewpub, 201 S. Boylan Ave., Raleigh; (919) 803-8927; www.boylanbridge.com.

Bruster's Real Ice Cream, 10450 Durant Rd., Raleigh; (919) 844-1120.

Players Retreat, 105 Oberlin Rd., Raleigh; (919) 755-9589; www.playersretreat.net.

15 Lake Lynn Trail

Lake Lynn Park has so much to offer the residents of Raleigh. A community center, tennis, baseball, bocce, playgrounds, and the fabulous Lake Lynn Trail provide entertainment for locals and visitors alike. The trail makes a loop around Lake Lynn the entire way. A mix of pavement and boardwalk makes up the surface, and the trail is quite wooded and shady. Several swimming spots make this popular trail great for hiking with your hound. Sparsely placed benches give you a place to sit and enjoy the view.

Start: The Lake Lynn trailhead is at the southwest end of the parking lot.
Distance: 2.65-mile loop
Hiking time: 1 hour, 30 minutes
Blaze color: None
Difficulty: Easy to moderate
Trailhead elevation: 300 feet
Highest point: 340 feet
Seasons: Year-round
Trail surface: Paved path and wooden boardwalks
Other trail users: Bicycles and roller blades
Canine compatibility: Leash required

Land status: City of Raleigh Parks, Recreation, and Cultural Resources
Fees and permits: None
Map: *DeLorme: North Carolina Atlas & Gazetteer*, page 40, C2–C3
Trail contact: Lynn Lake Park, 7921 Ray Rd., Raleigh; (919) 870-2911; www.raleighnc.gov/parks/content/ParksRec/Articles/Parks/LakeLynn.html
Nearest town: Raleigh
Trail tips: Bring lots of drinking water. There are several spots for the dogs to take a dip in the water, but no drinking water available.

Finding the trailhead: *From the junction of NC 50 (Creedmoor Road) and US 70 in Raleigh,* drive north on NC 50 for 2.0 miles to a left onto Lynn Road. Travel for 0.6 mile to a right onto Ray Road. Follow Ray Road for 1.3 miles to the entrance to Lake Lynn Park on the left. Enter the park and travel for 0.1 mile to a stop sign near the Community Center. Go left here and travel for less than 0.1 mile to the parking lot for the Lake Lynn Trail.

From I-440 in Raleigh, get off at exit 7 (Glenwood Ave./US 70). Travel on US 70 west for 0.7 mile to a right onto NC 50, and follow directions above.

From I-540 in Raleigh, get off at exit 9 and drive south on NC 50 (Creedmoor Road) for approximately 1.6 miles to a right onto Howard Road. Travel for 0.6 mile to a right onto Ray Road. Travel for 0.5 mile to the entrance to Lake Lynn Park on the left. GPS: N35 53.247'/W78 41.892'

The Hike

The Raleigh region has far greater lakes, with the likes of Falls Lake and Jordan Lake, but the trail around Lake Lynn is still quite appealing. Easy to access, the path alternates between pavement and long stretches of boardwalk. Several swimming spots make this an ideal place to bring your pooch. Popular with the locals, there is a large variety of waterfowl.

The dogs enjoy taking a break on the levee at the south end of Lake Lynn.

As you hike around this wonderful waterway, you can hear the honking sound of geese echoing across the lake. Your dogs will stay busy sniffing out the ducks, squirrels, and the many other dogs marking the trail. This is by far the most urban and busy trail in this book, but it's still very enjoyable for you and the dogs. It's surprisingly wooded,

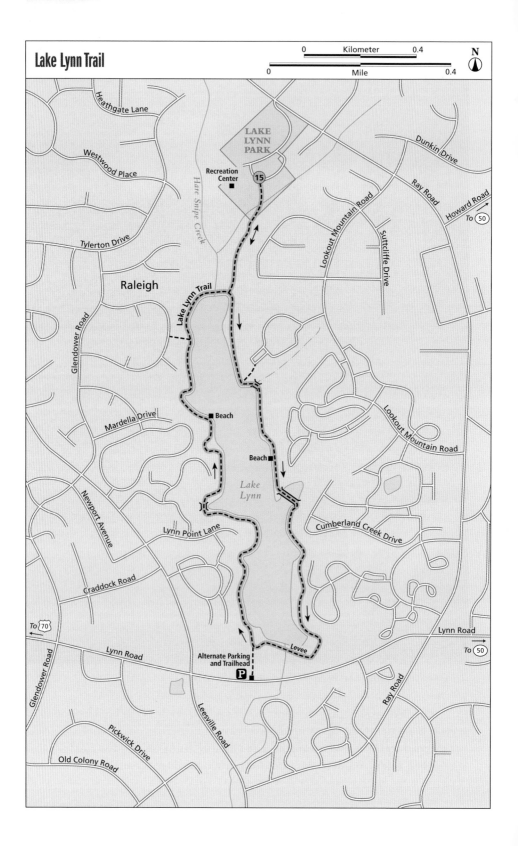

Lake Lynn Trail

Heathgate Lane

Westwood Place

Tylerton Drive

Raleigh

Glendower Road

Mardella Drive

Newport Avenue

Craddock Road

To 70

Glendower Road

Pickwick Drive

Old Colony Road

Lynn Road

Leesville Road

LAKE LYNN PARK

Recreation Center

15

Hare Snipe Creek

Lake Lynn Trail

Beach

Beach

Lake Lynn

Lynn Point Lane

Levee

Alternate Parking and Trailhead

P

Dunkin Drive

Ray Road

Howard Road

To 50

Lookout Mountain Road

Suttcliffe Drive

Lookout Mountain Road

Cumberland Creek Drive

Lynn Road

To 50

Ray Road

This family enjoys a leisurely stroll along the Lake Lynn Trail.

especially since it sits in the heart of the state's capital city. About a half a mile in, you reach a small gravel beach that makes a perfect puppy swimming hole.

As you continue around the lake, ducks greet you, insistently begging for food. Resist the temptation. You hike past many apartment complexes and houses, whose residents add to this hike's popularity. At the south end of the lake, you cross a levee, giving you the best view of the lake yet. After crossing the levee, you come to a T. The left leads to an alternate parking lot/trailhead off of Lynn Road. Go right, and the trail swings north as it loops back toward the trailhead.

The second half of the hike brings you past more apartments. You pass a few more swimming spots for the dogs, and you come to realize that each bird species has its own territory of Lake Lynn. More like gangs showing their colors, these flocks and gaggles have claimed their territory and seem to stand guard over it. Mallards meet you near the beginning of the loop, Canada geese hold the first footbridge, Muscovy ducks have their digs near the small dock, and more geese welcome you near the third footbridge. Take note of the small clay beach where locals keep their canoes and kayaks chained up. This a good spot for the dogs to easily enter and exit the water. Beyond this "beach" the trail leads you over two long boardwalks before you arrive at the fork where the loop began.

Miles and Directions

0.0 Hike south and downhill on the wide paved path.

0.25 Arrive at a fork in the boardwalk where the loop begins. Go left, and hike the loop clockwise.

0.45 Cross a footbridge, continue hiking south.

0.65 Pass a small gravel beach where the dogs enjoy a quick dip (N35 52.720'/W78 41.868').

0.75 Cross a footbridge, continue hiking generally south.

1.2 Hike west across a levee (N35 52.355'/W78 41.799').

1.3 Arrive at a T. The left leads south to an alternative parking area. Go right (north) as the trail loops back toward the trailhead.

1.45 A spur trail leads east about 75 feet down to a dock on the lake.

1.75 Cross a footbridge, continue hiking east.

2.05 Pass a small clay beach where locals keep canoes and kayaks chained up (N35 52.800'/ W78 42.013'). The dogs can easily access the water here.

2.1 Follow the long boardwalk generally north.

2.25 Follow a second long boardwalk north.

2.4 Arrive at the fork where you began the loop. Backtrack to the trailhead.

2.65 Arrive back at the trailhead.

Option: To shorten the hike, turn back at any time.

Resting up: Comfort Inn & Suites Crabtree Valley, 6209 Glenwood Ave., Raleigh; (919) 782-1112; two dogs any size, pet fee per dog per night.

Days Inn Raleigh Crabtree, 6619 Glenwood Ave., Raleigh; (919) 782-8650; two dogs any size, pet fee per dog per night, pets cannot be left unattended in the room.

Extended Stay America Raleigh Crabtree Valley, 4810 Bluestone Dr., Raleigh; (919) 510-855; two dogs any size, pet fee per dog per night.

Camping: William B. Umstead State Park Campground.

Fueling up: Boylan Bridge Brewpub, 201 S. Boylan Ave., Raleigh; (919) 803-8927; www.boylanbridge.com.

Bruster's Real Ice Cream, 10450 Durant Rd., Raleigh; (919) 844-1120.

Players Retreat, 105 Oberlin Rd., Raleigh; (919) 755-9589; www.playersretreat.net.

A variety of geese and ducks reside on Lake Lynn.

16 Pott's Branch Trail

Within the heart of the capital city of Raleigh, William B. Umstead State Park has lots to offer. With 20 miles of trails, your options are endless, but the Pott's Branch Trail is thoroughly enjoyable. The wooded path briskly leads you downhill and out to a little point alongside Pott's Branch. This is the first of several swimming holes where the dogs have a blast romping around in the rocky creek. The trail follows the creek upstream, before looping back through the picnic area where you began.

Start: Begin at the Sycamore trailhead at the southeast end of the parking lot. Follow the paved path south into the picnic area, and you'll immediately see the Pott's Branch trailhead on your right.
Distance: 1.3-mile loop
Hiking time: 50 minutes
Blaze color: Orange
Difficulty: Easy to moderate
Trailhead elevation: 333 feet
Highest point: 429 feet
Seasons: Year-round. December–February, 7:00 a.m.–6:00 p.m.; November, 7:00 a.m.–7:00 p.m.; March, April, September, October, 7:00 a.m.–8:00 p.m.; May–August, 7:00 a.m.–9:00 p.m. Closed Christmas Day.
Trail surface: Hard-packed dirt
Other trail users: Trail runners

Canine compatibility: Leash required
Land status: North Carolina Department of Natural Resources
Fees and permits: None
Map: *DeLorme: North Carolina Atlas & Gazetteer*, page 40, C2
Trail contact: William B. Umstead State Park, 8801 Glenwood Ave., Raleigh; (919) 571-4170; www.ncparks.gov/Visit/parks/wium/main.php
Nearest town: Raleigh
Trail tips: Take advantage of the watering holes and bring a towel to dry the dogs off afterward. Picnic tables and trash cans are located near the trailhead. Restrooms are 0.2 mile north of the trailhead. Trail maps are available at the visitor's center.

Finding the trailhead: *From I-440 in Raleigh,* get off at exit 7 and drive north on US 70 for approximately 5.8 miles to the entrance to the park on the left. Follow the park road for 1.8 miles to the end of the road.
From I-540 in Raleigh, get off at exit 4 and drive south on US 70 for 1.4 miles to the entrance to the park on the right. Follow the directions above. GPS: N35 52.294'/W78 45.662'

The Hike

With easy access to both Raleigh and Durham, William B. Umstead Park is a diamond in the rough. This surprisingly nice patch of forest encompasses more than 5,500 acres and is made up of wooded rolling hills. The park has trails for hiking, biking, and horseback. The campground offers wooded sites and makes a nice retreat from the busy city around it. A trio of man-made lakes give you options for fishing or paddling, and several creeks wind through the park, including Pott's Branch. The

Pott's Branch Trail, and its counterpart Sal's Branch, are preferred for hiking with your four-legged friend.

The hike begins in a large picnic area and immediately heads downhill. When you reach the bottom, head left and follow the creek east. The banks here are too steep to let the dogs play in the water, but not to worry. You'll quickly reach a fantastic flat, open area where Pott's Branch meets the creek you were following. This little point is a perfect place to let the dogs run, swim, and get some energy out. After they've had their fun, follow the trail upstream and uphill.

As you continue hiking north alongside Pott's Branch, you pass a few more places where the dogs can dip their paws in the rocky creek. You also cross a few footbridges and come to an intersection with the blue-blazed Sycamore Trail. Hike straight across, and again you reach another

Bracket fungi forms a row of "shelves" on the base of this oak tree.

fantastic place for the dogs to frolic and splash about in Pott's Branch. Small rocky ledges form cascades near this swimming hole, and the sound of rushing water fills the air. When you reach a stone wall, the trail heads away from the creek. You pass a large wooden overlook and come to a T at a paved path. Ignore the orange blazes to the right, and go left (south) on the pavement. After passing the restrooms the trail splits and circles around the picnic area. Go right (south), and you quickly arrive back at the trailhead. If you'd like to spend more time in the park, explore the Sal's Branch Trail. It's a moderate 2.8-mile hike that also follows the creek and a portion of Big Lake. The trailhead is behind the visitor's center.

Miles and Directions

0.0 Follow the paved path into the picnic area. You immediately come to a T with a paved path. Go right (south) on the pavement.

200' Arrive at the Pott's Branch trailhead on your right (N35 52.175' / W78 45.547'). Follow the dirt path south into the woods.

0.25 Come to a T at a creek that runs between Big Lake and Sycamore Lake. Go left (east) and hike downstream.

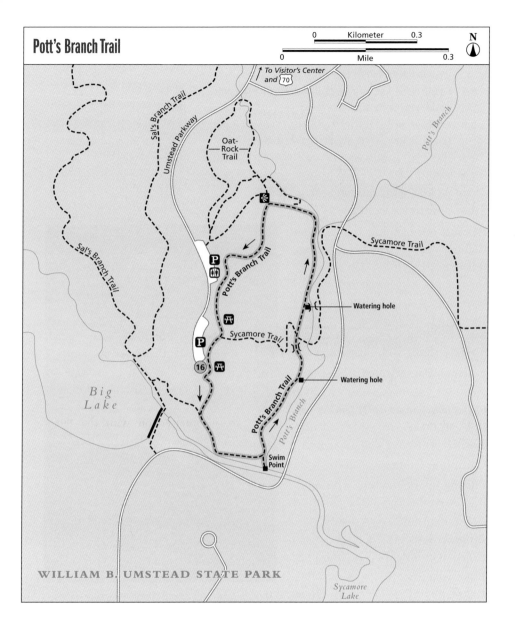

Pott's Branch Trail

0   Kilometer   0.3

N

0   Mile   0.3

To Visitor's Center
and 70

Sal's Branch Trail

Umstead Parkway

Oat-
Rock
Trail

Sycamore Trail

Sal's Branch Trail

Pott's Branch Trail

P

Watering hole

Sycamore Trail

Big
Lake

16

P

Pott's Branch Trail

Watering hole

Pott's Branch

Swim
Point

WILLIAM B. UMSTEAD STATE PARK

Sycamore
Lake

0.3 Come to another T at Pott's Branch. Go right (south) out onto a small point. The dogs can run and play in the water here. Return to the T and hike the other way (north) alongside the creek.

0.5 Enjoy a wonderful watering hole in the creek, and then cross a footbridge. Continue hiking north.

0.55 Cross a tiny footbridge, continue hiking north.

0.58 Hike across the Sycamore Trail. Continue following the orange blazes northeast.

0.6 Cross a footbridge over a gully, continue hiking northeast.

0.65 Come to another watering hole. This is the best spot yet for the dogs to splash in the creek. Continue hiking upstream and north.

0.8 Pass a stone wall as the trail climbs, bends left (northwest), and moves away from the creek.

0.9 Hike past an overlook and arrive at a T. The right is the Oak Rock Trail. Go left (south) on the pavement.

1.1 Hike past the restrooms.

1.2 Arrive at a fork that splits and circles around the picnic area. Go right (southwest) on the paved path.

1.3 Arrive back at the trailhead.

▶ **PUPPY PAWS AND GOLDEN YEARS: The large shady picnic area near the trailhead has a paved path that circles it. The dogs can enjoy sniffing around the picnic ground.**

Resting up: Comfort Inn & Suites Crabtree Valley, 6209 Glenwood Ave., Raleigh; (919) 782-1112; two dogs any size, pet fee per dog per night.

Days Inn Raleigh Crabtree, 6619 Glenwood Ave., Raleigh; (919) 782-8650; two dogs any size, pet fee per dog per night, pets cannot be left unattended in the room.

Extended Stay America Raleigh Crabtree Valley, 4810 Bluestone Dr., Raleigh; (919) 510-8551; two dogs any size, pet fee per dog per night.

Camping: Onsite.

Fueling up: Boylan Bridge Brewpub, 201 S. Boylan Ave., Raleigh; (919) 803-8927; www.boylanbridge.com.

Bruster's Real Ice Cream, 10450 Durant Rd., Raleigh; (919) 844-1120.

Players Retreat, 105 Oberlin Rd., Raleigh; (919) 755-9589; www.players retreat.net.

This chocolate lab, Diesel, thoroughly enjoyed the watering holes along the Pott's Branch Trail.

GREENSBORO

17 Woodland Trail

The town of Greensboro has outdone itself. The arboretum is one of several wonderful, dog-friendly gardens within the city limits. Gazebos, fountains, arbors, and artwork all add to the scenery as you follow the paved Woodland Trail through this spectacular greenway. While you explore the gardens, fragrances from the flowers and beautiful blossoms greet you at every turn. Bring a camera, and enjoy a leisurely stroll in this wonderful urban oasis.

Start: At the main entrance to the Greensboro Arboretum on Ashland Drive
Distance: 1.3-miles out and back
Hiking time: 40 minutes
Blaze color: None
Difficulty: Easy
Trailhead elevation: 738 feet
Highest point: 813 feet
Seasons: Year-round. May–August, 8:00 a.m.–8:00 p.m.; September, October, March, April, 8:00 a.m.–7:00 p.m.; November–February, 8:00 a.m.–5:00 p.m.
Trail surface: Paved path
Other trail users: Bicycles
Canine compatibility: Leash required

Land status: Greensboro Parks and Recreation Trails Division
Fees and permits: None
Map: *DeLorme: North Carolina Atlas & Gazetteer,* page 37, A8
Trail contacts: Greensboro Arboretum, 401 Ashland Dr., Greensboro; (336) 545-5961. Greensboro Beautiful; (336) 373-2199; www .greensborobeautiful.org.
Nearest town: Greensboro
Trail tips: There's a water fountain with a dog bowl at both ends of the trail, but bring water for the dogs along the way as well. A trash can and a stand with bags is found at 0.4 mile. A trail map and restrooms are located near the trailhead.

Finding the trailhead: *From I-40 in Greensboro,* get off at exit 214 and follow Wendover Avenue (US 70) northwest for 2.4 miles to a left onto South Holden Road. Travel for less than 0.1 mile to a right onto Ashland Drive. Travel for 0.3 mile to a stop sign at Walker Avenue. Drive straight across and drive less than 0.1 mile to a parking lot on the left.
   From the junction of US 70 (West Wendover Avenue) and US 220 in Greensboro, drive west on US 70 for approximately 3.0 miles to a right onto South Holden Road, and follow directions above. GPS: N36 04.200'/W79 50.543'

The Hike

With a name like the Woodland Trail, you'd expect this to be a narrow, dirt, hiking trail deep in the forest. On the contrary, this wide paved path is found in the heart of Greensboro. The trail leads through the glorious gardens of the Greensboro Arboretum. Showy blossoms, flowing fountains, and sculpted artwork add beauty to this

The Greensboro Arboretum is full of showy blossoms.

serene setting. The second you pass through the marvelous arched entrance you leave the hustle and bustle behind and enter a peaceful oasis.

The trail begins near the Education Center Building, and you immediately come to a fork. The Woodland Trail leads straight ahead, but I recommend strolling around every ounce of these gorgeous gardens. Go right (south) at the fork, and pass a water fountain with a dog bowl attached. As you begin exploring the greenway, benches, flowering plants, open lawns, arbors, and gazebos greet you. You can see why people host their weddings here. This short side trail crosses a few footbridges and then loops back onto the Woodland Trail.

Although there are massive powerlines and the highway passing by, you're in such a peaceful place, the beauty of the gardens outweighs any sounds from the city.

▶ **PUPPY PAWS AND GOLDEN YEARS: Visit the neighboring Bog Garden (hike 18) and Bicentennial Garden.**

The trail begins to follow a tiny creek, and several side paths lead to individual gardens. It's worth it to wander among the astonishing variety of trees, plants, and flowers that flourish here. Benches and trash cans are dispersed along the pathway, and trees are marked with small plaques so you can identify them. A footbridge to the right crosses the creek and leads to the Kaplan Family Rose Garden. This is a nice little side trip.

When the blooming bushes are full of rosebuds, they smell delicious! Please don't let your puppies pee on any of the plants in the arboretum. As the Woodland Trail makes a hard bend to the left, you'll see an alternate entrance and a stand with bags for doggy waste.

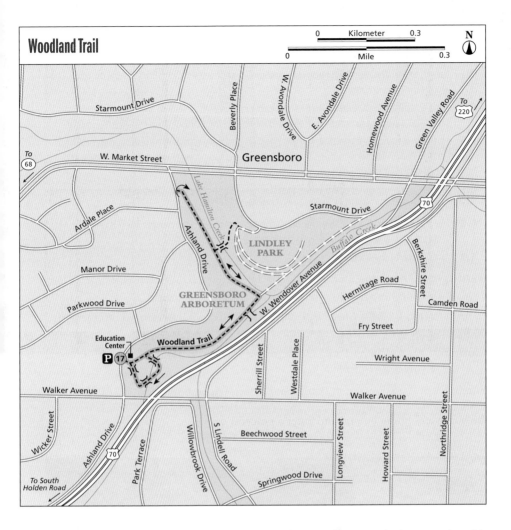

The trail now leads northwest alongside Lake Hamilton Creek. As you enjoy this leisurely stroll, you may hear the crack of a bat from the adjoining Lindley Park that sits on the other side of the creek. A pair of footbridges leads across the creek, so visitors can easily get from one park to the other. An abundance of trees offer shade. Take advantage of this, keeping the dogs cool while you stop to snap photos of the flora. Remember to bring drinking water for you both, as the only water fountains are the ends of the trail. The hike isn't long, but you may get carried away looking at the foliage, so it takes longer than it typically would. The trail comes to an abrupt end at Ashland Drive about 0.4 mile from where you parked.

Miles and Directions

0.0 Enter the arboretum and immediately come to a fork. Straight ahead leads east on the Woodland Trail. I recommend going right (south) and taking a detour around a small loop through some gardens. This route crosses three footbridges and brings you back to the Woodland Trail.

0.1 Return to the Woodland Trail from the detour. Go right (east) and follow the paved path alongside Buffalo Creek.

0.35 Pass a footbridge that leads right (southeast) and over the creek to the Kaplan Rose Garden. After stopping to smell the flowers, continue hiking northeast on the Woodland Trail.

0.4 As the trail bends left (northwest), you pass an alternate entryway into the arboretum from Lindley Park. A stand with bags to pick up after your dog is near this entrance. Follow the paved path left (northwest).

0.5 Bypass a footbridge over the creek that connects to Lindley Park. Continue hiking northwest.

0.65 The trail ends at Ashland Drive, about 0.4 mile from where you parked. There's a water fountain with a dog bowl here. Backtrack to the trailhead.

1.3 Arrive back at the trailhead.

Resting up: Drury Inn and Suites, 3220 High Point Rd., Greensboro; (336) 856-9696; www.druryhotels.com; two dogs any size, pet fee per night.

La Quinta Hotel, 1201 Canada Rd., Greensboro; (336) 316-0100; two dogs any size, no fee.

Camping: Hagen-Stone Park Campground; (336) 674-0472; www.greensboro-nc .gov/index.aspx?page=1193.

Fueling up: Brass Taps, 2506 Battleground Ave., Greensboro; (336) 570-6950.

Fishers Grille, 608 N. Elm St., (336) 275-8300.

Natty Green's Pub, 345 S. Elm St., Greensboro; (336) 274-1373.

Even the moths stop and smell the flowers in the Greensboro Arboretum.

18 Bog Garden Trail

Nestled in a neighborhood within the town of Greensboro is this amazing little piece of paradise. The heavily wooded area is more like a forest than a garden, but either way, it's remarkable and among my favorites. Wildlife and birdlife are abundant, and the variety of trees is phenomenal. Stunning views of a small lake are obtained from an overlook, and benches are built into the boardwalk so you can take it all in.

Start: The trailhead is off of Starmount Farms Drive.
Distance: 0.5-mile double loop
Hiking time: 20 minutes
Blaze color: None
Difficulty: Easy
Trailhead elevation: 816 feet
Highest point: 825 feet
Seasons: Year-round, sunrise to sunset
Trail surface: Boardwalk, sidewalk, hard-packed dirt
Other trail users: None
Canine compatibility: Leash required

Land status: Greensboro Parks and Recreation Trails Division
Fees and permits: None
Map: *DeLorme: North Carolina Atlas & Gazetteer*, page 37, A8
Trail contacts: Bog Garden, 1101 Hobbs Rd., Greensboro; (336) 545-5961. Greensboro Beautiful; (336) 373-2199; www.greensboro beautiful.org.
Nearest town: Greensboro
Trail tips: Trash cans are near the trailhead. There is no drinking water along the path. Bring a camera!

Finding the trailhead: *From I-40 in Greensboro*, get off at exit 214 and follow Wendover Avenue (US 70) northwest for 2.4 miles to a left onto Holden Road. Travel for 2.0 miles to a right onto Cornwallis Drive. Travel for 0.1 mile to a right onto Hobbs Road. Travel for 0.15 miles to a left onto Starmount Farms Drive. Park along the side of the road. The Bog Garden is on the corner of Starmount Farms Drive and Hobbs Road.
From the junction of Cornwallis Drive and US 220 in Greensboro, drive west on Cornwallis Drive for approximately 1.4 miles to a left onto Hobbs Road and follow directions above. GPS: N36 05.486'/W79 50.404'

The Hike

The Bog Garden Trail begins as a wide cement path and enters a thick, dense forested area that keeps you shaded the entire hike. Paths weave throughout this wonderful wooded nature preserve, so it's easy to get turned around. However, the area is small, so if you do get mixed up, you'll quickly regain your bearings.

This compact patch of forest truly is a hidden gem. Wildlife is abundant, and the property is a designated bird sanctuary. You may even spy the family of barred owls that has taken up residence here. A tiny creek runs through the property and leads out to a lovely lake. The creek is muddy, but you'll still see beautiful mallards swimming about, hoping a passerby will throw them a scrap. Please **do not** feed the ducks, or any

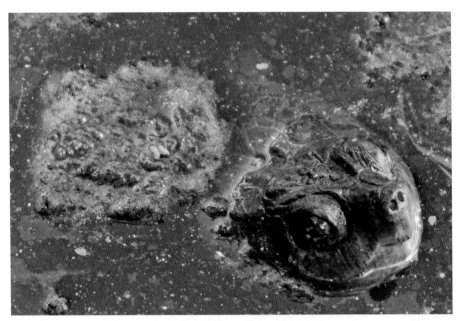

This friendly fellow lives in Greensboro's Bog Garden.

wildlife, including the adorable chipmunks. Feeding wildlife makes them dependent on people for food. Also, they cannot digest many types of "people food." The more often a wild animal associates people with food, the more likely they are to lose their fear, and they may end up biting someone. The bog itself provides plenty of food for all the wonderful creatures that live within it.

This preserve is a naturalist's dream. Although it's slight in size, the diversity of plant, animal, and birdlife is extraordinary. To protect these residents it's *imperative* that you keep your dogs on a leash *at all times*. Begin by bypassing a footbridge on the right, and hike south onto the wooden boardwalk. There's an impressive diversity of trees, but it's less structured than the neighboring Bicentennial Gardens or Greensboro Arboretum. There are no placards to tell you what's what, but bamboo, sycamore, and white oak are just a few. The boardwalk leads to a fantastic overlook with built-in benches to give you a stunning view of Starmount Farms Lake, especially at sunrise and sunset. You may see a soft-shell turtle, frogs, or a variety of wading birds as you take in the scenery. The boardwalk then swings around and leads you to a fork. You can follow the boardwalk, which cuts the loop in half and leads back toward the trailhead. Or you can follow the gravel path to a beautiful man-made waterfall. Beyond Serenity Falls the path climbs over an area known as "Melvin's Mountain." This stretch of trail parallels Northline Avenue, but the sound of frogs, crickets, birds, and nature drowns out the traffic.

▷ **PUPPY PAWS AND GOLDEN YEARS: Visit the neighboring Greensboro Arboretum (hike 17) and Bicentennial Gardens.**

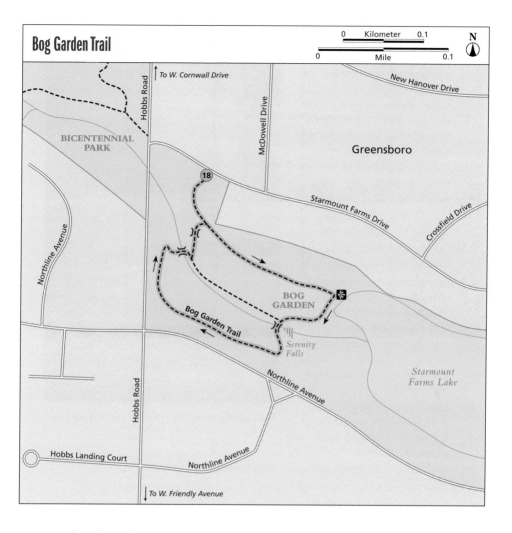

Bog Garden Trail

After descending back into the bog, you cross a footbridge and come to a T at a sidewalk. The right leads to the boardwalk that shortcuts through the bog. This is where you come out if you don't follow the trail over Melvin's Mountain. This boardwalk is also where you may see cute little chipmunks that reside here. To reach the trailhead go left and cross another footbridge. This is the one you bypassed at the beginning of the hike. Head left and return the trailhead.

Miles and Directions

0.0   Enter the garden off Starmount Farms Drive by walking west down the wide cement path.

0.1   Bypass a footbridge on the right (south). This is where the loop begins. Hike straight ahead (southeast) into the Bog Garden.

0.15 Arrive at an overlook of Starmount Farms Lake (N36 05.413'/W79 50.301'). Take a moment to enjoy the scenery. Hike southwest on the boardwalk.

0.2   Come to a fork. Straight ahead is a boardwalk that cuts through the middle of the bog and bisects the loop, splitting it into two loops. To shorten the hike, follow this boardwalk west. The left fork is a gravel trail that leaves the boardwalk and leads south toward a tiny creek. This is a perfect place for the pups to dip their paws.

0.22 Arrive at the base of Serenity Falls (N36 05.381'/W79 50.345'). Continue hiking past the falls.

0.25 Cross an ornamental footbridge. Continue hiking west uphill.

0.3   Pass an impressively large tree up on Melvin's Mountain (N36 05.403'/W79 50.427'). Immediately after the tree, pass a set of steps that lead to Hobbs Road. Continue hiking north down back-to-back stone steps that lead you back into the bog.

0.4   Cross a stone bridge and arrive at a fork. The right (southeast) is where you'd come out if you

Enjoying the view along the Bog Garden Trail.

skipped the dirt section and took the boardwalk shortcut. Chipmunks and a variety of birds frequent this section of the "trail." Go left (north) toward the trailhead.

0.42 Cross the footbridge you bypassed when you began the hike and arrive at a T. Go left (northwest) toward the trailhead.

0.5   Arrive back at the trailhead.

Resting up: Drury Inn and Suites, 3220 High Point Rd., Greensboro; (336) 856-9696; www.druryhotels.com; two dogs any size, pet fee per night.

La Quinta Hotel, 1201 Canada Rd., Greensboro; (336) 316-0100; two dogs any size, no fee.

Camping: Hagen-Stone Park Campground; (336) 674-0472; www.greensboro-nc.gov/index.aspx?page=1193.

Fueling up: Brass Taps, 2506 Battleground Ave., Greensboro; (336) 570-6950.

Fishers Grille, 608 N. Elm St.; (336) 275-8300.

Natty Green's Pub, 345 S. Elm St., Greensboro; (336) 274-1373.

TROY

19 Badin Lake Trail

Within the Uwharrie National Forest this is the only trail dedicated solely to hikers. The other perk is that this lengthy loop trail gives you the best of both worlds. It keeps you near the shoreline while the forest protects you from the sun's rays. The trail is easy to follow, and there are several swimming holes where both you and the dogs can enjoy a refreshing dip in the inviting Badin Lake.

Start: The Badin Lake trailheads are located in the parking lot for King's Mountain Point Day Use Area. The northern trailhead (clockwise) is at the northeast corner of the parking lot. The southern trailhead (counterclockwise) is at the southeast corner of the parking lot. The trail is described in a clockwise fashion, using the northern trailhead.

Distance: 5.4-mile loop

Hiking time: 3 hours

Blaze color: White

Difficulty: Easy

Trailhead elevation: 526 feet

Highest point: 644 feet

Seasons: Year-round

Trail surface: Hard-packed dirt, some rocky sections, rooty sections

Other trail users: None

Canine compatibility: Voice control

Land status: Uwharrie National Forest– Uwharrie Ranger District

Fees and permits: None

Map: *DeLorme: North Carolina Atlas & Gazetteer*, page 59, B6

Trail contact: Badin Lake Recreation Area; (910) 576-6391; www.fs.usda .gov/recarea/nfsnc/recreation/hiking/ recarea/?recid=49084&actid=50

Nearest towns: Troy and Albemarle

Trail tips: You may want to stop at the ranger station in Troy and purchase a map prior to hiking. Or you can print one from a pdf. The link is: www.fs.usda.gov/Internet/FSE_DOCUMENTS/ stelprdb5366057.pdf. Drinking water is found within the two campgrounds that you hike past. The campgrounds are at 3.05 and 4.6 miles, so bring lots of water along for you and the pooches.

Finding the trailhead: *From the junction of NC 109 and NC 24/NC 27 in Troy*, drive north on NC 109 for 10.6 miles to a left onto Mullinix Road (SR 1154). Travel for 1.5 miles to a where it ends at a T at FR 544 (McLeans Creek Road). Go right onto FR 544 and travel for 1.6 miles to where the road ends at FR 597 (Badin Lake Road). Turn right onto FR 597 and follow it for 0.2 mile to a fork. Go left at the fork onto FR597A. Follow FR 597A for 0.5 mile and you come to another fork. Go right at the fork and travel for 0.8 mile to the King's Mountain Point Day Use Area.

From the junction of NC 109 and NC 49 near Denton, drive south on NC 109 for approximately 8.4 miles to a right onto Mullinix Road (SR 1154) and follow the directions above. GPS: N35 27.255'/W80 04.782'

The Hike

The Badin Lake Trail closely follows the shoreline, with the exception of a 2.0-mile stretch in the middle of the hike that cuts through the forest. I recommend hiking the loop clockwise as is described. This gets you through the wooded portion and back to the waterfront faster. As you follow the trail north, you may pass a random person fishing, or see osprey soaring overhead, both hoping to make the catch of the day. The breeze is delightful, and at 0.3 mile you cross a small rocky bluff. The birds singing and the buzz from the occasional boat is all you hear. At 0.75 mile you pass a primitive campsite with a fire ring. This is a nice spot to let the dogs cool off in the water. Beyond the campsite take note of the stark-white quartz rock jutting out of the dirt path. At 0.8 mile you reach "the point," where the peninsula you've been hiking on literally juts out into Badin Lake. A little sandy beach offers great access for you and the dogs to take a dip and the views are fantastic.

Unfortunately this area also has a lot of litter. I *urge* you, please, to pack it in, pack it out. Hike around the point, and the trail leads south into a deep cove that's popular with boaters. As they pass by, waves lap on the shoreline. The sound of the pseudo-surf breaking on the shore drowns out any other, until the water settles back into silent stillness. About a third of the way into the cove, you pass some primitive campsites that are great for another dip in the lake. Beyond the campsites the trail gets a little confusing because there are many "social" trails coming and going from the woods to the water. As long as you stay near the water's edge, you'll soon pick up the white blazes again. As the cove narrows, you see houses across from you. This is your indication that the trail is about to leave the lake and head into the forest for the next 2.0 miles. Let the dogs swim one last time before continuing south. You come to two forks before reaching the forested part of the path. Stay left and with the water at both. The right leads up to the group camp.

▶ **PUPPY PAWS AND GOLDEN YEARS: Dogs of all ages enjoy King's Mountain Point. There's a large grassy field with plenty of room to let them run and play. Another option is to drive to the Cove Boat Ramp. The grassy banks near the boat ramp have an easy grade for the dogs to wade out into the water and simply enjoy the outdoors.**

The trail now follows a dried-up creek bed and crosses it. As you delve into the Uwharrie National Forest, the air seems cooler than you'd expect, even in summertime. You may see white-tail deer before they spook and run away, waving their white tails like a flag of surrender. Continue generally south through the forest and you cross a few forest roads and other trails. When you finally reach the Arrowhead Campground, it gives you hope that the lake is nearby. You can refill your water from spigots in the campground. When the lake comes into view, the trail leads down to the Cove Boat Ramp. To the right of the ramp, follow the sidewalk north. When it ends, the white-blazed trail continues north. Green grassy banks near the peaceful cove make this an

Badin Lake is simply stunning.

ideal place to let the dogs take a refreshing break by the water. When you resume, the remainder of the hike follows the water's edge north, and you'll pass a few good spots for the dogs to splash about. When you reach Badin Lake Campground, hike across the entrance road, unless you need to top your water off. Along the final leg of the trek the lake is more populated than before. Distracted by the boaters, and enjoying a gentle breeze, before you know it you arrive back at the trailhead.

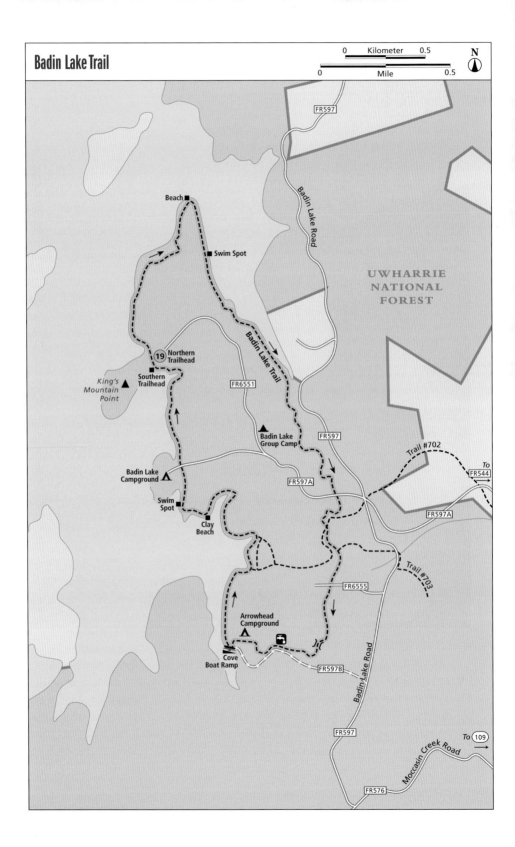

Badin Lake Trail

Kilometer 0.5

Mile 0.5

N

FR597

Badin Lake Road

UWHARRIE NATIONAL FOREST

Beach

Swim Spot

Badin Lake Trail

19 Northern Trailhead

King's Mountain Point

Southern Trailhead

FR6551

Badin Lake Group Camp

FR597

Trail #702

To FR544

Badin Lake Campground

FR597A

Swim Spot

Clay Beach

FR597A

Trail #703

FR6555

Arrowhead Campground

Cove Boat Ramp

FR597B

Badin Lake Road

FR597

Moccasin Creek Road

To 109

FR576

The Uwharrie National Forest has a multitude of camping opportunities.

Miles and Directions

0.0 From the northern trailhead, hike north into the woods following the shoreline of Lake Badin.

0.3 Cross a small rocky bluff, continue hiking northwest.

0.7 Pass a primitive campsite, continue hiking northwest.

0.8 Arrive at the sandy beach at the "point." This is a great place to let the dogs run, swim, and play. Continue hiking around the point and south.

Option: Return to the trailhead making this a 1.6-mile waterfront hike.

1.1 Pass some primitive campsites. Bypass the footpaths leading to and from the campsites and follow the shoreline south. There are some great swimming holes for the pups near here.

1.65 Arrive at a fork with some arrows painted on a rock. The right leads uphill southwest. Stay left and follow the water southeast.

1.75 Come to another fork with orange blazes leading west and uphill toward the group camp. Stay left (southeast) and downhill.

1.85 Cross a dried-up creek, continue hiking south and uphill.

2.25 Cross FR 597A, continue hiking south.

2.4 Come to a T at Trail 702. Go right (southwest), and the Badin Lake Trail merges with Trail 702. After 50 feet the narrow Badin Lake Trail veers off to the left (southeast) and into the woods.

Keep your eyes peeled.

2.55 Cross Trail 703, continue hiking south.

2.7 Cross FR 6555, continue hiking south.

2.9 Cross a footbridge over a dried-up creek. Continue hiking southwest.

3.0 Cross FR 597B, continue hiking west.

3.05 Cross the road at the entrance to Arrowhead Campground. Refill your water if need be as you hike through the campground on a paved path.

3.1 Come to a fork inside the campground, stay left, skirting west around the campground.

3.25 Come to another fork inside the campground, again stay left (west) on the paved path.

3.28 Come to a third fork inside the campground, again go left (west) on a dirt path.

3.35 Badin Lake comes into view. Hike down a wide set of steps to the Cove Boat Ramp. To the right of the ramp, follow the sidewalk north. This is a great place to give the dogs a well-deserved water break.

3.4 The sidewalk ends, follow the shoreline and white blazes north.

4.35 Bypass a clay-bottomed beach, a better beach is 0.15 mile away. Continue following the shoreline west.

4.5 Arrive at a swimming spot where the dogs can access the water without sinking into the clay. Continue following the water's edge north.

4.6 Hike across FR 597A, near the Badin Lake Campground. Top off your water, if need be. Continue hiking north along the shoreline.

5.4 The trail ends at the southern trailhead.

Resting up: Quality Inn Albemarle, 735 Highway 24/27 Bypass, Albemarle; (704) 983-6990; two dogs up to 50 pounds each, pet fee per pet per night.

Sleep Inn and Suites, 621 Highway 24/27 Bypass, Albemarle; (704) 983-2770; two dogs any size, pet fee per pet per night.

Camping: Within Uwharrie National Forest—Badin Lake Campground (no electric sites).

Arrowhead Campground (with electric sites). Canebrake Horse Camp (with electric sites).

October is spectacular for leaf peeping in the mountains of North Carolina.

Mountains Region

Peaceful valleys, breathtaking views, and towering trees greet you as you venture out to explore the magnificent mountains of North Carolina. With two national parks, two national forests, and countless state parks, this region really packs a punch! You can hike to the foot of Looking Glass Rock or to the summit of Stone Mountain. If you prefer a leisurely walk around Bass Lake, or a trip to Panthertown Valley, you and your four-legged friends are sure to enjoy some of the best hiking in the state. Take a scenic drive on the Blue Ridge Parkway or a subtle stroll through the gardens of the North Carolina Arboretum. Miles of trails traverse the western part of the state, just waiting for you to explore. Wildlife ranges from elk to owls and from beavers to bears. There are small mountain lakes like Cliffside and Bass, and the vast expanses of Lake Norman, Wylie, and James. This region has raging rivers to passive creeks. You can discover dozens of waterfalls as the crystal clear water of creek after creek flows freely down the mountainside. Lead your dog to a sandy beach along the river or to a pristine swimming hole tucked away at the base of a waterfall. See the white squirrels of Brevard, natural landmarks, historic sites, and stunning summits. Hike along a gravel "carriage road," or delve deep into the Pisgah National Forest. The possibilities are endless, and with you at their side, your puppies' tails will be wagging every step of the way.

It doesn't get any clearer than this (hike 33).

CHARLOTTE

20 Cove Trail

Following the edge of a long, narrow cove on the eastern edge of Lake Wylie, you'll enjoy stunning views while the dogs have several opportunities to splash around in the clear green water.

Start: The Cove trailhead is at the far left (northwest) corner of the parking lot
Distance: 1.2-miles out and back
Hiking time: 35 minutes
Blaze color: Blue
Difficulty: Moderate
Trailhead elevation: 606 feet
Highest point: 663 feet
Seasons: Year-round, 7:00 a.m.–dark
Trail surface: Hard-packed dirt
Other trail users: None
Canine compatibility: Leash required
Land status: Mecklenburg County Parks and Recreation

Fees and permits: None
Map: *DeLorme: North Carolina Atlas & Gazetteer*, page 57, F5
Trail contact: McDowell Nature Preserve, 15222 York Rd., Charlotte; (704) 583-1284; www.charmeck.org/mecklenburg/county/ ParkandRec/StewardshipServices/Nature Preserves/Pages/McDowell.aspx
Nearest town: Charlotte
Trail tips: Take advantage of the swimming spots halfway along the hike. The trail follows the shoreline, but often from high above, so the pups can't just pop in the water at any given point.

Finding the trailhead: *From the junction of NC 49 and the NC/SC state line*, drive east on NC 49 for 1.0 mile to the entrance to McDowell Nature Preserve on your left. After entering the nature preserve, travel for 0.5 mile to a right turn on the road that leads to the nature center. Follow this road for 0.1 mile to the nature center and parking lot. From here continue following the road to the right toward the 4-Seasons Trail for 0.25 mile to the end of the road.

From the junction of NC 49 and NC 160 (Steel Creek Road), drive west on NC 49 and travel for 2.1 miles to McDowell Nature Preserve on your right. Follow the directions above. GPS: N35 06.106'/W81 01.033'

The Hike

At the southeastern edge of the queen city of Charlotte, and nestled along the banks of Lake Wylie, the McDowell Nature Preserve gets you back to nature without you ever leaving the city. Visitors enjoy a nature center, campground, fishing piers, picnicking, and playgrounds. With 8.0 miles of hiking and two boat ramps at Copperhead Island, there's something for everyone. Of those hiking trails, the Cove Trail closely follows the banks of Lake Wylie most of the way. Follow the hard-packed dirt trail northwest into the woods. The trail follows a slow-moving creek and then swings around a marshy area. As you begin a steep climb, tree roots act as stairs that

The dogs have fun digging in the sand alongside Lake Wylie.

Mother Nature made for you. At the crest of the climb you get views of the cove on Lake Wylie.

The trail soon brings you near the water's edge, but the water's a bit murky here. Wait a little farther down the trail to let the pups jump in. As you continue hiking, views of the lake open up as you pass below a picnic shelter. A pair of footbridges lead you right back out on the edge of the water. Between 0.3 and 0.4 mile of the hike, you see several fantastic swimming holes where the dogs can dip their paws and claws in the clear green water. The lake is a man-made reservoir that was formed in the early 1900s when a local power company dammed off the Catawba River to generate hydroelectric power. Today it's heavily used for outdoor recreation and forms a portion of the North and South Carolina border.

The trail now follows the water's edge from high above. The path is easy to follow and peaceful. With the exception of the occasional plane flying overhead, it certainly doesn't feel like you're hiking within the biggest city in the state. The trail continues to climb higher and higher above the lake and eventually moves away from the water, leading to the park road where it

▶ **PUPPY PAWS AND GOLDEN YEARS:** Shorten the hike by returning after the dogs cool off in Lake Wylie. Another option is the 4-Seasons Trail. The trailhead is at the northeast corner of the parking lot. This 0.4-mile paved path is handicap accessible and follows Porter Branch.

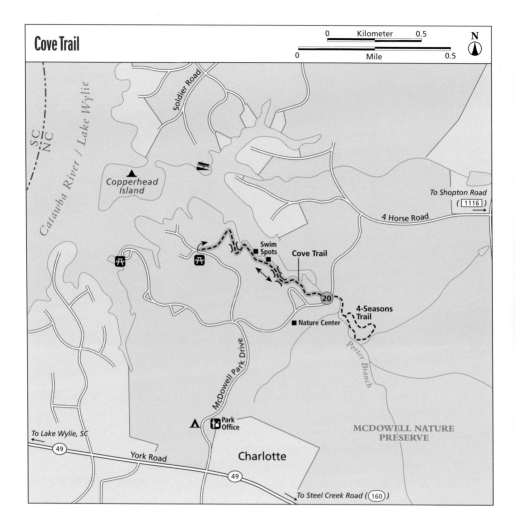

Cove Trail

abruptly ends. There's a wooded picnic area across from the trail's end if you want to enjoy a picnic. The trail offers shade the entire way, except in winter when the leaves have fallen. In spring, wildflowers greet you; in autumn, the full colors of fall are magnificent.

Miles and Directions

0.0 Hike northwest into the woods. The trail swings around a marshy area before climbing steeply.

0.2 Cross a footbridge, hike north toward the water.

0.23 Cross another footbridge, hike north toward the water.

0.3 Over the next 0.1 mile you pass several fantastic swimming spots for the dogs to splash around in Lake Wylie. Continue hiking northwest along the water.

0.45 Cross a tiny footbridge, continue hiking northwest.

The Cove Trail follows a long narrow cove of Lake Wylie.

0.6 The trail ends at the park road near a picnic area. Backtrack to the trailhead.

1.2 Arrive back at the trailhead.

Resting up: Double Tree Suites by Hilton, 6300 Morrison Blvd., Charlotte; (866) 676-3077.

La Quinta Hotel, 4900 Styron St., Charlotte; (800) 531-5900; two dogs up to 45 pounds, no fee.

Camping: Onsite.

Fueling up: Angry Ale's, 1518 Montford Dr., Charlotte; (704) 525-3663; www .angryales.com. Icehouse.

The Dog Bar, 3307 N. Davidson St., Charlotte; (704) 370-3595; www.dogbarcharlotte .com.

South End Bar & Grill, 2100 South Blvd., Charlotte; (704) 375-1128; www.icehouse charlotte.com.

MOORESVILLE TO STATESVILLE

21 Lake Shore Trail

Among my favorites, the Lake Shore Trail offers stunning views and gives the dogs ample opportunities to splash around in the clear green water of Lake Norman. The trail closely follows the water's edge most of the way around a peninsula that resembles the shape of a white oak leaf. Dipping in and out of small coves, you'll enjoy a gentle breeze from the lake, while a variety of trees shade you from the sun.

Start: At the southeast end of the parking area

Distance: 5.05-mile loop

Hiking time: 2.5 hours

Blaze color: White

Difficulty: Moderate

Trailhead elevation: 821 feet

Highest point: 846 feet

Seasons: Year-round. Trail hours—November–February, 8:00 a.m.–5:30 p.m.; March, April, September, October, 8:00 a.m.–7:30 p.m.; May–August, 8:00 a.m.–8:30 p.m. Closed Christmas Day.

Trail surface: Hard-packed dirt

Other trail users: None

Canine compatibility: Leash required

Land status: North Carolina Department of Natural Resources

Fees and permits: None

Map: *DeLorme: North Carolina Atlas & Gazetteer,* page 35, F6

Trail contact: Lake Norman State Park, 759 State Park Rd., Troutman; (704) 528-6350; www.ncparks.gov/Visit/parks/lano/main.php

Nearest town: Troutman

Trail tips: Grab a trail map from the kiosk near the trailhead. There are lots of swimming spots, and you can access drinking water by hiking the spur trails to the campground (0.6 mile) and group camp (3.9 miles). This is a long hike and the last mile is challenging. Bring lots of drinking water.

Special considerations: The gate near the trailhead closes one hour before the main park gate year-round. Make sure you're off the trail in time.

Finding the trailhead: *From I-77 in Mooresville,* travel north to exit 42 and get off onto US 21/NC 115. Drive north on US 21 for 2.8 miles to a left onto Wagner Street (SR 1303). Follow Wagner Street for 1.5 miles to a right onto State Park Road (SR 1321). Follow State Park Road for 2.1 miles to the entrance to the park. Enter the park and travel 2.9 miles to a left onto Shortleaf Drive. Travel 0.1 mile to a stop sign. Turn right, and the trail head is immediately on the left.

From I-77 in Statesville, travel south to exit 42 and get off onto US 21/NC 115. Drive north on US 21 and follow the directions above. GPS: N35 38.967'/W80 56.646'

The Hike

A trail map stands near the trailhead, and the park provides brochures so you can take one with you. The trail begins as a steep descent down to the level of the lakeshore and leads you to a fork. The left leg is the Short Turn Trail, which cuts the loop in half.

Sunsets are magnificent along Lake Norman.

If you want to short-cut the hike, it would come back out here. Go right (south), and within 0.1 mile you're greeted with fantastic views of Lake Norman. The trail juts in and out around small coves as it closely follows the shoreline. At 0.25 mile you come to the first of many beachy swimming areas where the dogs enjoy digging in the sand and wading in the water. The trail follows the lake, sometimes right beside it and other times from above. Shaded by the forest, the only sounds you hear are birds singing and the occasional hoot of an owl.

▶ **PUPPY PAWS AND GOLDEN YEARS: Drive to the park's group camp on Group Camp Lane. A spur trail leads down to one of the best swimming beaches on the lake. The dogs can play on the sand or wade out into the clear green water of Lake Norman.**

At 0.4 mile you pass a few spur trails that lead to the campground near a nice point in the lake. Continue following the water's edge, and you come to the best sandy beach you've seen yet. You can smell campfires in the air while the dogs romp around. An amazing contrast of color is created from the clear green water and clay earthen banks as the trail swings around one gorgeous cove after another. The trail repeatedly dips into the forest and then back out to the banks of the water as you hike around these little coves. Mile markers keep track of your progress, and benches give you a place to sit and enjoy the view. The trail is shaded and has a gentle breeze, but you still need to bring lots of drinking water.

You'll pass this fantastic root burl on the Lake Shore Trail.

Almost a mile from the last swim beach, you come to another splendid swimming hole. Deer, squirrels, birds, and bunnies are among the more common wildlife in the park. With the exception of these swimming holes, keep the dogs on a leash. At 2.6 miles you come to a fork. The Short Turn Trail leads left (southwest) back toward the first fork you encountered. This shortcut takes 2.0 miles off the hike. To follow the loop trail, continue straight ahead (north). Just past the 3.0-mile mark, cross a park road that leads to the boat launch. Over the next mile, the trail seems hillier and leads past a few more swimming spots. Take advantage of these water breaks, because the last mile of the trail leads away from the water, where it stays for the remainder of the hike. Just before reaching the 4.0-mile mark, bypass a spur trail that heads to the group camp and stay left cutting northwest across the peninsula. The climbs and descents now seem more dramatic and take more effort. Cross the park road once more, and the trail flattens, leading you back to the trailhead.

Miles and Directions

0.0 Hike down some steps and head southwest into the forest.

0.1 Cross a footbridge and come to a fork. The left (northwest) is the red-blazed Short Turn Trail. This is where you come back if you only hike the first half of the loop and return on the Short Turn Trail. Go right (east) toward the lake.

0.2 Cross a footbridge, follow the shoreline south.

0.25 Come to the first of several beachy areas that are perfect for the dogs to hop in the lake.

0.3 Cross a footbridge, continue hiking southwest.

0.4 Pass an obscure trail to the left (south), stay right, continue hiking west along Lake Norman.

0.5 Arrive at another swimming beach out on a lovely little point that juts into the lake. Continue hiking southwest.

0.55 Come to a fork where a red-blazed trail goes straight ahead (south) out to a point before looping back to the other side of the point. The white-blazed Lake Shore Trail heads left

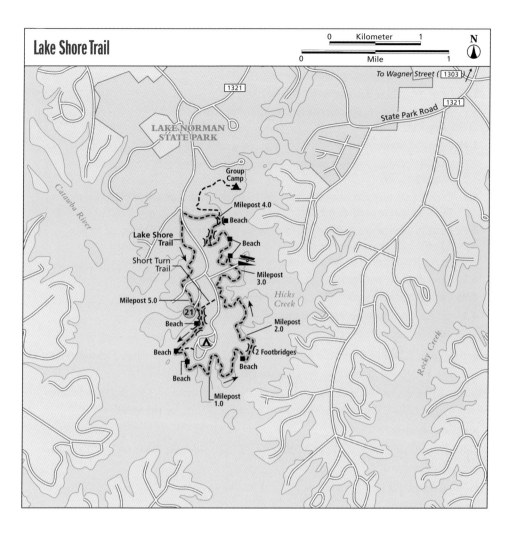

0   Kilometer   1

0   Mile   1

N

To Wagner Street (1303)

1321

State Park Road

1321

LAKE NORMAN STATE PARK

Group Camp

Milepost 4.0

Beach

Lake Shore Trail

Beach

Short Turn Trail

Milepost 3.0

Milepost 5.0

Hicks Creek

21

Milepost 2.0

Beach

Rocky Creek

Beach

2 Footbridges

Beach

Beach

Milepost 1.0

Catawba River

and shortcuts west across the point. These two trails intersect again on the other side of the point.

0.6   Arrive at the second intersection on the other side of the point. The Lake Shore Trail crosses over the red-blazed spur trail. Follow the white-blazed Lake Shore Trail, and it immediately bends left (east). This spur trail leads to the campground where you could top off your drinking water.

0.65 Pass a fantastic sandy beach. This is the most populated beach, because it sits below the campground, but it's big enough to play fetch in and out of the water. Continue hiking along the lakeshore.

1.6   Come to another great beach in a little cove, and you're likely to have this one to yourself.

1.75 Cross two footbridges. Continue hiking north.

2.25 Come to a T at a service road. The trail follows the service road north.

2.3 The white-blazed Lake Shore Trail veers off the service road to the right (north).

2.6 The red-blazed Short Turn Trail shoots off to the left (southwest). To shorten the hike, take this trail as a shortcut. It leads 0.3 mile to the first fork you encountered and onto the trailhead. Continue hiking north on the Lake Shore Trail.

3.05 Cross a road near the boat ramp, continue hiking north.

3.1 Pass a so-so beach. The next one is 0.35 mile away and much better. Continue hiking over rolling hills.

3.45 Arrive at a wonderful sandy beach, continue hiking north near the water.

3.7 Cross a footbridge next to a gully and then a second one over a gully. Continue hiking toward the water.

3.9 Cross a footbridge and arrive at a small swimming beach. Take advantage of this beach. This is the last opportunity the dogs have to get in the water.

3.92 Come to a fork with a spur trail that leads to the group camp. If you need to top off your water, there's a spigot near the group camp. Follow the Lake Shore Trail around a hard bend left (southwest) as you move away from the lake and begin to climb steadily.

4.3 Cross the main park road, and the trail widens. Hike south and downhill.

4.85 Cross under some power lines, continue hiking south.

4.9 Cross the park road, continue hiking south.

5.05 Arrive back at the trailhead.

Resting up: Candlewood Suites Mooresville, 3247 Charlotte Hwy., Mooresville; (704) 360-4899; two dogs up to 80 pounds, pet fee per stay.

Holiday Inn Express Hotel & Suites Mooresville Lake Norman, 130 Norman Station Blvd., Mooresville; (704) 662-6900; two dogs any size, pet fee per stay.

Camping: Onsite.

Fueling up: Blue Parrot Grill, 169 Pinnacle Ln., Mooresville; (704) 663-1203; www .lknblueparrot.com.

Brooklyn Boys Pizza, 119 Market Place Ave., Mooresville; (704) 696-2697; www .brooklynsouthpizzeria.com.

Bruster's Real Ice Cream, 252 Williamson Rd., Mooresville; (704) 799-9898.

LEXINGTON TO SALISBURY

22 Cottonwood Tree Trail

Boone's Cave Park is famous for its notable namesake: Boone's Cave. But when you visit the park, you realize there's more to see. The Yadkin River borders the park to the west, and a canoe launch offers access to explore the waterway. There's a campground, a picnic shelter, and an eighteenth-century log cabin. Over 5.0 miles of hiking trails lead through the forest and along the river's edge. And the feature trail leads to the tallest Eastern Cottonwood Tree in the state. At 169 feet tall and 16 feet around, it's an impressive sight.

Start: At the northwest corner of the parking lot, to the left of the picnic shelter
Distance: 1.2-miles out and back (including 0.1 mile if you visit Boone's Cave)
Hiking time: 35 minutes
Blaze color: Pink, gray
Difficulty: Easy to moderate
Trailhead elevation: 736 feet
Highest point: 736 feet
Seasons: Year-round. May 1–September 30, Monday–Saturday 8:00 a.m.–8:00 p.m., Sunday 1:00 p.m.–8:00 p.m.; October 1–April 30, Monday–Saturday 8:00 a.m.–5:30 p.m., Sunday: 1:00 p.m.–5:30 p.m.
Trail surface: Gravel and mulch path; steep wooden stairs if you visit Boone's Cave
Other trail users: None

Canine compatibility: Leash required
Land status: Davidson County Parks and Recreation
Fees and permits: None
Map: *DeLorme: North Carolina Atlas & Gazetteer*, page 36, D2
Trail contact: Boone's Cave Park, 3552 Boones Cave Rd., Lexington; (336) 242-2285 or (336) 752-2322; www.visitdavidsoncounty .com/recreation.html#
Nearest towns: Salisbury and Lexington
Trail tips: Bring plenty of water; there's a water fountain next to the trailhead, so you can fill up there. Although the trail is next to the river, you can't access it. The first 0.2 mile is mulch and gravel. If your puppy is tender-footed, use booties.

Finding the trailhead: *From the junction of NC 150 and US 64 near Reeds Crossroads,* drive south on NC 150 for 7.3 miles. Turn right onto Boone's Cave Road and travel for 3.4 miles to the park on the left. Enter the park and travel 0.4 mile to the end of the road.
From I-85 near Salisbury, get off at exit 83 and drive north on NC 150 for 5.0 miles to a left turn onto Boone's Cave Road and follow the directions above. GPS: N35 47.958'/W80 28.065'

The Hike

As you enter Boone's Cave Park, you're immediately greeted by beautiful flowers and a trail map near the restrooms. Take a peek at the map and continue to the trailhead. The trail begins high on a bluff overlooking the Yadkin River, and a water fountain is perfectly placed near the trailhead. Once you're topped off, follow the wide

Sunflowers can grow to be 9 feet tall.

canoe and kayak launch trail downhill. Along the mulch and gravel path you'll see signs identifying different trees and plants such as jack-in-the-pulpit.

After 0.2 mile you come to a marked T. Although there's no mention of the Cottonwood Tree Trail, go right, and in another 0.1 mile the trail leads you to another marked T alongside the Yadkin River. The left leads south to the Cottonwood Tree Trail, Red Oaks Trail, and Wilderness Walk. Before you go that way, take a detour to see the park's namesake: Boone's Cave. Along the way you'll pass Baptism Rock, a large, flat, open-faced rock along the edge of the river. The drop-off from the rock is steep, and the current is strong, so there's *no swimming allowed* for you, or the dogs. Beyond Baptism Rock, the trail continues along the river and leads up some steep steps to Boone's Cave. The cave is named for Daniel Boone, who reportedly lived near the park in the mid-1700s.

After appreciating this unique geological feature, return to the T and follow the river downstream and south. The blazes are now blue, and the trees form a canopy overhead, providing plenty of shade. After 0.2 mile you come to a fork. Although the Ts and forks are well marked, several trails intertwine, so it's a good idea to bring a trail map. You can get one online, or take a photo of the map near the park's entrance. At this fork, the left leads toward a boardwalk and Boone's Peak Trail. Go right, following the trail west over rolling hills. You reach another fork. Here, the left is green blazed and leads to the Red Oak Trail and Wilderness Walk. Again go right (north), continuing to follow the gray-blazed Cottonwood Tree Trail. Beyond this fork the trees seem a little bigger, the air a little cooler, and you soon find yourself standing at the foot of the massive Eastern Cottonwood Tree (Populus deltoids). The tree is the tallest of its species in the state! At 169 feet tall, and 16 feet around, you can't help but stare in awe at the power and beauty of Mother Nature. When you've recovered from the reverie, backtrack to the trailhead.

Miles and Directions

0.0 Follow the wide gravel Canoe & Kayak Trail downhill to the river.

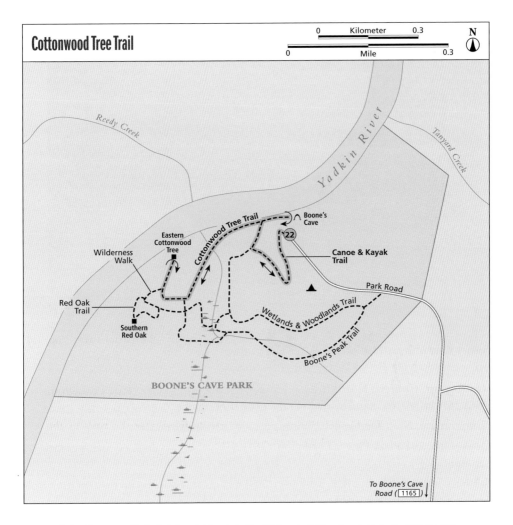

0.2 Come to a T, the left (south) leads to the Wetlands & Woodlands Trail, go right (north) toward the river and Boone's Cave.

0.25 Come to another T near the Yadkin River. The right leads north on a side trip past Baptism Rock to Boone's Cave. The left leads south and is the beginning of the gray-blazed Cottonwood Tree Trail. Go right for now and follow the river upstream toward the cave.

0.3 Arrive at Boone's Cave (N35 47.987'/W80 28.057'. Return to the T.

0.35 Arrive back at the T from the cave. Hike south on the Cottonwood Tree Trail.

0.54 Come to a fork. The left leads southeast toward the boardwalk, Boone's Peak, and the main entrance. Go right (west), following the gray-blazed Cottonwood Tree Trail.

0.57 Come to another fork. The left leads south to the Wilderness Walk and the Red Oak Trail. Go right, continue hiking northwest.

0.65 Arrive at the magnificent Eastern Cottonwood Tree (N35 47.926'/W80 28.275'). Backtrack to trailhead.

1.2 Arrive back at the trailhead.

Boone's Cave is worth a visit while you're hiking in Boone's Cave Park.

Resting up: Country Hearth Inn and Suites, 1525 Cotton Grove Rd., Lexington; (336) 357-2100; two dogs any size, pet fee per pet per night.

Hampton Inn, 1001 Klumac Rd., Salisbury; (704) 637-8000; no fee.

Quality Inn, 101 Plaza Pkwy., Lexington; (781) 861-0850; two dogs any size, pet fee per night.

Salisbury Inn, 825 Klumac Rd., Salisbury; (704) 411-3436; two dogs up to 20 pounds each, pet fee per pet per night.

Camping: Primitive camping onsite.

Lake Norman State Park Campground, 159 Inland Sea Ln., Troutman; (704) 528-6350; www.ncparks.gov/Visit/parks/lano/main.php; for reservations visit www.reserveamerica.com or call (877) 722-6762.

Tanglewood Park, 4201 Manor House Circle, Clemmons; (336) 778-6300; www.forsyth.cc/Parks/Default.aspx?StoryID=17574; RVs only, no tents.

Fueling Up: Hot Diggity Dog, 125 W. Kerr St., Salisbury; (704) 636-9933. There are no dog-friendly restaurants nearby. Locally owned and operated, this pet store sells a variety of raw food lines and pet products that are made in the United States.

DANBURY

23 Lower Cascades Trail

Hanging Rock State Park is full of natural wonders, from waterfalls to unique geological features, from rocky cliffs where birds of prey roost to the wonderful Dan River. Hike, or mountain bike, on nearly 20.0 miles of trails, or take a dip in the park's marvelous mountain lake. Among these trails Lower Cascades leads to one of the most pristine waterfalls in the park with a picture-perfect swimming hole at the base. Bring a towel, book, or picnic and stay for a while at the stunning Lower Cascades.

Start: At the northwest end of the parking lot

Distance: 0.8-mile out and back

Hiking time: 45 minutes

Blaze color: No blazes

Difficulty: Moderate

Trailhead elevation: 1,015 feet

Highest point: 1,038 feet

Seasons: Year-round. January and February, 7:00 a.m.–7:00 p.m.; March and April, 7:00 a.m.–9:00 p.m.; May–September, 7:00 a.m.–10:00 p.m.; October, 7:00 a.m.–9:00 p.m.; November, 7:00 a.m.–8:00 p.m.; December, 7:00 a.m.–7:00 p.m. Closed Christmas Day.

Trail surface: Wide, hard-packed sandy path, steep stone steps

Other trail users: None

Canine compatibility: Leash required

Land status: Hanging Rock State Park

Fees and permits: None

Map: *DeLorme: North Carolina Atlas & Gazetteer,* page 16, C4

Trail contact: Hanging Rock State Park, 1790 Hanging Rock Park Rd., Danbury; (336) 593-8480; www.ncparks.gov

Nearest towns: Danbury, Walnut Cove, and Pilot Mountain

Trail tips: Trash cans are located at the trailhead.

Finding the trailhead: *From the northernmost junction of NC 8 and NC 89 north of Danbury,* drive south on NC 8/NC 89 for 1.4 miles. Turn right onto Hanging Rock Park Road and travel 1.5 miles. Turn right onto Moore's Springs Road (SR 1001) and continue for 0.25 mile to a left onto Hall Road. Travel for 0.4 mile to a parking area on the right.

From the southernmost junction of NC 8 and NC 89 south of Danbury, drive north on NC 8/ NC 89 for 5.1 miles. Turn left onto Hanging Rock Park Road and follow the directions above. GPS: N36 24.887'/W80 15.896'

The Hike

As you explore Hanging Rock State Park, you'll see it's broken into free-standing sections not found within the main body of the park. The Lower Cascades trailhead is one such area. The easy-to-follow trail begins as a wide roadlike path west. You'll pass some oddly placed split-rail fencing that adds a bit of scenery to the otherwise mundane hike. When you begin to see the typical waterfall warning signs, you know

Lower Cascades is exquisite.

you're growing near. I *urge* you to heed all warnings, for your safety and your dogs' as well. From the wooden deck overlook you catch a glimpse of the falls from high above and enjoy long-range views downstream. The drop-offs are extremely steep, so please use extra caution, and keep the dogs leashed up.

▶ **PUPPY PAWS AND GOLDEN YEARS: If your pooch is unable to hike down the steep stairs, hike to the "overlook" and return to the trailhead. This portion is easy and gives you a glimpse of the falls from above. Keep the pups leashed, the drop-offs are steep.**

Follow the steep stone steps down to the base of Lower Cascades. Up until these stairs, this hike is easy, but the steep steps make this trail moderate. As you begin down them, you see the rocky ledges they were built upon and realize you're literally hiking down the side of a cliff. At the bottom, large flat rocks near the base of the falls are perfect for having a picnic or simply sitting to enjoy the sound of the falls. This one is favored by locals, so you may have company here. The waterfall is spectacular. Massive cliffs loom overhead, dwarfing the falls that are nestled in their own private cove. Although the hike is humdrum, the waterfall certainly is a favorite. When you've had your fill of the falls, begin the steep ascent up the steps. As you do, you'll work up a sweat even in wintertime.

Miles and Directions

0.0   Hike west on the old roadbed.

0.3   Arrive at an overlook of the falls (N36 24.960'/W80 16.118'). Hike south down the steps.

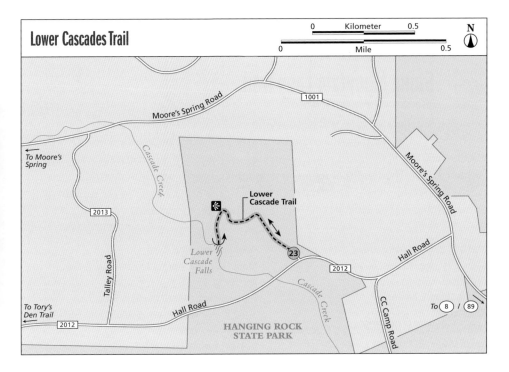

Lower Cascades Trail

0   Kilometer   0.5

0   Mile   0.5

N

To Moore's Spring

Moore's Spring Road

1001

Moore's Spring Road

Cascade Creek

Lower Cascade Trail

2013

Lower Cascade Falls

Talley Road

23

2012

Hall Road

Cascade Creek

To Tory's Den Trail

Hall Road

2012

HANGING ROCK STATE PARK

CC Camp Road

To 8 / 89

0.4   Arrive at the base of Lower Cascades (N36 24.883'/W80 15.893'). Backtrack to the trailhead.

0.8   Arrive back at the trailhead.

Resting up: Econo Lodge, 711 S. Key St., Pilot Mountain; (336) 368-2237.

Indian Creek Cabin, 3466 Moore Springs Rd., Westfield; (336) 593-2583.

Southwyck Farm Bed & Breakfast, 1070 Southwyck Farm Rd., Lawsonville; (336) 593-8006 or (336) 408-7058; www.southwyckfarm .com.

Camping: Onsite.

Fueling up: Green Heron Ale House, 1110 Flinchum Rd., Danbury; (336) 593-4733; www.green heronclub.com. They serve beer, wine, soda, and snacks. On occasion there's a food truck on location.

This little guy, Dash, is ready for a splash at Lower Cascades.

24 Stone Mountain Loop Trail

Stone Mountain State Park will leave you in awe! The 600-foot-tall granite dome is the highlight, but the park is also home to fabulous waterfalls, meadows filled with wildflowers, a campground, fishing, picnicking, and over 18.0 miles of trails for hiking and horseback. The loop trail follows a delightfully active creek leading to the spectacular Stone Mountain Falls. You'll then hike past the brink and up to the summit of Stone Mountain. The breathtaking views from here are unmatched.

Start: At the southwest corner of the lower parking lot near the restrooms

Distance: 4.4-mile loop

Hiking time: 3 hours

Blaze color: Orange

Difficulty: Moderate to strenuous; moderate to Stone Mountain Falls and back

Trailhead elevation: 1,641 feet

Highest point: 2,305 feet

Seasons: Year-round. November–February, 7:00 a.m.–7:00 p.m.; March, April, October, 7:00 a.m.–9:00 p.m.; May–September, 7:00 a.m.–10:00 p.m. Closed Christmas Day.

Trail surface: Wide dirt and sandy gravel

Other trail users: None

Canine compatibility: Leash required

Land status: North Carolina Department of Natural Resources

Fees and permits: None

Map: *DeLorme: North Carolina Atlas & Gazetteer*, page 15, C5

Trail contact: Stone Mountain State Park, 3042 Frank Pkwy., Roaring Gap; (336) 957-8185; www.ncparks.gov

Nearest towns: Elkin and Sparta

Trail tips: Most of the footbridges give the dogs a place to play in the creek. Parts of the trail are hard packed and sandy. If your dogs have soft pads, you may want to bring booties. The descent from the summit is steep. If your dog pulls, a harness with the leash clipped in the front helps alleviate the pulling. Restrooms, trash cans, and a soda machine that only sells water are located near the trailhead.

Finding the trailhead: *From I-77 in Elkin*, take exit 83 and follow US 21 north approximately 10.7 miles. Turn left onto Traphill Road and travel 4.3 miles to a right onto John P. Frank Parkway. Travel 2.3 miles to the entrance to Stone Mountains State Park. From the gate, travel 2.9 miles to a parking area on the left.

From the junction of US 21 and the Blue Ridge Parkway near Sparta, drive south on US 21 for 4.4 miles. Turn right onto Oklahoma Road (SR 1100) and travel 3.0 miles to where it ends at John P. Frank Parkway. Turn right onto John P. Frank Parkway, and the entrance to Stone Mountain State Park is directly in front of you. Then follow the directions above. GPS: N36 23.858'/W81 03.098'

The Hike

Less than 0.1 mile from the trailhead, you reach a fork where this long loop begins. The left leads to the summit first, but I recommend hiking counterclockwise. This route follows the creek and leads to the falls, before climbing over the summit of Stone Mountain. The stoic granite dome has a 4.0-mile circumference and is over 360 million years old. Rock climbers and rappellers travel from near and far to explore the face of this National Natural Landmark. You'll hike past the Wolf Rock Trail and out to an open area with some benches for the weary. If you're weary now, only hike to the falls and back. The climb over the summit is much more strenuous. You soon pass a spur trail that leads to the historic Hutchinson Homestead. This farm site dates back to the mid-1800s. Beyond the spur trail you pass a water spigot; fill up if you need a refill. Beyond the spigot you hike across a meadow at the foot of Stone Mountain. Enjoy the phenomenal views of this massive monolith before heading back into the cover of the forest. Bypass the Cedar Rock Trail and continue following Big Sandy Creek upstream and over several more footbridges. Each footbridge gives the dogs an opportunity to play in the creek. Take advantage of the water while you can; once you begin the hearty climb over the summit, you'll lose the creek. Bypass the trail

The views from the summit of Stone Mountain are hard earned, but worth every step.

to Middle and Lower Falls while you have the dogs with you. The trail leads to the brink of both falls and requires a steep muddy scramble with drop-offs to reach the base. Instead, stay left at the fork, following the creek past several splendid cascades.

After climbing some steps, you reach another fork in the boardwalk. Take the side trip to the right (southeast) down some stairs to the base of Stone Mountain Falls. Large boulders at the base are ideal for sunning yourself while the dogs play in the water. When you return to the fork, if you or your dog are not in tip-top shape, backtrack to the trailhead. The hike ahead is strenuous. If you're up for the challenge, continue climbing and you pass an overlook for the falls. Keep the dogs on a tight leash here since you're now at the brink of the falls. Continue to climb and you reach a marked fork near a free-standing chimney. The right leads to the Upper Parking Lot if you need a "bailout." To reach the summit, continue following the wide gravel path north. You eventually hike over patches of flat stone that offer outstanding views. Keep the dogs on a tight leash here. As the trail flattens, you follow orange dots painted on the stone that lead you across the summit. When you reach the precipice, a split-rail fence reminds you of the steep drop-offs beyond it, and the long-range views are unmatched! When you've had your fill, follow the blazes over this mammoth monadnock. When the path returns to a traditional trail, it makes a long steady descent down stairs and switchbacks and along guy-wires before leading you back to the very first fork.

> **PUPPY PAWS AND GOLDEN YEARS:** The Widow's Creek Falls Trail (hike 25) is suitable for dogs of all ages. It's an easy 0.2-mile hike leading to a lovely waterfall, and it's also found within Stone Mountain State Park.

Miles and Directions

0.0 Hike south into the forest.

0.05 Come to a fork where the loop begins. The left (south-southwest) leads to the summit. I recommend hiking counterclockwise, so go right (southeast).

0.1 Cross a footbridge.

0.2 Come to a fork. The right is the Wolf Rock Trail. Stay left (south), following the orange blazes.

0.28 Cross a footbridge, continue hiking southeast.

0.30 Cross a footbridge, continue hiking southeast.

0.35 Cross a footbridge, continue hiking southeast.

0.6 Bypass a spur trail that leads left (east) to the Hutchinson Homestead (N36 23.495'/ W81 02.953'). Continue hiking southeast.

0.62 Pass a water spigot.

0.65 Cross a beautiful meadow at the foot of Stone Mountain. Continue hiking south and back into the woods.

0.7 Come to a fork. The Cedar Rock Trail leads right (southwest) and uphill. Stay left, continuing hiking southeast.

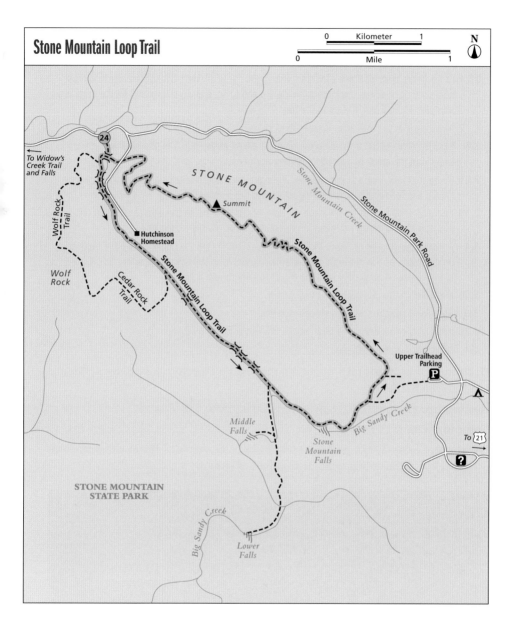

0   Kilometer   1

0   Mile   1

N

0.8 Bypass some steps, continue hiking southeast.

0.9 Cross a footbridge, continue hiking southeast.

1.2 Cross a footbridge, continue hiking southeast.

1.22 Cross a footbridge, continue hiking southeast.

1.3 Cross a footbridge, continue hiking southeast.

1.4 Come to a fork. The right leads south to Middle and Lower Falls. Neither of these falls are good for dogs, so stay left and continue hiking southeast toward Stone Mountain Falls.

1.65 Climb the steps.

1.7 Come to a fork. The right leads down some steps to the base of Stone Mountain Falls. The left leads steeply up more steps. Go right toward the falls.

1.71 Arrive at the base of Stone Mountain Falls (N36 22.860'/W81 02.138'). Large boulders and a sandy beach at the base is an ideal place to sit, enjoy a picnic, and let the dogs run and play in the water. Return to the fork.

1.72 Arrive back at the fork. Hike up the steep steps.

1.8 Pass the brink of the falls; keep the dogs on a tight leash here. The trail begins to move away from the creek and climbs east and northeast.

2.05 Come to a fork near a stone chimney. The right leads south to the upper trailhead parking lot. Go left, following the trail northeast toward the summit.

2.15 Come to another fork, where a service road heads downhill to the right (east). Stay left and continue climbing northeast on the wide, gravel, orange-blazed trail.

3.4 Arrive at the summit of Stone Mountain (N36 23.620'/W81 02.630'). Keep the dogs on a tight leash, as the drop-offs are extremely steep. After taking in the scenery, follow the orange blazes northwest across the top of the mammoth monolith.

3.55 A guy-wire helps you down off the summit.

3.6 Steps and switchbacks lead steeply downhill.

4.35 Arrive at the fork where the loop began. Backtrack to the trailhead.

4.4 Arrive back at the trailhead.

Option: To shorten the hike, or cut out the strenuous portion, hike to Stone Mountain Falls and back.

Resting up: Elk Inn, 1101 N. Bridge St., Elkin; (336) 835-7780.

Camping: Onsite.

Fueling up: Sonic Drive-in Restaurant, 1425 N. Bridge St., Elkin; (336) 835-2681. Eat in the car at this 1950s-style drive-in burger joint.

The bright colors of the red spotted newt serve as a warning that these creatures are poisonous to predators.

25 Widow's Creek Trail

Abruptly rising from the earth, Stone Mountain is certainly the highlight of the park, a park so large that it spans two counties. This magnificent state park also houses a little hidden gem known as Widow's Creek Falls. A short, easy hike leads to this two-tiered waterfall. An inviting swimming hole at the base makes this one ideal for the entire family to splash about in the clear mountain water of Widow's Creek.

Start: In the parking area
Distance: 0.2-mile out and back
Hiking time: 15 minutes
Blaze color: None
Difficulty: Easy
Trailhead elevation: 1,230 feet
Highest point: 1,287 feet
Seasons: Year-round. November–February, 7:00 a.m.–7:00 p.m.; March, April, October, 7:00 a.m.–9:00 p.m.; May–September, 7:00 a.m.–10:00 p.m. Closed Christmas Day.
Trail surface: Gravel

Other trail users: None
Canine compatibility: Leash required
Land status: North Carolina Department of Natural Resources
Fees and permits: None
Map: *DeLorme: North Carolina Atlas & Gazetteer*, page 15, C5
Trail contact: Stone Mountain State Park, 3042 Frank Pkwy., Roaring Gap; (336) 957-8185; www.ncparks.gov
Nearest towns: Elkin and Sparta

Finding the trailhead: *From I-77 in Elkin,* take exit 83 and follow US 21 north for approximately 10.7 miles. Turn left onto Traphill Road and travel 4.3 miles to a right onto John P. Frank Parkway. Continue 2.3 miles to the entrance to Stone Mountain State Park. From the gate, travel 3.9 miles to a pull-off on the right.

From the junction of US 21 and the Blue Ridge Parkway near Sparta, drive south on US 21 for 4.4 miles. Turn right onto Oklahoma Road (SR 1100) and travel 3.0 miles to where it ends at John P. Frank Parkway. Turn right onto John P. Frank Parkway, and the entrance to Stone Mountain State Park is directly in front of you. Then follow the directions above. GPS: N36 23.791'/W81 04.018'

The Hike

This fabulous state park boasts over 18.0 miles of hiking and bridle trails and 20.0 miles of streams. You can fish, picnic, camp, hike, horseback ride, and even climb or rappel on the face of Stone Mountain. A number of waterfalls are among the park's natural treasures, including Widow's Creek Falls. The obvious wide gravel path leads west and begins a slight climb. Halfway to the falls you'll see a trash can, reminding you to dispose of any waste properly.

As soon as you enter the forest, you find yourself standing at the base of Widow's Creek Falls. This small but powerful waterfall is loaded with character. The lower portion of the falls acts as a mini sliding rock. You may see local families picnicking or literally sliding down the rock face. A trail to the left of the falls leads to the "Upper

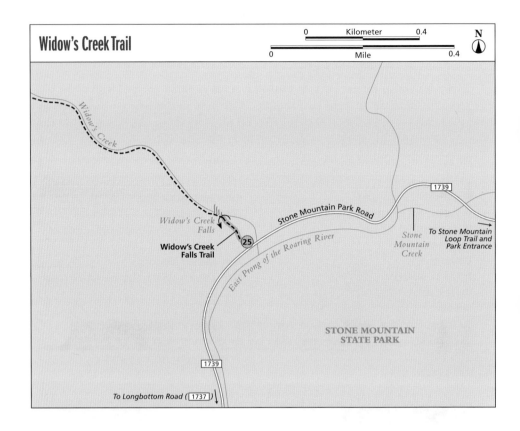

Widow's Creek Trail

0 — Kilometer — 0.4

0 — Mile — 0.4

N

Widow's Creek

1739

Widow's Creek Falls

Stone Mountain Park Road

25

Widow's Creek Falls Trail

East Prong of the Roaring River

Stone Mountain Creek

To Stone Mountain Loop Trail and Park Entrance

STONE MOUNTAIN STATE PARK

1739

To Longbottom Road (1737)

Deer are abundant throughout Stone Mountain State Park.

Everyone can enjoy the quick trip to Widow's Creek Falls.

Falls." This portion of the waterfall has a completely different look, but is just as gorgeous. Beyond the upper falls, the trail continues a strenuous trek for over 2.0 miles to some backcountry campsites. Near this camping area the Widow's Creek Trail also connects with the renowned Mountains-to-Sea Trail. This trail spans over 900 miles, and literally leads from the Great Smoky Mountains all the way to the sea, where it ends at the Atlantic Ocean.

Miles and Directions

0.0 Hike west on the wide gravel path.

0.1 Arrive at the base of Widow's Creek Falls (N36 23.833'/W81 04.073'). Backtrack to the trailhead.

0.2 Arrive back at the trailhead.

Resting up: Elk Inn, 1101 N. Bridge St., Elkin; (336) 835-7780.

Camping: Onsite.

Fueling up: Sonic Drive-in Restaurant, 1425 N. Bridge St., Elkin; (336) 835-2681. Eat in the car at this 1950s-style drive-in burger joint.

WILKESBORO TO BLOWING ROCK

26 Cascades Trail

Within E. B. Jeffress Park, a small recreation area off the Blue Ridge Parkway, this hike is advertised as a leisurely walk, but that's simply not so. It begins as a stroll through the forest with interpretive signs identifying a variety of flora. You then cross a footbridge near some cascades, which is a great place for the dogs to play in the creek. Beyond the footbridge keep them on a tight leash. The trail leads past the brink of Cascades Falls and then *steeply* down to a pair of overlooks amid this 200-foot waterfall.

Start: At the north end of the parking lot near the restrooms
Distance: 0.9-mile out and back
Hiking time: 30 minutes
Blaze color: None
Difficulty: Moderate
Trailhead elevation: 3,489 feet
Highest point: 3,498 feet
Seasons: Year-round
Trail surface: Gravel
Other trail users: None
Canine compatibility: Leash required
Land status: National Park Service–Blue Ridge Parkway
Fees and permits: None

Map: *DeLorme: North Carolina Atlas & Gazetteer,* page 14, E1
Trail contact: (828) 298-0398; www.nps.gov/blri
Nearest towns: Boone, Jefferson, Glendale Springs, and Wilkesboro
Trail tips: Restrooms and a water fountain are located near the trailhead. Bring enough drinking water for you and the dogs, as there's only one spot at 0.35 mile where they can play in the water. If you or your dogs are not good with stairs, hike to the footbridge, let the dogs play in the creek, and return to the trailhead from there.

Finding the trailhead: *From the junction of the Blue Ridge Parkway (BRP) and US 421 near Deep Gap,* drive north on the BRP for 4.5 miles to a right into Cascades Parking Area of E. B. Jeffress Park.
From the junction of the BRP and NC 16 near Glendale Springs, drive south on the BRP for approximately 10.8 miles to a left into Cascades Parking Area of E. B. Jeffress Park.
Note: The Cascades Parking Area is on the east side of the BRP between Milepost 271 and 272. GPS: N36 14.733'/W81 27.471'

The Hike

As the trail leads back into the woods, you almost immediately come to a fork where the Mountains-to-Sea Trail heads left (northwest). Stay right at the fork and follow the Cascades Trail northeast. Along the way, signs help you identify some of the plant life such as mountain laurel, poplar, witch hazel, and more. Because you're so high up on the Blue Ridge Parkway, a steady breeze keeps you cool, and a variety of trees

The boys wait patiently on the trail.

offer shade. The trail leads down some stone steps and crosses a footbridge near some beautiful small cascades. Here the dogs can safely dabble in the water for a bit. Beyond the footbridge, the path gets a little rocky and a little muddy and leads downstream to the brink of the falls. Use *extreme caution* here, and keep the dogs on a tight leash. The rocks are slippery, and the drop-offs are sheer. Even with four legs your pups could easily be swept off their feet. Beyond the brink, steep stone steps lead down to an overlook in the middle of the 200-foot Cascades Falls. Again, use caution and *do not* let your dogs, or children, up on the wall that forms the overlook. After getting a glimpse of the falls and seeing how tall they are, another set of stone steps continues steeply down to another overlook of the falls where the trail ends. As you watch the water flow over the sheer rock face of the mountain, it's amazing to think that when this park was established in the late 1960s, someone actually laid out each of the stone steps, leading you safely down the mountainside to give you this view. It's hard to fathom the work and ingenuity required to complete such a project, and yet here you stand. A sign near the trailhead calls this a leisurely stroll taking about 30 minutes to complete. That sign is deceiving!

▶ **PUPPY PAWS AND GOLDEN YEARS: The Tomkins Knob Trail is at the south end of the parking lot. This 1.0-mile hike (one way) follows easy terrain. Another option is the Lump Overlook at milepost 264.4 on the Blue Ridge Parkway. Wind sweeps over a tall grassy hill, and a narrow path leads up "the lump," giving the dogs a unique place to stretch their legs.**

Miles and Directions

0.0 Hike north back into the woods.

0.03 Come to a fork. The left (northwest) is the white-blazed Mountains-to-Sea Trail, go right and follow the gravel path northeast.

0.3 Hike down some stone steps.

0.35 Cross a footbridge near some small beautiful cascades. This is the only place where the dogs can enjoy the creek, so take advantage of it. Continue hiking east, downstream toward the brink of the falls.

0.38 Hike down some steep stone steps.

0.4 Arrive at an overlook in the middle of the falls (N36 14.968'/W81 27.317'). Please use caution here! Keep your dogs on a leash and off the wall. Continue hiking down more steep stone steps.

0.45 Arrive at another overlook of Cascades Falls (N36 14.969'/W81 27.304'). Backtrack to the trailhead.

0.9 Arrive back at the trailhead.

Option: To lengthen the hike, follow the Mountains-to-Sea Trail as far as you'd like. The trail leads west to Cherokee and east all the way out to the Atlantic Ocean.

Resting up: La Quinta Inn & Suites, 165 Highway 105 Extension, Boone; (828) 262-1234; two dogs any size, no fee.

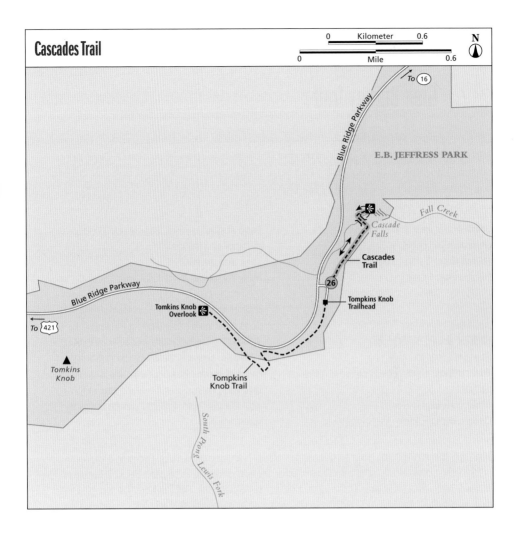

Camping: New River State Park has full-service camping at the US 221 Access Area and tent camping at the Wagoner Access Area; for more information visit www.ncparks.gov/Visit/parks/neri/main.php or call (336) 982-2587.

Stone Mountain State Park Campground, 3042 Frank Pkwy., Roaring Gap; (336) 957-8185; www.ncparks.gov/Visit/parks/stmo/main.php; for reservations call (877) 722-6762.

Fueling up: Café Portofino, 970 River St., Boone; (828) 264-7772; www.cafeportofino.net.

Hob Knob Farm Café, 506 W. King St., Boone; (828) 262-5000; www.hobnobfarmcafe.com.

Murphy's Restaurant & Pub, 747 W. King St., Boone; (828) 264-5117; www.murphysboonenc.com/home.html.

BLOWING ROCK

27 Glen Burney Trail

Found within a wonderful garden-style park in the heart of Blowing Rock, the Glen Burney Trail makes a bee line nearly due south as it follows New Years Creek downstream. The trail leads you past "The Ruins" and then on to view three wonderful waterfalls, each a bit bigger than the last.

Start: At the west end of the parking lot
Distance: 2.3-miles out and back
Hiking time: 1 hour, 30 minutes
Blaze color: None
Difficulty: Strenuous; moderate to Cascades and back
Trailhead elevation: 3,550 feet
Highest point: 3,550 feet
Seasons: Year-round
Trail surface: Hard-packed dirt with rocky sections
Other trail users: None
Canine compatibility: Leash required

Land status: Town of Blowing Rock Department of Parks and Recreation
Fees and permits: None
Map: *DeLorme: North Carolina Atlas & Gazetteer*, page 13, F7
Trail contact: Annie Cannon Memorial Gardens, 229 Laurel Ln., Blowing Rock; (828) 295-5222 or (828) 295-4636; www.blowingrock.com/services/hiking-biking-climbing/
Nearest towns: Blowing Rock and Boone
Trail tips: There's a well-marked trail map near the trailhead. The trail can be buggy in summertime.

Finding the trailhead: *From the junction of US 321 and the Blue Ridge Parkway*, drive south on US 321 for 1.1 mile to a right onto Sunset Drive. Travel 0.3 mile to a left onto US 321 Business (Main Street). Travel less than 0.1 mile to a right onto Laurel Lane. Follow Laurel Lane for 0.1 mile to a stop sign at Wallingford Road. Go to the stop sign and immediately turn left into Annie Cannon Park and Memorial Gardens.

From the junction of US 321 Business (Main Street) and US 321 Bypass in Blowing Rock, drive north on US 321 Business for approximately 1.1 miles to a left onto Laurel Lane and follow the directions above. GPS: N36 07.946'/W81 40.833'

The Hike

The exact origins of the Glen Burney Trail are unknown, but it's been used for over 100 years. Despite its longevity, it doesn't see much traffic, due to its difficulty. It begins as a wide gravel path, but the majority of the trail is hard-packed dirt that's easier on the paws. The cool air from the creek and shade from the trees make this hike enjoyable year-round.

As the path leads you around a switchback, you'll pass the first of four landmarks—the "Ruins." These cement and stone walls are the remnants of a sewage plant that once served the city of Blowing Rock up until 1929. About 0.1 mile past the ruins,

Along a country road, you're often treated with wonderful sights like these.

you come to a fantastic watering hole for the dogs. Although the trail follows New Years Creek the entire way, sometimes it's from high above. Walls of rhododendron line the path with their showy blossoms in full bloom throughout the summer. As the trail slowly descends, it leads to a small waterfall known as "the Cascades." Enjoy the view and continue downstream and downhill. If you're not very steady on your feet, turn back now. The next 0.2 mile is very rocky.

When you reach a fork, stay left, bypassing an overlook made of boulders with a very steep drop-off; the area is overgrown anyway, so you don't get a great view. As you head left (south), the trail leads downhill to a T. The right leads north to the base of Glen Burney Falls, and the left leads south to Glen Marie Falls. Hiking toward Glen Burney Falls, you get your first taste of uphill on this entire hike. When you reach the falls, it's spectacular! The tall, beautiful, steady flow offers a perfect place to stop for lunch, and the dogs can play

▶ **PUPPY PAWS AND GOLDEN YEARS: Enjoy wandering around the grounds of Annie Cannon Memorial Gardens. Another option is the Bass Lake Loop Trail (hike 28). It's an easy 1.0-mile stroll around Bass Lake and is suitable for dogs of all ages.**

around at the base. Return to the T and hike south and downstream toward Glen Marie Falls. As you near the falls, the descent gets steeper and a few tight switchbacks help you navigate the terrain. The trail puts you in the middle of the falls. Although Glen Marie Falls is pretty to see, Glen Burney is a better place for the dogs to romp around in the water. Returning to the trailhead, you climb, climb, climb, and then climb some more. You'll work up a sweat, even in winter, so make sure you bring lots of drinking water for you and the dogs.

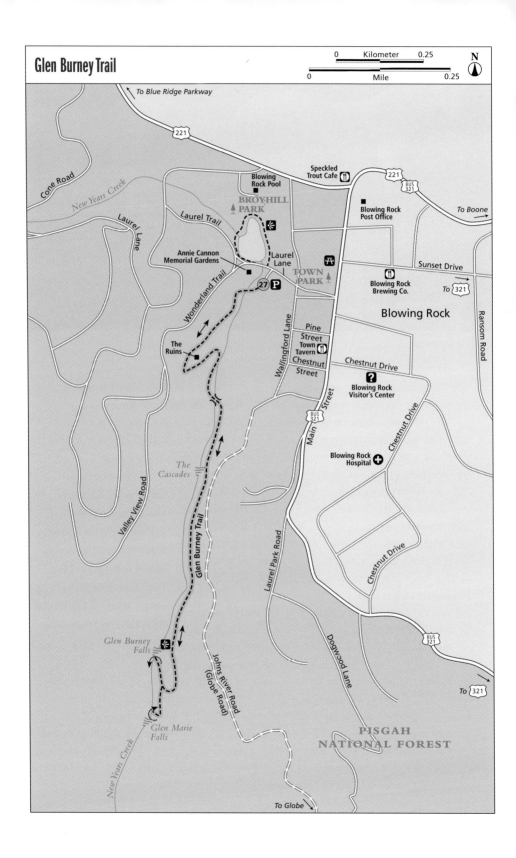

Glen Burney Trail

N

Kilometer		
0		0.25
0	Mile	0.25

To Blue Ridge Parkway

221

Cone Road

New Years Creek

Laurel Lane

Laurel Trail

Blowing Rock Pool

BROYHILL PARK

Speckled Trout Cafe

Blowing Rock Post Office

221

BUS 321

To Boone

Annie Cannon Memorial Gardens

Wonderland Trail

Laurel Lane

TOWN PARK

Sunset Drive

Blowing Rock Brewing Co.

To 321

Blowing Rock

27 P

The Ruins

Wallingford Lane

Pine Street

Town Tavern

Chestnut Street

Chestnut Drive

Blowing Rock Visitor's Center

Main Street

BUS 321

Ransom Road

Valley View Road

The Cascades

Glen Burney Trail

Blowing Rock Hospital

Chestnut Drive

Chestnut Drive

Laurel Park Road

Glen Burney Falls

Johns River Road (Globe Road)

Dogwood Lane

BUS 321

To 321

Glen Marie Falls

New Years Creek

PISGAH NATIONAL FOREST

To Globe

Miles and Directions

0.0 Hike southwest, downhill on the wide gravel path.

0.05 Cross a land bridge, near a sewer lift station. Continue hiking south.

0.25 Bypass a narrow trail to the right (west). Continue hiking south on the overgrown dirt trail, which begins to lead you around some switchbacks.

0.4 Pass the "Ruins" and continue hiking south following New Years Creek downstream.

0.45 Pass a good watering hole, then cross a footbridge over the creek. Continue hiking south and downstream.

0.7 Arrive at "the Cascades" (N36 07.549'/W81 40.997'). Continue hiking south on the steep, muddy path.

0.9 Come to a fork. The right leads to an overlook of Glen Burney Falls. Bypass the overlook and continue hiking steeply downhill and south.

1.0 Come to a T. The right leads north to Glen Burney Falls, the left leads south to Glen Marie Falls. Go right toward Glen Burney Falls.

1.05 Arrive at the spectacular Glen Burney Falls (N36 07.397'/ W81 41.056'). The dogs can run and play at the base. Backtrack to the T.

1.1 Arrive back at the T. Hike south around the steep switchbacks en route to Glen Marie Falls.

1.2 When you near Glen Marie Falls, scramble down a steep muddy path leading to the falls (N36 07.311'/W81 41.058').

Option: If you don't have steady feet, or to make this a moderate hike, turn back at the Cascades.

Resting up: The Village Inn, 7876 Valley Blvd., Blowing Rock; (828) 295-3380; multiple dogs allowed up to 50 pounds, pet fee per night.

Camping: Julian Price Campground, on the Blue Ridge Parkway at milepost 297; (828) 298-0398; www.nps.gov/blri/planyour visit/camping-on-the-blue-ridge -parkway.htm. For reservations visit www .recreation.gov or call (877) 444-6777.

Fueling up: Blowing Rock Brewing Co. (also a restaurant), 152 Sunset Dr., Blowing Rock; (828) 414-9600.

The Speckled Trout, 922 Main St., Blowing Rock; (828) 295-9819.

Town Tavern, 1182 Main St., Blowing Rock; (828) 295-7500.

Daylilies blossom in a variety of colors.

28 Bass Lake Loop Trail

Just outside the quaint little town of Blowing Rock, in a remote access area of Moses Cone Memorial Park, is the Bass Lake Loop Trail. As the name implies, the trail makes a circle around the lake. The wide gravel roadlike path is flat and easy to follow, and with each season that passes, the lake paints a new portrait for you to enjoy.

Start: At the Bass Lake Recreation Area, which is a remote section of Moses Cone Memorial Park off US 221 near Blowing Rock. The trailhead is at the southeast corner of the lakeshore parking lot.
Distance: 1.0-mile loop
Hiking time: 30 minutes
Blaze color: None
Difficulty: Easy
Trailhead elevation: 3,576 feet
Highest point: 3,645 feet
Seasons: Year-round, daylight hours
Trail surface: Finely chopped gravel path

Other trail users: Trail runners
Canine compatibility: Leash required
Land status: National Park Service–Blue Ridge Parkway
Fees and permits: None
Map: *DeLorme: North Carolina Atlas & Gazetteer*, page 13, F7
Trail contact: (828) 295-7938 or (828) 295-3782; www.blueridgeheritage.com/attractions-destinations/moses-cone-manor
Nearest town: Blowing Rock
Trail tips: Restrooms and a water fountain are located near the trailhead.

Finding the trailhead: *From the Blue Ridge Parkway between milepost 294 and 295,* access US 221. Drive north on US 221 toward Blowing Rock for 1.0 mile to a left into the Bass Lake Area of Moses Cone Memorial Park. Travel for 0.2 mile to the parking area at the bottom of the hill.

From the junction of US 221 and US 321 Business in Blowing Rock, drive south on US 221 for 0.55 mile to a right into the Bass Lake Area of Moses Cone Memorial Park and follow the directions above. GPS: N36 08.451'/W81 41.212'

The Hike

The hike begins near the restrooms, which is convenient, because there's a water fountain here, so you could fill up your drinking water. A trail map gives you a good picture of the other trails in the area, but if you're staying on the Bass Lake Loop Trail, you don't really need a map. The trail literally makes a loop around the lake, following the shoreline the entire way. The map shows that this is one of the original "carriage trails." These trails were used in the early 1900s for carriages to tote visitors around the Cone family estate. Moses and Bertha Cone were naturalists who built their summer home, the Flat Top Manor (Moses Cone Manor), off the Blue Ridge Parkway. You can visit the manor, but only service dogs are allowed inside. The Cones extensively planted the grounds and built a tower to overlook them. About 25.0 miles of carriage trails remain. They are all open to hikers, and some are open to equestrians. No bicycles allowed.

Tranquility at its best is found along the Bass Lake Trail.

You can go either way on the trail, but it's described here hiking clockwise. As you begin hiking, you can easily picture a carriage with horses trotting around the lake on the wide gravel path. This hike is very popular with locals. On any given day you'll see trail runners, families out for a stroll, birders, and people walking their dogs. At 0.2

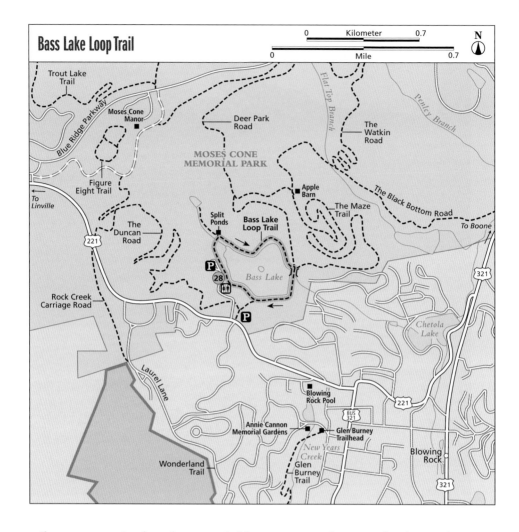

0   Kilometer   0.7

0   Mile   0.7

N

Trout Lake Trail

Blue Ridge Parkway

Moses Cone Manor

Deer Park Road

Flat Top Branch

Penley Branch

The Watkin Road

MOSES CONE MEMORIAL PARK

Figure Eight Trail

To Linville

Apple Barn

The Black Bottom Road

The Maze Trail

Split Ponds

Bass Lake Loop Trail

The Duncan Road

221

To Boone

P

28

Bass Lake

321

Rock Creek Carriage Road

P

Chetola Lake

Laurel Lane

Blowing Rock Pool

221

BUS 321

Annie Cannon Memorial Gardens

Glen Burney Trailhead

New Years Creek

Glen Burney Trail

Wonderland Trail

Blowing Rock

321

mile you pass a pair of ponds surrounded by moss-covered stone walls. The ponds are split in the middle by a narrow waterway that runs between them. It's quite unique and momentarily draws your attention away from the lake. A variety of birds happily sing for you as they flit about from tree to tree, and at the west end of the lake, you notice a large area covered with lily pads. On my last visit I was lucky enough to see a beaver swimming here, so keep your eyes peeled. The surface of the trail is finely chopped gravel, but the dogs can walk on the soft grass that lines the trail if they have sensitive feet. A small island in the center of the lake adds character. Big beautiful trees lining the path offer shade, and an occasional bench gives you a place to sit and take it all in. Continuing around the lake, you'll cross a stone bridge and pass "The Maze" trail. This trail swirls around like a maze and leads 2.3 miles to the park's apple barn. Bypass it and continue circling around the lake. You'll pass what looks like a small boat launch, but there is no swimming, wading, boating, or buoyant devices allowed

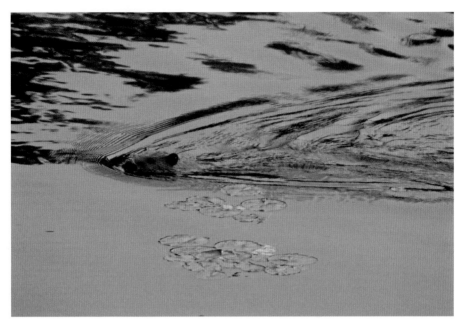

A beaver explores the depths of Bass Lake.

on Bass Lake. Between the birdlife, a beaver, wildflowers, waterfront views, and majestic trees lining the path, before you know it you're back at the trailhead.

Miles and Directions

0.0 To hike clockwise, go left (northwest) on the wide gravel path.

0.15 Bypass a spur trail that heads off to the left and leads toward the Manor House. Continue hiking north around the lake.

0.2 Appreciate the "split ponds," and continue hiking east.

0.6 Cross a stone bridge, bypass the Maze Trail (east), continue hiking south.

0.75 Pass what looks like a small boat ramp, continue hiking west.

1.0 Arrive back at the trailhead.

Resting up: The Village Inn, 7876 Valley Blvd., Blowing Rock; (828) 295-3380; multiple dogs allowed up to 50 pounds, pet fee per night.

Camping: Julian Price Campground, on the Blue Ridge Parkway at milepost 297; (828) 298-0398; www.nps.gov/blri/planyourvisit/camping-on-the-blue-ridge -parkway.htm. For reservations visit www.recreation.gov or call (877) 444-6777.

Fueling up: Blowing Rock Brewing Co. (also a restaurant), 152 Sunset Dr., Blowing Rock; (828) 414-9600.

The Speckled Trout, 922 Main St., Blowing Rock; (828) 295-9819.

Town Tavern, 1182 Main St., Blowing Rock; (828) 295-7500.

29 Boone Fork Trail

Whether you have an RV, school bus, or are an individual wanting to hike, the lovely Julian Price Picnic Area has plenty of parking. The trail follows Bee Tree Creek and Boone Fork for a few miles. If you're not up for hiking the full loop, you can make this an out and back. Either way, you and the dogs are sure to enjoy it. Within the recreation area you can camp, hike, paddle, or fish from the banks of the glorious Price Lake.

Start: On the west side of the parking lot near the restrooms in the Price Lake Picnic Area

Distance: 5.2-mile loop (including a side trip to Hebron Falls)

Hiking time: 3 hours

Blaze color: Orange

Difficulty: Moderate to strenuous

Trailhead elevation: 3,303 feet

Highest point: 3,506 feet

Seasons: Year-round

Trail surface: Hard-packed dirt, muddy in some spots, rooty sections, gravel sections

Other trail users: None

Canine compatibility: Leash required

Land status: National Park Service–Blue Ridge Parkway

Fees and permits: None

Map: DeLorme: North Carolina Atlas & Gazetteer, page 13, F7

Trail contact: (828) 298-0398; www.nps.gov/blri/upload/price-park.png

Nearest town: Blowing Rock

Trail tips: Bring a towel, as you may want to take a dip. Bring lots of drinking water. Bring a few dog treats along, in case you need to coax a pooch down the "ladder." If your dogs don't like getting their feet wet, skip this hike and head over to the Bass Lake Trail (hike 28) instead. A trail map is located near the first fork where the loop begins. Restrooms, trash cans, picnic tables, and charcoal grills are all located in the picnic area.

Finding the trailhead: *From the junction of the Blue Ridge Parkway (BRP) and US 221 near Moses Cone, drive south on the BRP for 1.8 miles to a right into the Price Lake Picnic Area and drive 0.1 mile to the restrooms on the left.* **Note:** *The picnic area is on the BRP between mileposts 296 and 297.*

From the junction of the BRP and US 221 near Linville Falls, drive north on the BRP for 9.5 miles to a left into the Price Lake Picnic area and follow the directions above. GPS: N36 08.378'/ W81 43.655'

The Hike

If you hike the entire loop, you'll pass through meadows, dense forest, rocky outcroppings, and wonderful waterfalls. I recommend hiking clockwise, which is technically backward according to the mileposts provided along the way. But to shorten the hike, follow it counterclockwise alongside Boone Fork and return to the trailhead whenever you choose. On the full loop (clockwise) there is one obstacle at 3.35 miles where the dogs will have to climb down a ladder-type stairway. The steps are

Your canine companions will love this large swimming hole along the Boone Fork Loop Trail.

wide, but steep, so it may take some coaxing. If you think this may be a problem, hike counterclockwise to Hebron Falls and back. Aside from this obstacle, you and your pups will enjoy spending hours in the forest.

Begin by crossing the grassy field and entering the woods. The second you step into the forest, the air cools and rhododendron thickets line the path. Bypass a spur trail that leads to Price Lake, and then hike through the campground where you could refill your water. At 1.0 mile, stay right (west northwest) at a fork, bypassing the Tanawha Trail. Not far from the fork, the trail leads to a split-rail fence. Depending on the size of your dogs, they should have no problem going over, or under. Just past the fence is another well-marked fork. Continue straight ahead (west), and the Boone Fork Trail merges with the Mountains-to-Sea Trail. You'll now follow orange and white blazes for the next 3.1 miles. Beyond the fork the trail leads across a beautiful hilly meadow. Wildflowers and blackberries line the path in the warmer months, and a strong breeze blows by. About three-quarters of the way across the field, bypass a spur trail that continues straight ahead (west) and climbs. Go right (north) and follow the orange markers downhill. When you reenter the forest, the trail begins to follow Bee Tree Creek. Bypass a blue-blazed spur trail to the left, and over the next 0.6 mile

▶ **PUPPY PAWS AND GOLDEN YEARS: Puppies and seniors will enjoy playing in the grassy field near the trailhead and elsewhere in the large picnic area. Another option is to hike counterclockwise alongside the creek and turn back whenever you feel appropriate.**

you'll cross the creek and tributaries several times. These crossings are great for the dogs to get in the water, while you enjoy some shade and a cool breeze.

Because you are hiking clockwise, the mileposts are counting down rather than up. The trail weaves back and forth across the creek as you follow it downstream. At 3.3 miles, you come to a T near the creek. The left leads north toward the creek, where large boulders make a perfect place to sit and relax while enjoying the thunderous sound of water rushing by. As the trail moves away from the creek, you notice some amazingly huge rock formations. About 0.1 mile past the T is the "ladder" obstacle. After coaxing or carrying your dogs down it, you come to a spur trail that leads down a steep, muddy slope to the middle of Hebron Falls. The boulders that form the creek here are exceptional, and water flows through every crevice. Beyond Hebron Falls the loop trail leads past another small waterfall with a pristine pebble beach at the base. The dogs will love this one. At 4.2 miles, you finally leave the Mountains-to-Sea Trail and continue hiking downstream. The water seems alive with cascade after cascade. After passing the 0.5 milepost, and crossing a footbridge, the trail turns to gravel nearing the picnic area. As you hike across a large field near the finish, keep your eyes peeled for hummingbirds, and you soon reach the end of the loop.

Miles and Directions

0.0   Immediately cross a footbridge over a small brook, and come to a fork where the loop begins. If you're only hiking to the waterfalls and back, go right (north) through the picnic area. If you're hiking the whole loop as described below, go straight ahead (west) across a field and into the woods.

0.4   Bypass a spur trail that leads toward Price Lake. Continue hiking west, and the trail skirts by the Julian Price Campground.

0.6   Cross the road near the entrance to the campground.

0.7   Cross a road inside the campground. Top off your water, if need be.

0.9   Cross another road inside the campground, pass the restrooms, and continue hiking west.

0.95 Come to a fork. The left (south) is the Tanawha Trail. Go right, following the Boone Fork Trail northwest.

1.1   Step over the single rail of a fence blocking the trail.

1.12 Come to a fork. The left (south) accesses the Tanawha Trail again. Go right (west) and merge with the Mountains-to-Sea Trail, now following both orange and white blazes.

1.4   Hike across a meadow.

1.5   Bypass a spur trail that goes straight (west) and climbs. Go right (north), downhill, and follow the orange blazes.

1.65 Bypass a blue-blazed spur trail to the left (south southwest). Continue hiking northwest.

1.7   Rock hop a tributary, continue hiking northwest.

1.8   Rock hop a tributary, continue hiking northwest.

1.82 Rock hop a tributary, continue hiking northwest.

1.97 Cross a footbridge, continue hiking northwest.

2.05 Rock hop a tributary, continue hiking north.

Boone Fork Trail

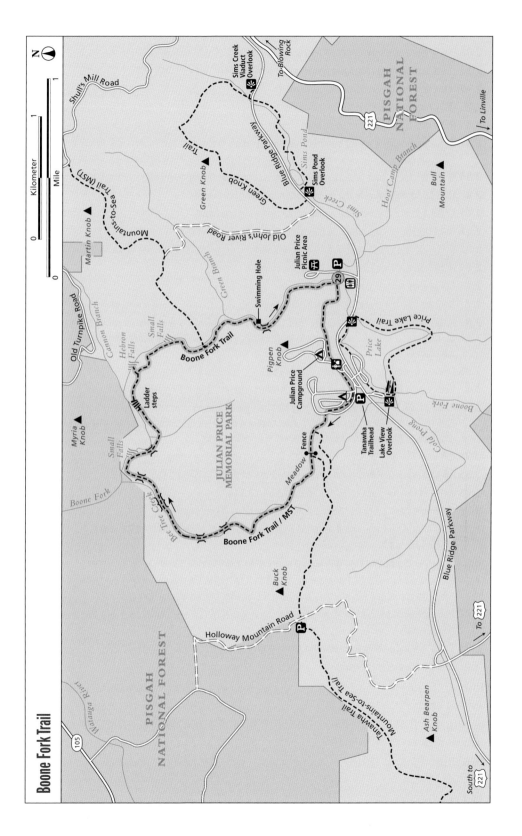

2.08 Rock hop a tributary, continue hiking north.

2.1 Cross a footbridge, continue hiking north.

2.15 Rock hop the creek, continue hiking north.

2.2 Rock hop the creek, continue hiking north.

2.3 Rock hop a tributary, continue hiking north.

2.32 Come to the creek again, but this time do not cross. Instead, go left (north) and follow it downstream.

2.35 Cross the creek over perfectly placed stones. Continue hiking northeast.

2.4 Cross a footbridge over the creek, continue hiking northeast.

2.45 Cross a footbridge over the creek, continue hiking northeast.

2.51 Rock hop the creek, continue hiking northeast.

2.52 Rock hop the creek, continue hiking northeast.

2.55 Rock hop the creek, continue hiking northeast.

2.6 Cross a log bridge, continue hiking north.

2.7 Boulder hop the creek, continue hiking northeast.

2.8 Pass a small, beautiful waterfall (N36 09.289'/W81 44.625'). A wonderful sandy beach at the base is ideal for a picnic or to let the dogs run and play in the water. Continue hiking south.

2.95 Cross a footbridge, the trail bends left (east).

3.1 Rock hop a tributary, the trail bends left (northeast).

3.3 Arrive at a T. The left leads about 100 feet to a great spot for a picnic alongside Boone Fork (N36 09.276'/W81 44.385'). After taking a break on the boulders, follow the white and orange blazes south as you move away from the creek.

3.35 Come to the only obstacle on the trail: the steep ladder-like steps.

3.55 Take the spur trail to the left that leads northeast down to Hebron Falls.

3.65 Arrive at Hebron Falls (N36 09.297'/W81 44.139').

3.75 Scramble back up to the Boone Fork Trail. Continue hiking southeast.

4.05 Pass another pristine small waterfall with a beach at the base (N36 09.121'/W81 43.994').

4.1 Return to the Boone Fork Trail after a side trip to the waterfall. Continue hiking south.

4.2 Arrive at a marked fork. The Mountains-to-Sea Trail heads left (south) across the creek. Stay straight ahead (southwest), following the orange-blazed Boone Fork Trail.

4.65 Pass one final fantastic watering hole for the dogs (N36 08.749'/W81 43.908'). Continue hiking south.

4.75 Cross a wooden bridge. Follow the gravel path southeast.

5.2 Arrive back at the trailhead.

Option: To shorten this hike to 3.1 miles, follow it counterclockwise to Hebron Falls and back.

Resting up: The Village Inn, 7876 Valley Blvd., Blowing Rock; (828) 295-3380; multiple dogs up to 50 pounds each, pet fee per night.

Camping: Julian Price Campground; (828)298-0398; www.nps.gov/blri/

The dogs may need some coaxing to overcome this ladder-type stairway along the Boone Fork Loop Trail.

planyourvisit/camping-on-the-blue-ridge-parkway.htm; for reservations visit www .recreation.gov or call (877) 444-6777.

Fueling up: Blowing Rock Brewing Co. (also a restaurant), 152 Sunset Dr., Blowing Rock; (828) 414-9600.

The Speckled Trout, 922 Main St., Blowing Rock; (828) 295-9819.

Town Tavern, 1182 Main St., Blowing Rock; (828) 295-7500.

LENOIR TO LINVILLE FALLS

30 Hunt Fish Falls Trail

The Hunt Fish Falls trail makes a steady descent all the way to the falls. You don't realize how challenging it is until you come back out. But the prize is well worth the effort! This little beauty is located within the Lost Cove Wilderness Study Area. The cove is a black bear sanctuary, although it's more notably known for the Lost Cove Cliffs. The cliffs are home to roosting peregrine falcons, rare mosses, and stunted pitch pine trees. To view the cliffs, visit the Blue Ridge Parkway overlook at milepost 310.

Start: At the south end of the parking lot
Distance: 1.8-miles out and back
Hiking time: 1 hour, 10 minutes
Blaze color: White
Difficulty: Strenuous
Trailhead elevation: 2,387 feet
Highest point: 2,387 feet
Seasons: Year-round
Trail surface: Hard-packed dirt, rocky sections
Other trail users: None
Canine compatibility: Voice control
Land status: Pisgah National Forest–Grandfather Ranger District

Fees and permits: None
Maps: DeLorme: North Carolina Atlas & Gazetteer, page 33, B6. National Geographic Trails Illustrated Map #779 Linville Gorge & Mount Mitchell: J13, Trail #263.
Trail contact: Pisgah National Forest, Grandfather Ranger District; (828) 652-2144; www.fs.fed.us
Nearest town: Linville
Trail tips: Bring a towel and a picnic, as this is a great place to spend the day swimming and sunning on the rocks near this spectacular two-tiered waterfall.

Finding the trailhead: *From the junction of the Blue Ridge Parkway (BRP) and the northernmost US 221 (to Linville),* drive south on the BRP for 6.1 miles to a left onto State Road 1518 (SR 1518—Old Jonas Ridge Road). After turning onto SR 1518, travel 1.7 miles to a fork at Mortimer Road (with the Long Ridge Baptist Church on your left). At this fork proceed straight ahead onto FR 464 (Edgemont Road). Follow FR 464 for 6.25 miles to the parking area on the left.
From the junction of the BRP and NC 181, drive north on the BRP for 0.8 mile to a right onto SR 1518 and follow the directions above. **Note:** SR 1518 is between milepost 311 and 312 on the BRP. GPS: N36 00.450'/W81 48.058'

The Hike

Among the waterfalls within the Lost Cove, Hunt Fish is by far my favorite. The white-blazed trail leads southeast into the forest and begins to make a steady descent. You don't quite realize how steep the trail is until you're returning to the trailhead. A few switchbacks ease the descent, and the coolness of the forest keeps you refreshed. You don't hear an inkling of moving water as you continue down, down, down, but don't be discouraged. The prize at the end is well worth the journey. At last you come

The whole family will enjoy the expansive swimming hole at the base of Hunt Fish Falls.

alongside a trickling tributary that doesn't offer much hope for the waterfall. Be patient, the falls are phenomenal!

As the trail finally flattens, you cross a rock bridge. Continue hiking downstream and the welcome sounds of big water moving come into earshot. With the creek encouraging you, continue downhill around a few more switchbacks. At 0.75 mile you reach Lost Cove Creek. Head right (east) and pass a primitive campsite near the brink of the falls. Keep the dogs leashed near the brink. They'll be running free near the base of the falls in no time. Continue hiking east, and the trail leads out onto the large flat rocks near Hunt Fish Falls. The falls are flawless! Two distinct drops over smooth-faced stone add a perfect touch to the picturesque setting. The stone surface wraps around the falls and is ideal for a picnic or sunning yourself. To top it off, the large swimming hole at the base is fun for the entire family. If your dogs love the water, they're in for a real treat here. The swimming hole is deep and big enough to throw a stick well out into the water. You could easily spend an entire day enjoying this one.

▶ **PUPPY PAWS AND GOLDEN YEARS:** The dogs can enjoy playing in Lake James either along the Paddy's Creek Trail (hike 34) or near the park's picnic area. Another option is the Duggers Creek Falls Trail. The trailhead is in the Linville Falls Recreation Area, near the Linville Falls Trailhead. This easy 0.2-mile hike leads to a creek and a small lovely waterfall.

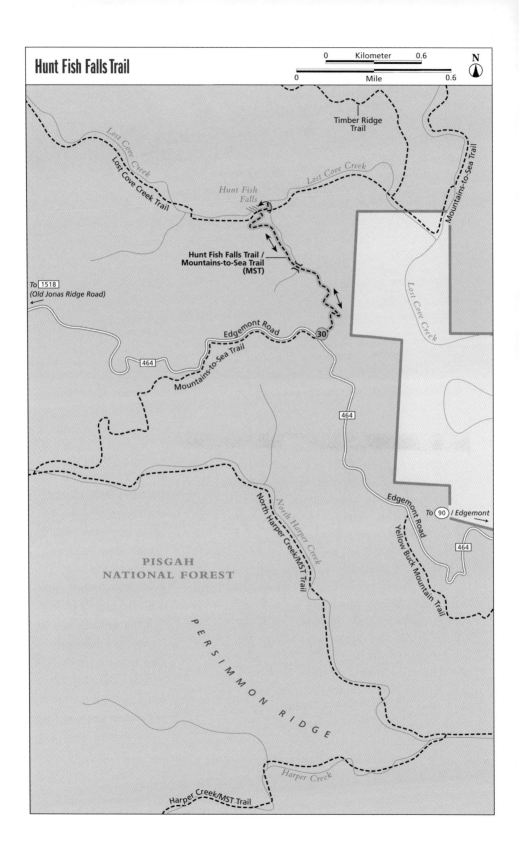

Hunt Fish Falls Trail

0   Kilometer   0.6

0   Mile   0.6

N

Timber Ridge Trail

Lost Cove Creek

Lost Cove Creek

Lost Cove Creek Trail

Hunt Fish Falls

Mountains-to-Sea Trail

Hunt Fish Falls Trail /
Mountains-to-Sea Trail
(MST)

Lost Cove Creek

To 1518
(Old Jonas Ridge Road)

Edgemont Road

30

Mountains-to-Sea Trail

464

464

Edgemont Road

To 90 / Edgemont

464

North Harper Creek

North Harper Creek/MST Trail

Yellow Buck Mountain Trail

PISGAH
NATIONAL FOREST

PERSIMMON RIDGE

Harper Creek

Harper Creek/MST Trail

Miles and Directions

0.0 Hike southeast into the forest, making a steady descent.

0.5 Cross a rock bridge over a tributary.

0.8 Arrive at Lost Cove Creek. Go right (east), downstream past the brink of the falls.

0.9 Arrive at the base of Hunt Fish Falls (N36 00.842'/W81 48.246'). Backtrack to the trailhead.

1.8 Arrive back at the trailhead.

Resting up: Gable Haus Country Inn and Cottages, 154 Ruffin St., Linville; (828) 733-9535; www.gablehausinn.com; two dogs any size, no fee.

Red Carpet Inn Lenoir, 142 Wilkesboro Blvd. SE, Lenoir; (828) 758-4403; two dogs any size, pet fee per dog per stay.

Camping: Linville Falls Campground; (828) 298-0398; www.nps.gov/blri/planyour visit/camping-on-the-blue-ridge-parkway.htm; for reservations visit www.recreation .gov or call (877) 444-6777.

Mortimer Campground, on NC 90 in the town of Edgemont; (828) 675-5616; www.fs .usda.gov/recarea/nfsnc/recreation/camping-cabins/recarea/?recid=49006&actid =29; no electric sites.

Black bears have a healthy population in the coastal and mountain regions of North Carolina.

31 Harper Creek Trail

The Harper Creek Trail begins with a steep and strenuous climb, but then flattens out to a leisurely stroll through the Pisgah National Forest. You'll navigate a few forks before arriving at an overlook of the magnificent Harper Creek Falls. Massive cliffs loom above the falls, adding to the scenery. On your way to the falls, the dogs can run and play and get some energy out in a large primitive camping area near the creek. But when you reach the falls overlook, keep them leashed up.

Start: In the center of the parking lot
Distance: 3.0-miles out and back
Hiking time: 1 hour, 30 minutes
Blaze color: Orange and white
Difficulty: Easy to moderate
Trailhead elevation: 1,579 feet
Highest point: 1,812 feet
Seasons: Year-round
Trail surface: Hard-packed dirt
Other trail users: None
Canine compatibility: Voice control
Land status: Pisgah National Forest–
Grandfather Ranger District

Fees and permits: None
Maps: *DeLorme: North Carolina Atlas & Gazetteer*, page 33, B6. National Geographic Trails Illustrated Map #779 Linville Gorge & Mount Mitchell, I13, Trail #260.
Trail contact: Pisgah National Forest, Grandfather Ranger District; (828) 652-2144; www.fs.fed.us
Nearest towns: Linville and Lenoir
Trail tips: Bring a hiking stick; the first quarter mile climbs steeply.

Finding the trailhead: *From the junction of the Blue Ridge Parkway (BRP) and NC 181 near Linville*, drive north on the BRP for 4.0 miles. Turn right onto SR 1511 and travel for 4.3 miles to where SR 1511 becomes FR 981. Continue straight ahead onto FR 981 and travel for 4.5 miles to a stop sign. This road is SR 90. Turn right onto SR 90 and travel for 2.0 miles. Turn right onto SR 1328 (Brown Mountain Beach Road) just past the Mortimer Recreation Area and travel for 1.4 miles to a pull-off on the right.

From the junction of the BRP and the northernmost intersection with US 221 (to Linville), drive south on the BRP for 2.8 miles. Turn left onto SR 1511 and follow the directions above.

Note: SR 1511 is between mileposts 307 and 308 on the BRP. GPS: N35 58.656'/W81 45.993'

The Hike

The trail to Harper Creek Falls immediately challenges you and your furry friends on a steep climb. At the top of the hill, as you start to catch your breath, you notice you're standing at a fork. A red-blazed trail heads right (north). Go straight ahead (west) on the orange-blazed Harper Creek Trail while appreciating the flat terrain. Walls of rhododendron line the path and in some places form a tunnel for you to hike through. Sparsely placed blazes guide you, but the path is heavily trodden and easy to follow.

You'll get a great view of Harper Creek Falls from the overlook.

The forest offers a pleasant diversity of holly and hemlock, poplar and pine. Ignore the sound and sight of some falls in the distance and continue following the wide footpath. At 0.8 mile, bypass a spur trail that leads left toward the creek and campsite, and continue straight ahead (west). Bypass the narrow footpaths that lead to primitive

Come back another day, without the dogs, to see Harper Creek Falls from the base.

campsites, and continue hiking on the well-trodden trail. You'll hike alongside a large, flat primitive campsite with a fire pit in the middle. Logs surrounding the fire pit form a natural seating area. At the far west end of this campsite, you reach another fork where an obscure trail heads left and crosses the creek and the obvious trail you've been hiking on goes right and uphill.

▶ **PUPPY PAWS AND GOLDEN YEARS: The dogs can enjoy playing in Lake James either near the Paddy's Creek Trail (hike 34) or near the park's picnic area. Another option is the Duggers Creek Falls Trail. The trailhead is in the Linville Falls Recreation Area, near the Linville Falls trailhead. This easy 0.2-mile hike leads to a creek and a small lovely waterfall.**

Although you want to follow the trail to the right, take a side trip to the creek, giving the dogs a chance to run and play and get some energy out. After the dogs have had their fun, return to the fork and you see a sign indicating the trail leads 8.3 miles to NC 181. The sign is white blazed because you're now merging onto the Mountains-to-Sea Trail for a short distance. Hike uphill and cross a rocky obstacle. This is the only tricky spot on the trail, and you may need to help your pups here. Beyond the rocks, the trail leads to another fork. The white-blazed Mountains-to-Sea Trail goes right (northeast) and uphill. Go left (northwest) on a spur trail marked with pink surveyor's tape. Bypass several narrow muddy paths leading steeply down to Harper Creek and continue hiking upstream. Soon the giant cliffs looming above Harper Creek Falls come into view. Keep the dogs leashed up, as the trail dead-ends at an overlook. The scenery before

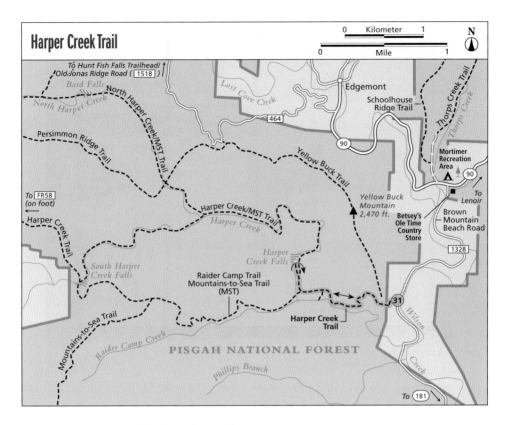

Harper Creek Trail

you is absolutely stunning! Massive cliffs seem to dwarf the two-tiered waterfall, which flows over smooth sleek stone. The view from here is unparalleled, but some experienced hikers like to hike to the base of the falls. I highly recommend you save that for another day when the dogs aren't with you.

Miles and Directions

0.0 Hike west and steeply climb.

0.25 Arrive at a fork at the top of the hill. A red-blazed trail heads right (north). Continue straight ahead (west) on the Harper Creek Trail.

0.8 Bypass a spur trail that leads left (southwest) toward the creek and primitive campsite. Continue hiking straight ahead (west).

1.1 At the far west end of a large primitive campsite, arrive at a marked fork. An obscured trail heads left (west) and crosses the creek which is a great watering hole for the dogs. Go right and now follow the white-blazed Mountains-to-Sea Trail north and uphill.

1.3 Climb over a rock obstacle. Continue hiking north.

1.35 Come to a fork; the white-blazed Mountains-to-Sea Trail continues northeast to the right. You want to go left (north northwest) on an obscure spur trail that follows Harper Creek upstream.

Your pups will enjoy hiking in North Carolina year-round.

1.5 Arrive at an overlook of Harper Creek Falls (N35 58.876'/W81 46.845') Once you've enjoyed the falls, backtrack to the trailhead.

3.0 Arrive back at the trailhead.

Option: To lengthen the hike continue hiking on the Mountains-to-Sea Trail.

Resting up: Gable Haus Country Inn and Cottages, 154 Ruffin St., Linville; (828) 733-9535; www.gablehausinn.com; two dogs any size, no fee.

Red Carpet Inn Lenoir, 142 Wilkesboro Blvd. SE, Lenoir; (828) 758-4403; two dogs any size, pet fee per dog per stay.

Camping: Linville Falls Campground, on the Blue Ridge Parkway at milepost 316; (828) 298-0398; www.nps.gov/blri/planyourvisit/camping-on-the-blue-ridge -parkway.htm; for reservations visit www.recreation.gov or call (877) 444-6777.

Mortimer Campground, on NC 90 in the town of Edgemont; (828) 675-5616; www.fs .usda.gov/recarea/nfsnc/recreation/camping-cabins/recarea/?recid−49006&actid =29; no electric sites.

32 Lower Falls of Upper Creek Trail

The Lower Falls of Upper Creek trail leads you on a steady downhill trek all the way to the falls. Once you reach the base, you're greeted with a charming waterfall that flows between large rounded rocks. The rock face continues alongside the creek and gives the dogs a perfect place to sit, run, play, or swim while the water rushes by.

Start: At the northeast corner of the parking lot (The Upper Falls of Upper Creek trailhead is on the west side of the parking lot.)
Distance: 1.6-miles out and back
Hiking time: 1 hour, 30 minutes
Blaze color: Yellow
Difficulty: Moderate to strenuous
Trailhead elevation: 3,166 feet
Highest point: 3,172 feet
Seasons: Year-round
Trail surface: Hard-packed dirt, very rooty
Other trail users: None
Canine compatibility: Voice control

Land status: Pisgah National Forest—Grandfather Ranger District
Fees and permits: None
Maps: DeLorme: North Carolina Atlas & Gazetteer, page 33, B5. National Geographic Trails Illustrated Map #779 Linville Gorge & Mount Mitchell, H12, Trail #268B.
Trail contact: Pisgah National Forest, Grandfather Ranger District; (828) 652-2144; www .fs.fed.us
Nearest towns: Linville, Pineola, and Morganton
Trail tips: Bring a hiking stick and lots of drinking water.

Finding the trailhead: *From the junction of NC 181 and the Blue Ridge Parkway near Linville,* drive south on NC 181 for 5.6 miles. Turn left at the sign for Upper Creek Falls and follow the road until it ends at the parking area.
From the junction of NC 181 and US 64 in Morganton, drive north on NC 181 for 20.9 miles. Turn right at the sign for Upper Creek Falls and follow the directions above. GPS: N35 57.610'/ W81 51.657'

The Hike

The trail begins by leading you across a small grassy field, and then takes you on a long, steady downhill trek around several switchbacks. If your dogs are well behaved under voice control, keep them off the leash; this prevents them from pulling you down the mountain or tripping you up on the rooty path. You'll hear a variety of birds, chirping and singing as you pass them by, and at 0.6 mile you come to a T. Go right (northeast), and continue your slow descent toward the falls. You'll pass a huge cliff overhang, where people have camped and sought shelter. After admiring this natural feature, continue on the trail downhill to the creek and falls. Large, smooth, rounded rocks line banks, and pools of water are formed here and there. Be smart about where you let the dogs hop in; the current is swift. The flat stone surface at the base of the falls is perfect for a picnic, to dip your feet in the water, or to simply sit

The dogs enjoy a leash-free hike at Lower Falls of Upper Creek.

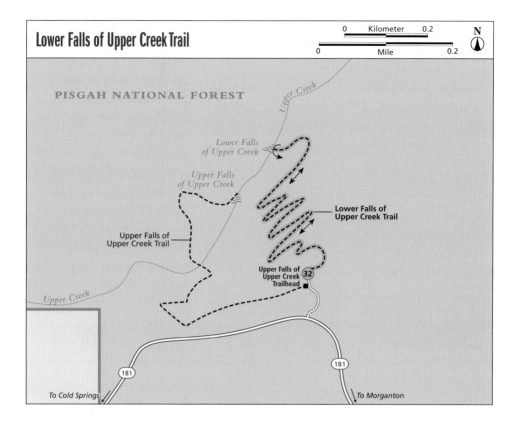

Lower Falls of Upper Creek Trail

PISGAH NATIONAL FOREST

Upper Creek

Lower Falls
of Upper Creek

Upper Falls
of Upper Creek

Lower Falls of
Upper Creek Trail

Upper Falls of
Upper Creek Trail

Upper Creek

Upper Falls of
Upper Creek 32
Trailhead

181

181

To Cold Springs

To Morganton

and breathe in the fresh mountain air. While you enjoy the tranquility, the dogs enjoy the crisp water and laying on the cool face of the stone.

As you return to the trailhead, switchbacks ease the incline, and the cool damp forest air helps keep you refreshed. But you'll still need plenty of drinking water. If you're here late in the day, after the hike drive 2.0 miles south on NC 181 to the Brown Mountain Overlook. On a clear night the mysterious "Brown Mountain Lights" can be seen wavering in the distance. This strange phenomenon has mystified people for hundreds of years. Cherokee legend says the lights are the spirits of Indian maidens searching for their loved ones lost in battle. Others say the ghosts of Civil War veterans are doomed to carry candles across the mountain forever. Whether they are ghosts, spirits, foxfire, or a mirage, the lights do exist and have yet to be scientifically explained.

Miles and Directions

0.0 Cross a small grassy field. Follow the trail downhill around several switchbacks.

0.6 Come to a T, left leads southwest to a rocky outcropping. Go right (northeast), continuing your descent.

0.75 Pass a cliff overhang. Continue downhill and west.

0.8 Arrive at Lower Falls of Upper Creek (N35 57.751'/ W81 51.713'). When you're finished enjoying the falls, backtrack to the trailhead.

1.6 Arrive back at the trailhead.

Option: Hike to Upper Falls of Upper Creek. The trailhead is on the west side of the parking lot and the hike is a strenuous 1.4 miles out and back. Keep the dogs on a leash until you safely cross the brink of the falls at 0.4 mile.

Resting up: Gable Haus Country Inn and Cottages, 154 Ruffin St., Linville; (828) 733-9535; www.gable hausinn.com; two dogs any size, no fee.

Quality Inn, 2400 S. Sterling St., Morganton; (828) 437-0171; two dogs up to 35 pounds, pet fee per dog per stay.

Red Carpet Inn Lenoir, 142 Wilkesboro Blvd. SE, Lenoir; (828) 758-4403; two dogs any size, pet fee per dog per stay.

Camping: Linville Falls Campground; (828) 298-0398; www.nps.gov/blri/plan yourvisit/camping-on-the-blue-ridge-parkway.htm. For reservations visit www .recreation.gov or call (877) 444-6777.

Fueling up: The Grind Café and Coffee House, 136 W. Union St., Morganton; (828) 430-4343.

▶ **PUPPY PAWS AND GOLDEN YEARS: The dogs can enjoy playing in Lake James either along the Paddy's Creek Trail (hike 34) or near the park's picnic area. Another option is the Duggers Creek Falls Trail. The trailhead is in the Linville Falls Recreation Area, near the Linville Falls trailhead. This easy 0.2-mile hike leads to a creek and a small lovely waterfall.**

Mikey loves the waterfalls as much as his mom does.

MORGANTON TO MARION

33 High Shoals Falls Loop Trail

Comprised of more than 18,000 acres you could spend weeks exploring the vast terrain of this state park. There's a campground, equestrian camping, and an astonishing 47.0 miles of trails for hiking, mountain biking, and horseback riding. The South Mountain Range is equally as expansive. It encompasses three counties and once served as a buffer between the Cherokee and Catawba Tribes and early white settlers.

Start: At the Hemlock Nature Trail trailhead, located at the southwest corner of the parking lot
Distance: 2.4-mile loop
Hiking time: 1 hour, 30 minutes
Blaze colors: White and blue
Difficulty: Moderate to strenuous; moderate to High Shoals Falls and back
Trailhead elevation: 1,361 feet
Highest point: 1,885 feet
Seasons: Year-round. December–February, 7:00 a.m.–7:00 p.m.; November, 7:00 a.m.–8:00 p.m.; March, April, October, 7:00 a.m.–9:00 p.m.; May–September, 7:00 a.m.–10:00 p.m. Closed Christmas Day.
Trail surface: Hard-packed dirt, gravel road, man-made steps

Other trail users: Mountain bikers and equestrians
Canine compatibility: Leash required
Land status: North Carolina Department of Natural Resources
Fees and permits: None
Map: *DeLorme: North Carolina Atlas & Gazetteer*, page 33, F7
Trail contact: South Mountains State Park, 3001 South Mountain Park Ave., Connelly Springs; (828) 433-4772; www.ncparks.gov
Nearest towns: Morganton and Laurel Hill
Trail tips: If you're afraid of heights, turn back at 0.75 mile. Bring a hiking stick and lots of drinking water. Trail maps may be available in a box at the west end of the parking area. Restrooms, trash cans, and a picnic area are near the trailhead.

Finding the trailhead: *From I-40 in Morganton*, take exit 105 and drive south on NC 18 for 11.0 miles to a right onto Sugar Loaf Road (SR 1913). Travel for 4.2 miles to where Sugar Loaf Road ends at Old NC 18 (SR 1924). Turn left and travel for 2.6 miles to a right onto Wards Gap Road (SR 1901). Travel for 1.3 miles to a fork and bear right onto South Mountain Park Avenue. Travel for 1.0 mile to the park gate. Continue another 2.4 miles to the end of the road.
From the junction of NC 18 and NC 10 in Laurel Hill, drive north on NC 18 for 0.6 mile. Turn left onto Old NC 18 (SR 1924) and travel for 6.0 miles. Turn left onto Wards Gap Road (SR 1901) and follow the directions above. GPS: N35-36.129'/W81-37.762'

The Hike

The hike begins as a leisurely stroll along the Hemlock Nature Trail. You pass interpretive signs about streamside birds, minnows, and animal tracks. You may learn a

High Shoals Falls is simply stunning.

thing or two while following the shallow rocky river. You'll see families wading in the water, and the dogs can too. Hike past an outdoor amphitheater, and the nature trail ends at a T. The right leads back to the parking lot. Go left and follow the gravel road over a bridge and into Shinny Creek Picnic Area. Once inside the picnic area, stay left at the first fork, and the loop begins at the second fork where a double staircase leads up in opposite directions.

To see the falls first, go left (south). The trail leads across a few footbridges, and you pass several places where the dogs can play in the water. Near the base you can't really see the falls, but massive boulders piled up on top of one another create a wonderland where water flows through every crack and crevice. A steep climb up some wooden steps leads to an overlook of High Shoals Falls. Freely flowing over a smooth stone-faced wall, with brilliant green moss clinging to the rock, the scenery is simply stunning. If your dogs are not in tip-top shape, turn back now. The loop continues to steeply climb up more stairs, leading past the upper portion of the falls. Beyond the falls, cross another footbridge. Upstream from the footbridge is a fantastic place for the pups to play in the creek. The water is crystal clear, and it's shallow enough for them to romp around. The loop continues through another picnic area and climbs some more. You come to a T and a fork. Stay right at both. On the way to the falls you'll see several people; beyond the falls you're likely to have the trail to yourself. The remainder of the hike is a long, steep, slow descent until you arrive at the double staircase where the loop began.

Miles and Directions

0.0 Hike west on the Hemlock Nature Trail alongside Jacob Fork.

0.2 Bypass an outdoor amphitheater (N35 36.069'/W81 37.935').

0.3 Come to a T at a service road. The right leads east to the parking lot. Go left (west).

0.4 Cross a footbridge over Jacob Fork.

0.45 Arrive at a fork in the Shinny Creek Picnic Area. The right (north) is the Headquarters Trail. Go left (south), following High Shoals Falls Loop Trail.

0.5 Come to another fork, where the loop begins. Go left (south) up the steps.

0.52 Cross a footbridge. Continue hiking south and upstream.

0.65 Cross a footbridge. Continue hiking upstream.

0.75 Cross a footbridge and climb up the steep steps.

0.9 Arrive at the High Shoals Falls overlook (N35 35.667'/W81 38.125'). Continue climbing up more stairs.

1.0 Pass the upper part of the falls (N35 35.643'/W81 38.113').

1.05 Cross a footbridge. Hike north through the picnic area and continue climbing.

▶ **PUPPY PAWS AND GOLDEN YEARS: The Hemlock Nature Trail is suitable for all dogs.**

1.3 Come to a T. Left leads south toward the Raven Rock Trail and Upper Falls campsites. Go right (north), following blue and white blazes.

1.45 Come to a fork. The left leads south and uphill. Go right (west) and hike downhill around a few switchbacks.

1.9 Arrive at the double set of steps where the loop began. Backtrack to the trailhead.

2.4 Arrive back at the trailhead.

High Shoals Falls Loop Trail

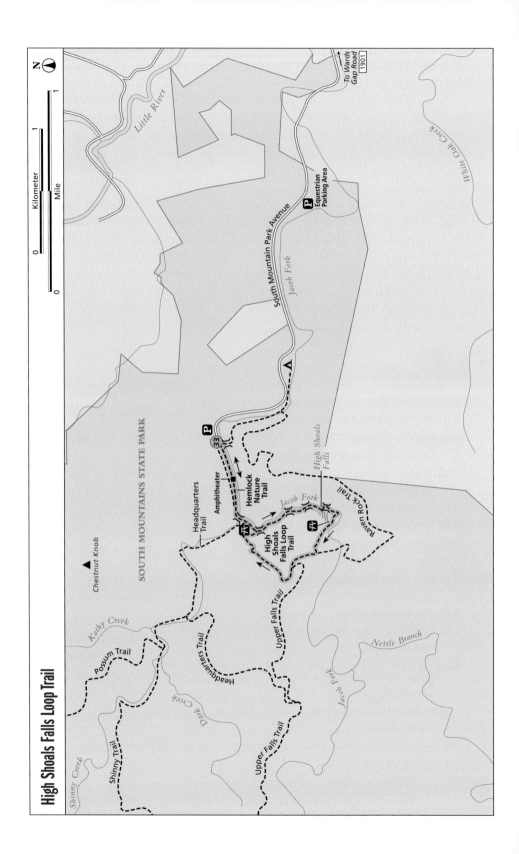

SOUTH MOUNTAINS STATE PARK

Chestnut Knob

Shinny Creek

Possum Trail

Shinny Trail

Kathy Creek

Dark Creek

Headquarters Trail

Upper Falls Trail

Upper Falls Trail

Jacob Fork

Nettle Branch

Headquarters Trail

Amphitheater

Hemlock Nature Trail

High Shoals Falls Loop Trail

Jacob Fork

High Shoals Falls

Raven Rock Trail

Little River

South Mountain Park Avenue

Jacob Fork

Equestrian Parking Area

To Wards Gap Road

1901

White Oak Creek

N

Kilometer

Mile

0   1

0   1

You and your furry friends will get a workout hiking the High Shoals Falls Loop Trail.

Option: If you or your dogs are not in tip-top shape, hike to the falls overlook and back, shortening the hike to 1.9 miles round trip.

Resting up: Quality Inn, 2400 S. Sterling St., Morganton; (828) 437-0171; two dogs up to 35 pounds, pet fee per dog per stay.

Sleep Inn, 2400A S. Sterling St., Morganton; (828) 433-9000; two dogs up to 35 pounds, pet fee per dog per stay.

Camping: Primitive camping onsite.

Fueling up: The Grind Café and Coffee House, 136 W. Union St., Morganton; (828) 430-4343.

34 Paddy's Creek Trail

Lake James State Park is made up of two separate sections along the shores of this magnificent reservoir. Each has miles of trails, a fishing pier, and boat ramps within easy reach. The Catawba River Area is home to the park's campground, and Paddy's Creek houses the park's fabulous swimming beach and the Paddy's Creek Trail. Dogs are not allowed within the public swimming area, but don't fret: The Paddy's Creek Trail leads to some of the most pristine sandy beaches on the lake.

Start: At the west end of the parking lot, west of the visitor's center

Distance: 2.3-miles out and back

Hiking time: 1 hour, 35 minutes

Blaze color: Orange

Difficulty: Easy

Trailhead elevation: 1,216 feet

Highest point: 1,237 feet

Seasons: Year-round. November–February, 7:00 a.m.–6:00 p.m.; March–May, September, October, 7:00 a.m.–8:00 p.m.; June–August, 7:00 a.m.–9:00 p.m. Closed Christmas Day.

Trail surface: Smooth compact clay, hard packed dirt

Other trail users: None

Canine compatibility: Leash required

Land status: North Carolina Department of Natural Resources

Fees and permits: None

Map: *DeLorme: North Carolina Atlas & Gazetteer*, page 33, E5

Trail contact: Lake James State Park, Paddy's Creek Area, NC Highway 126, Nebo; (828) 584-7728 or (828) 584-7730; www.ncparks .gov/Visit/parks/laja/main.php

Nearest towns: Nebo, Marion, and Morganton

Trail tips: Restrooms, a water fountain, and trail maps are available at the visitor's center.

Finding the trailhead: *From I-40 in Morganton*, get off at exit 94 and drive north for 0.5 mile to a stop sign at US 70. Turn left and travel approximately 1.6 miles to a right onto Bridgewater Road. Travel for 1.3 miles to a left onto Benfields Landing Road. Travel for 2.2 miles to a right onto NC 126 in Nebo. Travel for 0.7 mile to the entrance to Paddy's Creek Area of Lake James State Park on your right. Enter the park and drive 2.0 miles to the end of the road. **Note:** Bypass the Catawba River Area of Lake James State Park.

From the junction of NC 126 and US 70 in Nebo, drive northeast on NC 126 for approximately 5.3 miles to a right into the Paddy's Creek Area of Lake James State Park and follow the directions above. GPS: N35 45.066'/W81 52.701'

The Hike

This one is a trail for all seasons. A variety of wildflowers flourish in the spring and summer; in autumn the full color of fall glimmers off the water; and snow cleanses the earth and covers the trees in winter, giving visitors breathtaking views of the lake. The trail begins as a paved path and quickly transforms into traditional hard-packed dirt as it enters the woods. Looping around a small cove, you arrive at the first of several swim spots where the dogs enjoy splashing around in Lake James. A soft breeze and

Enjoy hiking alongside Lake James on the Paddy's Creek Trail.

the shade of the trees keeps you cool year-round as you hike generally west. The lake is in view for most of the hike, and at 0.3 mile you come to a fork. Stay left, following the shoreline north.

As you and your canine companions stretch your legs on this lovely wooded hike, you realize a fabulous forest surrounds Lake James. The forest is home to deer, foxes, minks and rabbits, but because you're hiking near the water, you may see frogs, turtles, or snakes as well. At the half-mile mark you come to a wonderful sandy beach where you can have a picnic and the dogs can take a dip. This piece of paradise sits at the halfway point, which is perfect for stopping on the way back too. Continue following the water's edge; cross a footbridge over a tiny, narrow creek; and you come to a second fork. The Homestead Trail leads away from the water. Again stay left, following the shoreline west. Less than a half mile from this fork, a spur trail makes a hairpin turn east over your left shoulder while the main path continues straight ahead (west). If you kept going straight here, you'd cross a grassy field and arrive at an alternate parking area. Instead, go left, following the spur trail east and it leads to a pristine point jutting out into the lake. A sandy beach with an island just off shore adds to the view. A variety of ferns form the underbrush, while holly, pine, and maple saplings stand amid them.

Miles and Directions

0.0   Follow the paved path past the handicap accessible picnic area toward Lake James. Before reaching the lake, follow the dirt trail north and into the woods.

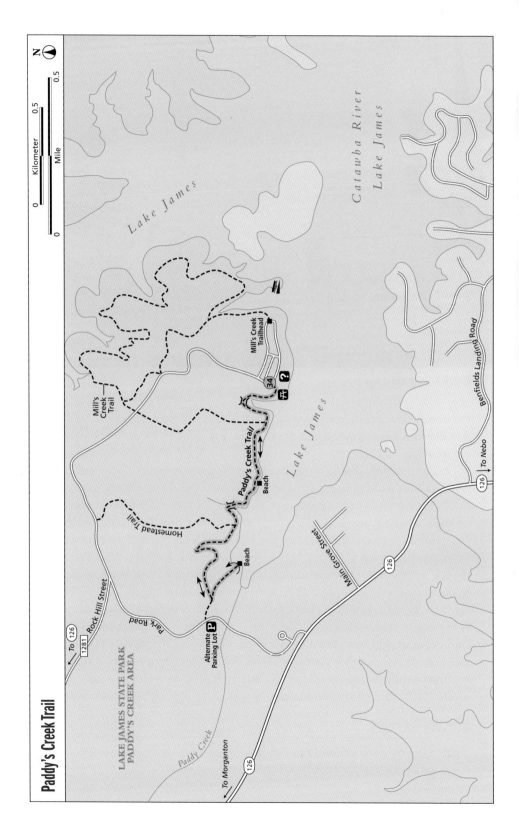

Paddy's Creek Trail

LAKE JAMES STATE PARK
PADDY'S CREEK AREA

Lake James

Catawba River
Lake James

Lake James

Mill's Creek Trail

Mill's Creek Trailhead

Paddy's Creek Trail

Homestead Trail

Beach

Beach

Alternate Parking Lot

Park Road

Rock Hill Street

To (126)

1281

34

Main Grove Street

126

To Nebo

Benfields Landing Road

126

To Morganton

Paddy Creek

N

0   Kilometer   0.5

0   Mile   0.5

0.15 Cross a footbridge, the trail follows the shoreline.

0.3 Come to a fork. The right (east) is the Mill's Creek Trail. Go left (north).

0.5 Arrive at a wonderful little sandy beach (N35 45.118'/W81 53.032'). Continue hiking west.

0.6 Cross a footbridge over a tiny creek.

0.75 Come to a fork. The right (north) is the Homestead Trail. Go left (west) following the lakeshore.

1.15 Arrive at a fork. The main trail leads west, away from the water 0.1 mile to an alternative parking lot. Go left here on a spur trail that leads east toward the water.

1.3 Arrive at a peaceful beach (N35 45.185'/W81 53.330'). Backtrack to the trailhead.

2.3 Arrive back at the trailhead.

Option: To shorten the hike, begin at the alternative parking lot, hike in, and follow the spur trail to the "beach." Then backtrack, making this a 0.5-mile out and back.

Resting up: Americas Best Value Inn, 4248 US 221 S., Marion; (828) 659-2567; two dogs up to 40 pounds, pet fee per dog per stay.

Comfort Inn, 178 US 70 W., Marion; (828) 652-4888; one dog up to 50 pounds, pet fee per stay.

Quality Inn, 2400 S. Sterling St., Morganton; (828) 437-0171; two dogs up to 35 pounds, pet fee per dog per stay.

Camping: Tent camping onsite; requires a 0.25-mile hike.

South Mountains State Park Campground, 3042 Frank Pkwy.

Roaring Gap; (336) 957-8185; www.ncparks.gov/Visit/parks/ stmo/main.php; primitive camping only, no hike required; for reservations visit www.reserveamerica.com or call (877) 722-6762.

Jaz wears a badge, just like her partner, and helps patrol Lake James.

Fueling up: The Grind Café and Coffee House, 136 W. Union St., Morganton; (828) 430-4343.

Switzerland Café and General Store, 9440 Highway 226A, Little Switzerland; (828) 765-5289; www.switzerlandcafe.com.

MARION TO LITTLE SWITZERLAND

35 Crabtree Falls Loop Trail

To reach Crabtree Falls is challenging, leading you on a steady descent, but the falls are absolutely gorgeous and well worth the effort. A single tree stands at the base of the falls, while the bold creek swiftly passes it by. A bench built into a footbridge at the base is a perfect place to take in the scenery while the dogs enjoy sniffing and playing around in the creek.

Start: At the east end of the small parking lot for the gift shop

Distance: 3.3-mile loop

Hiking time: 1 hour, 30 minutes

Blaze color: No blazes

Difficulty: Strenuous; moderate to strenuous to Crabtree Falls and back

Trailhead elevation: 3,780 feet

Highest point: 3,806 feet

Seasons: Year-round. Campground is open April 30–October 30.

Trail surface: Hard-packed dirt with rocky sections

Other trail users: None

Canine compatibility: Voice control, but keep them on a leash until you cross the campground road.

Land status: National Park Service–Blue Ridge Parkway

Fees and permits: None

Map: *DeLorme: North Carolina Atlas & Gazetteer*, page 32, D3

Trail contact: Blue Ridge Parkway; (828) 298-0398; www.nps.gov/blri

Nearest towns: Little Switzerland, Marion, and Burnsville

Trail tips: Bring a hiking stick and lots of drinking water. The full loop is strenuous.

Finding the trailhead: *From the junction of the Blue Ridge Parkway (BRP) and NC 80 in Busick,* drive north on the BRP for 4.5 miles. Turn left into Crabtree Meadows and park at the east end near the gift shop.

From the junction of the BRP and NC 226 near Spruce Pine, drive south on the BRP for 8.5 miles. Turn right into Crabtree Meadows and follow the directions above. Crabtree Meadows is between mileposts 339 and 340 on the BRP. GPS: N35 48.755'/W82 08.598'

The Hike

Crabtree Meadows has changed a bit in the last few years. The trailhead has moved from the campground entrance to the parking lot near the gift shop, and the gift shop is currently closed indefinitely. This new addition to the hike is quite pleasant and leads you past an outdoor amphitheater, through a field of flowers, and onto a fork. Stay right, and the trail leads northwest up to the campground road. Cross the road, pass the registration booth, and you'll see a large trail map posted near the former trailhead. Follow the dirt path north into the forest, and it begins a slow descent while

Daylilies line the roadways in spring and summer.

a variety of birds chirping and singing welcome you to the woods. When you reach a T, the loop begins. Go right (north) and the rocky path continues to descend. You'll pass a variety of impressively large trees as the sound of the falls grows stronger and the path gets rockier. While the dogs handle the rocks masterfully, watch your footing. A few benches are randomly placed if you need a breather.

At last, almost out of nowhere, you look up and see the glorious Crabtree Falls. A footbridge across the base has a bench built into it, giving visitors a perfect place to sit and enjoy the view. The dogs can explore the rocky creek near the base, while you take photos from the footbridge. If you're afraid of heights, turn back now. Beyond the falls the loop steeply climbs to a bench at the crest of the climb. Steep drop-offs are intimidating as you look across the valley from high above the falls. Giant boulders and rock formations add to the scenery. From the apex the loop descends to the creek and passes by a beautiful little cascade. Hiking past the Hoover Meadow, you cross several footbridges. The meadow is overgrown and more like chaos than a peaceful open area. These crossings give the dogs plenty of places to cool off in the creek. When you reach a marked fork, go left (north), and finish the loop on an easy peaceful stroll back to the T where the loop began. This trail is especially enjoyable in springtime. It's home to more than forty species of wildflowers waiting to show off their brilliant blossoms for any passersby.

▶ **PUPPY PAWS AND GOLDEN YEARS:** The Paddy's Creek Trail in Lake James State Park (hike 34) is suitable for all dogs. Or hike to Setrock Creek Falls, an easy 0.8 mile round trip hike leading to a wonderful waterfall. The trailhead is inside the Black Mountain Campground off FR 472, north of the Blue Ridge Parkway.

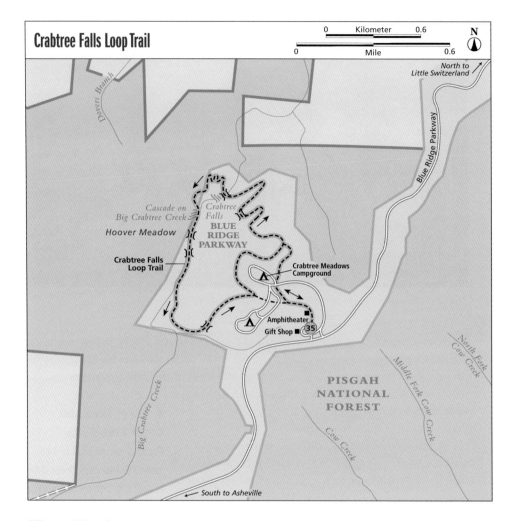

Miles and Directions

0.0 From the gift shop, hike north up the paved path.

0.1 Pass an outdoor amphitheater.

0.2 Come to a fork. The left leads west to the campground B-loop. Go right, hiking north toward the campground entrance. When you reach the road, hike north across the road to the small parking lot behind the campground registration booth.

0.3 Arrive at the former trailhead near a large trail map. Hike north into the forest and begin a slow descent.

0.5 Come to a T where the loop begins. The left is a narrow dirt path. Go right (north) on the wider rocky path that leads to the falls.

0.8 Cross a footbridge over a trickling tributary.

1.2 Arrive at the base of Crabtree Falls (N35 49.186'/W82 08.952'). Continue hiking past the falls, and the trail steeply climbs for 0.3 mile. *Option:* If you're afraid of heights, backtrack to the trailhead.

Cooling off in a crisp mountain creek.

1.5 Arrive at a bench at the crest of your climb. Continue hiking generally south on a steady descent.

1.6 Pass a lovely cascade on Big Crabtree Creek (N35 49.139'/W82 09.062').

1.7 Cross a footbridge, continue hiking south.

1.75 Cross a footbridge, continue hiking south.

2.25 Cross a footbridge, and the trail begins to loop north.

2.5 Come to a fork. The right leads southeast to the B-loop of the campground. Go left, continue hiking north.

2.8 Arrive back at the T where the loop began. Backtrack to the trailhead.

3.3 Arrive back at the trailhead.

Crabtree Falls has seating for you and a clear running creek to explore for your playful pooch.

Resting up: Americas Best Value Inn, 4248 US 221 S., Marion; (828) 659-2567; two dogs up to 40 pounds, pet fee per dog per stay.

Comfort Inn, 178 US 70 W., Marion; (828) 652-4888; one dog up to 50 pounds, pet fee per stay.

Camping: Primitive camping onsite; April 30–October 30.

Fueling up: Switzerland Café and General Store, 9440 Highway 226A, Little Switzerland; (828) 765-5289; www.switzerlandcafe.com.

36 Roaring Fork Falls Trail

The tall, narrow Roaring Fork Falls is outstanding! Brilliant green moss covers the rocks that form the falls, as the water tap dances from one tier to the next. To reach this beauty, you'll be following a wide grassy forest road for most of the way. The road gently climbs before heading into the forest. When you reach the falls, the dogs enjoy climbing on the rocks in the creek, while you sit upon streamside stones and take in the scenery.

Start: Hike south and uphill on FR 552
Distance: 1.1-miles out and back
Hiking time: 50 minutes
Blaze color: None
Difficulty: Easy
Trailhead elevation: 2,919 feet
Highest point: 2,986 feet
Seasons: Year-round
Trail surface: Grassy and gravel roadbed, hard-packed dirt
Other trail users: None
Canine compatibility: Voice control

Land status: Pisgah National Forest—Appalachian Ranger District
Fees and permits: None
Map: *DeLorme: North Carolina Atlas & Gazetteer*, page 32, D2
Trail contact: Pisgah National Forest, Appalachian Ranger District; (828) 682-6146; www.fs.fed.us
Nearest towns: Busick, Little Switzerland, and Marion
Trail tips: In summertime look for blackberries growing near the edge of the parking lot and along the trail.

Finding the trailhead: *From the junction of the Blue Ridge Parkway (BRP) and NC 80 in Busick, drive north on NC 80 for 2.2 miles. Turn left onto South Toe River Road and drive across the bridge. Immediately after crossing the bridge, turn left onto Busick Work Center Road and travel for 0.2 mile to the gate in front of the work center. Park here, but don't block the gate.* **Note:** *NC 80 is located between mileposts 344 and 345 on the BRP. GPS: N35 46.103'/W82 11.713'*

The Hike

The tiny town of Busick sits peacefully at the foot of Black Mountain. If you're coming from the south, you'll get fantastic views of the massive mountain looming above it. From the parking "lot" next to the Busick Work Center, follow the gated FR 552 generally south. As the "trail" gently climbs, all you hear is the sound of your own footsteps—and the jingling of your dogs' tags. A strip of grass in the center of the gravel "road" is soft on your puppies' paws, and though you're following a forest road, tall trees keep you shaded. Blackberry bushes are dispersed alongside the trail, and in summertime you can pluck the plump fruit and enjoy a tasty little treat. *Never* eat a berry or any vegetation unless you know exactly what it is.

As the trail continues to climb, you'll pass a pair of small abandoned buildings. These once held explosives for the work center. Not to worry: TNT hasn't been

Character oozes from Roaring Fork Falls.

stored here for years. At the half-mile mark, as the wide grassy road makes a hard bend left (north), you'll see a footbridge that leads south into the woods. Follow this footpath upstream, and you quickly arrive at the base of Roaring Fork Falls. The falls are magnificent! Multiple tiers allow the water to drop from one level to the next. Brilliant-green moss covers the rocks that rest on each side of the narrow waterfall. Large rocks give visitors a seating platform near the perfect pool at the base, and the dogs appreciate this one as much as you do.

Miles and Directions

- **0.0** Hike south up FR 552.
- **0.2** Pass an abandoned building.
- **0.25** Pass another empty explosive bunker.
- **0.5** As the forest road bends left, follow the narrow trail to the right (south) into the woods over a footbridge.
- **0.55** Arrive at Roaring Fork Falls (N35 45.609'/W82 11.510'). Backtrack to the trailhead.
- **1.1** Arrive back at the trailhead.

Resting up: America's Best Value Inn, 4248 US 221 S., Marion; (828) 659-2567; two dogs up to 40 pounds, pet fee per dog per stay.

Comfort Inn, 178 US 70 W., Marion; (828) 652-4888; one dog up to 50 pounds, pet fee per stay.

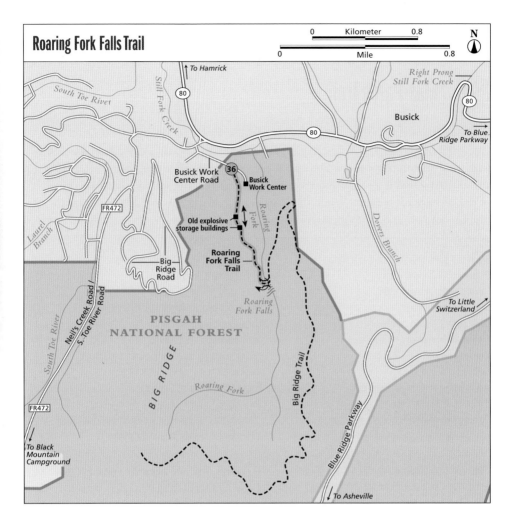

Roaring Fork Falls Trail

Camping: Black Mountain Campground, off FR 472, north of the Blue Ridge Parkway; (828) 675-5616; www.fs.usda.gov/recarea/nfsnc/recreation/camping-cabins/recarea/?recid=48522&actid=29; no electric sites; open April 14–October 31.

Carolina Hemlocks Campground, about 5 miles north of Busick on NC 80; (828) 682-6146 or (828) 675-5509; www.fs.usda.gov/recarea/nfsnc/recreation/camping-cabins/recarea/?recid=48596&actid=29; no electric sites; open April 14–October 31.

Fueling up: Switzerland Café and General Store, 9440 Highway 226A, Little Switzerland; (828) 765-5289; www.switzerlandcafe.com.

HOT SPRINGS

37 Max Patch Trail

From the moment you stand at the foot of Max Patch, to the time you reach the top, you'll be in awe of the stunning views around you. The dogs enjoy running free while you take in the scenery. The trail is extremely popular among dog owners. On any given day you'll see several dogs romping around on the summit. It's truly a slice of doggy heaven on Earth. While the dogs enjoy making new friends, you have the privilege of hiking on the Appalachian Trail.

Start: At the north end of the parking lot
Distance: 1.2-mile loop
Hiking time: 45 minutes
Blaze color: White
Difficulty: Easy to moderate
Trailhead elevation: 4,350 feet
Highest point: 4,629 feet
Seasons: Year-round
Trail surface: Hard-packed dirt
Other trail users: None
Canine compatibility: Voice control

Land status: Pisgah National Forest—Appalachian District
Fees and permits: None
Map: *DeLorme: North Carolina Atlas & Gazetteer*, page 30, C3
Trail contact: (828) 675-5616; www.fs.usda.gov/recarea/nfsnc/recreation/recarea/?recid=48620&actid=50
Nearest town: Hot Springs
Trail tips: Bring a camera and a picnic. Also bring plenty of drinking water and a bowl. The trail can be buggy in summertime.

Finding the trailhead: *From I-40*, get off at exit 7, Harmon Den, and follow Cold Springs Creek Road (FR 148) northeast for 6.3 miles to a hard left onto Max Patch Road (SR 1182). Travel for 1.8 miles to the parking area on the right.

From the junction of NC 209 and US 25 North/US 70 West in Hot Springs, drive south on NC 209 for 7.1 miles to a right onto Meadowfork Road (SR 1175). Travel for 5.2 miles to a right onto Little Creek Road (SR 1181). Travel for 3.5 miles to a right onto Max Patch Road (SR 1182) and follow the directions above. **Note:** FR 148 is a bumpy forest road, so high-clearance vehicles are recommended. GPS: N35 47.788'/W82 57.747'

The Hike

Standing at the foot of Max Patch Mountain, you can almost see the entire trail as it loops around the summit. Wildflowers grow freely, and everywhere you look you see pristine mountain views. It's no wonder this is one of my favorite places to bring the boys (Mikey and Bandit). You can hike either way, but clockwise has a gentler climb, and the views seem more dramatic. There's not much tree cover, but you're at such a high elevation the air feels cool even when the sun's out.

As you begin the hike, you hear the birds singing and the wind blowing through the tall grass, and the views are absolutely breathtaking! You pass through a small patch of forest. Enjoy the shade while you can, and ignore the narrow footpath to the right (south). The wide muddy trail continues to climb and quickly leads you back into the open on the backside of the summit. You'll come to a T on the famed Appalachian Trail (AT). The minute you stand here, you understand why people hike the AT. It's truly heaven! The mountain views are staggering. You literally have to stop and catch your breath as you take in the beauty before you. If you were to go left, you could hike all the way to Mount Katahdin, Maine, but save that for

Mikey patiently waits for me to catch up.

another day. Instead, go right and follow the white-blazed trail southwest up to the summit of Max Patch. At the top of this 4,629-foot bald, you get 360-degree views of pristine scenery for as far as the eye can see. In the center of the summit you'll see a US Coast & Geodetic Survey Marker letting you know you've reached your destination.

▶ **PUPPY PAWS AND GOLDEN YEARS: Dogs of all ages will enjoy frolicking around the grassy trails at the foot of Max Patch Mountain.**

While people picnic, socialize, and take photos, their dogs run free and enjoy some playtime. On my last visit there were eight dogs on the summit at once, running, romping, and making new friends as if they were at a free-range dog park. Bring lots of water and a bowl. They're going to work up a thirst with all this playtime. It's so heavenly on top of Max Patch, you and your canine compadres may find it hard to depart. You can see the parking lot from the top, so when you're ready to leave you really can't get lost. On your descent you'll pass wildflowers, and the birds and crickets chirp as you pass them by.

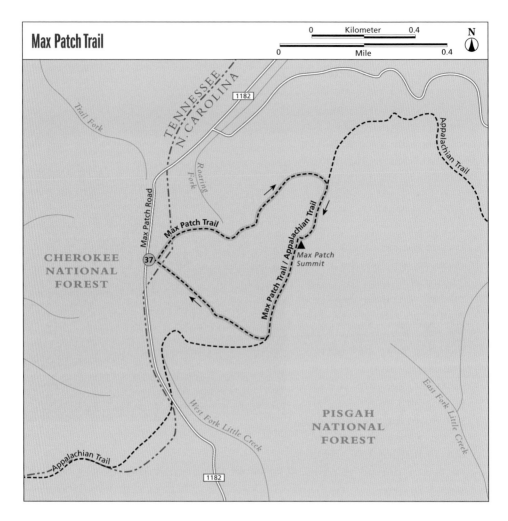

Max Patch Trail

CHEROKEE
NATIONAL
FOREST

PISGAH
NATIONAL
FOREST

TENNESSEE
N. CAROLINA

Max Patch Trail

Max Patch Road

Max Patch Trail / Appalachian Trail

Appalachian Trail

Max Patch
Summit

Trail Fork

Roaring Fork

West Fork Little Creek

East Fork Little Creek

Appalachian Trail

1182

37

Kilometer

Mile

N

The summit of Max Patch is like a free-range dog park for all to enjoy.

The dogs will have a blast running free along the Max Patch Trail, while you enjoy breathtaking views.

Miles and Directions

0.0 Several routes lead to the summit. Go left (north) to hike the loop clockwise.

0.2 Pass through a patch of woods. Ignore the spur trail to the right (south), continue hiking east-northeast.

0.5 Come to a T at the white-blazed Appalachian Trail (AT). Go right (southwest) toward the summit.

0.65 Arrive at the summit of Max Patch (N35 47.838'/W82 57.410'). To finish the loop continue hiking south on the AT as you head back to the trailhead.

1.2 Arrive back at the trailhead.

Option: To lengthen the hike, go left at the T and spend a little more time on the Appalachian Trail.

Camping: Big Creek Campground—Great Smoky Mountains National Park; (828) 486–5910; www.nps.gov/grsm/planyourvisit/frontcountry-camping.htm; tents only; dogs are not allowed on the national park trails in North Carolina.

Rocky Bluff Campground; (828) 682–6146; www.fs.usda.gov/recarea/nfsnc/recreation/camping-cabins/recarea/?recid=48602&actid=29; no electric sites; open May 1–October 1.

Fueling up: Spring Creek Tavern, 145 Bridge St., Hot Springs; (828) 622-0187.

ROBBINSVILLE

38 Joyce Kilmer Loop Trail

This trail is comprised of two loops resembling a figure eight. The lower loop leads to the Joyce Kilmer Memorial, embedded in a large rock where the loops meet in the middle. The upper loop then continues on, leading past even taller trees, towering overhead as you hike through Poplar Cove. The dogs enjoy several creek and tributary crossings, while you appreciate the sheer size of these massive trees.

Start: At the south end of the parking lot
Distance: 2.0-mile double loop
Hiking time: 1 hour
Blaze color: None
Difficulty: Easy to moderate
Trailhead elevation: 2,161 feet
Highest point: 2,543 feet
Seasons: Year-round
Trail surface: Hard-packed dirt
Other trail users: None
Canine compatibility: Leash required
Land status: Nantahala National Forest–
Cheoah Ranger District

Fees and permits: None
Maps: *DeLorme: North Carolina Atlas & Gazetteer*, page 50, B2. National Geographic Trails Illustrated Map #784 Fontana & Hiawassee Lakes, J8, Trail #43.
Trail contact: (828) 479-6431; www .fs.usda.gov/recarea/nfsnc/null/ recarea/?recid=48920&actid=70
Nearest town: Robbinsville
Trail tips: Picnic tables, charcoal grills, trash cans, and restrooms are located near the trailhead.

Finding the trailhead: *From the junction of NC 143 W and US 129 in Robbinsville,* drive west on NC 143 (Massey Branch Road) for 3.3 miles to a stop sign and right turn onto Snowbird Road (NC 143). Travel for 6.9 miles to a left onto Santeetlah Road (SR 1127). Follow this road for 2.3 miles to a left onto FR 416 and follow it to the trailhead at the end of the road.

From the junction of US 129 (Tapaco Road) and NC 28 near Tapaco, drive south on US 129 for approximately 9.6 miles to a right onto Joyce Kilmer Road (SR 1134). Travel west on Joyce Kilmer Road for 6.0 miles to a stop sign. Drive straight across the intersection onto FR 416 and continue 0.5 mile to the end of the road. **Note:** After 0.5 mile on Joyce Kilmer Road, the road makes a hard bend to the right over a bridge. GPS: N35 21.518'/W83 55.740'

The Hike

A map near the trailhead helps you navigate the figure eight that forms this double loop trail. You'll also find a kiosk with historical information about the trail's namesake. Joyce Kilmer was a poet, most famous for his poem "Trees." How apropos that years after his death the forest service would honor his name with a patch of forest filled with massive trees nearly 500 years old. The loops are described hiking clockwise. You'll immediately cross a footbridge over Little Santeetlah Creek, making

Little Santeetlah Creek rumbles by.

your first introduction to the forest. As you look up- and downstream, the views are phenomenal.

Beyond the bridge the trail follows a steady incline, crossing over several more footbridges. As you hike the lower loop, you don't realize how high you've climbed, because the birds are singing, the creek is flowing, and the tall trees around you are so enjoyable. A mix of ferns, blackberries, holly, and rhododendron line the understory, and if you just stop to look up, you realize how big the trees truly are. Footbridge #7 crosses a small tributary and is a good place for the dogs to take a water break. When

▶ **PUPPY PAWS AND GOLDEN YEARS: Dogs of all ages will enjoy strolling around the picnic area near the trailhead.**

you arrive at a crossroads, you'll see the Joyce Kilmer Memorial, a plaque embedded in a large rock. Continue clockwise onto the upper loop, as you get deeper into Poplar Cove, named for the predominant species in this area. These towering trees are even bigger than those on the lower loop. As the trail continues to climb, these mammoth trees offer shade, and the damp, cool forest keeps you comfortable year-round. You cross a

few tributaries, where the dogs can dip their paws. As you pause to look up at these giant poplars, reaching to the sky, you can see why Joyce Kilmer wrote about them. You reach a pair of trees that stand out above all others, like the twin towers. If you can get the dogs to sit still near these mighty behemoths, it makes a good photo op. As you make your way downhill, toward the memorial, you rock hop a few tributaries. The dogs enjoy these crossings, and you soon arrive back at the memorial. The remainder of the lower loop crosses a few more footbridges and leads to a fork. Stay right, following the creek downstream for the remainder of the hike.

Miles and Directions

0.0 Immediately cross a footbridge over Little Santeetlah Creek. Follow the path east and uphill.

0.05 Cross a footbridge.

0.14 Cross a footbridge.

0.18 Cross a footbridge.

0.3 Cross a footbridge.

0.4 Cross a footbridge.

0.48 Cross a footbridge.

0.5 Arrive at the Joyce Kilmer Memorial (N35 21.323'/W83 56.004'). This is also where the loops meet in the middle. To return on the lower loop, stay right (west northwest). To hike the upper loop, hike south and you'll see where the upper loop begins. Go left (southeast) and cross the footbridge.

0.53 Cross a footbridge.

0.8 Arrive at a pair of trees I call the "Twin Trees" (N35 21.233'/W83 56.142'). Continue hiking west.

0.85 Rock hop a tributary. The trail soon bends right (northwest).

1.0 Rock hop a tributary.

1.25 Arrive back at the Joyce Kilmer Memorial. Go left (west northwest) to finish the remainder of the lower loop.

1.3 Cross a footbridge.

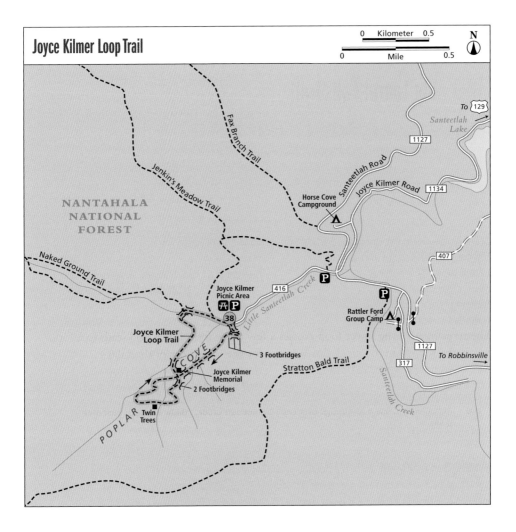

1.7 Cross a footbridge, and come to a fork. The left leads west on the Naked Ground Trail. Go right (north).

1.72 Cross a footbridge.

2.0 Arrive back at the trailhead.

Options: Hike either loop clockwise or counterclockwise. You could also hike just the lower loop, but the trees seem bigger on the upper loop.

Resting up: Microtel Inn & Suites, 111 Rodney Orr Bypass, Robbinsville; (828) 479-6772; two dogs any size, pet fee per stay.

Camping: Cheoah Point Campground; (828) 479-6431; www.fs.usda.gov/recarea/nfsnc/recreation/camping-cabins/recarea/?recid=48928&actid=29. Open April 15–October 31. For reservations visit www.recreation.gov or call (877) 444-6777.

39 Big Laurel Falls Trail

Running parallel with a lively creek, you'll find cascades, moss-covered rocks, and downed trees keep you entertained. As you hike through the damp forest, you'll pass over rolling hills, with a few quick climbs. Once you reach Big Laurel Falls, you'll be stunned at how beautiful it is. The falls beckon you to brave the chilly water and take a dip in the inviting pool.

Start: At the southwest end of the parking area

Distance: 1.2-miles out and back

Hiking time: 40 minutes

Blaze color: Blue

Difficulty: Easy to moderate

Trailhead elevation: 3,639 feet

Highest point: 3,784 feet

Seasons: Year-round

Trail surface: Hard-packed dirt

Other trail users: None

Canine compatibility: Voice control

Land manager: Nantahala National Forest— Nantahala District

Fees and permits: None

Maps: *DeLorme: North Carolina Atlas & Gazetteer*, page 51, B5. National Geographic Trails Illustrated Map #785 Nantahala & Cullasaja Gorges, C5, Trail #29.

Trail contact: (828) 524-6441; www.fs.usda .gov/recarea/nfsnc/recreation/hiking/ recarea/?recid=48856&actid=50

Nearest towns: Franklin and Hayesville

Trail tips: Bring a towel; this is a fantastic swimming hole for both you and the dogs.

Finding the trailhead: *From the junction of US 64 and Business 441 in Franklin,* drive west on US 64 for 11.7 miles to a left onto West Old Murphy Road, at the sign for "Wallace Gap." Travel 1.9 miles to a right onto FR 67, at the sign for the "Standing Indian Campground." Travel 6.8 miles to the pull-off on the right.

From the junction of US 64 and NC 175, drive east on US 64 for 16.2 miles to a right onto West Old Murphy Road, at the sign for "Wallace Gap," and then follow the directions above. **Note:** When driving west on US 64, be sure to drive the full distance to the westernmost West Old Murphy Road. GPS: N35 01.323'/W83 30.215'

The Hike

The second you step out of the car, you can hear the creek flowing strong, luring you into the forest. The trail leads you down some log steps and across the lively creek to a T. The left is the Timber Ridge Trail. Go right, following the wide muddy path west and downstream. The creek is full of character, with tiny waterfalls, rapids, and cascades. Moss-covered rocks and downed trees all add to the scenery. Along the path you can't help but notice there are several amazing massive trees. Some have intricate root systems or giant burl formations. These trees are as unique as the creek. The trail

You never do know what you'll see along a country road.

also has a large variety of mushrooms. Make sure your pups don't eat them! Many are poisonous and can be very dangerous or even fatal. Be diligent if your puppies are prone to putting everything in their mouths. If you're confident they won't try nibbling on any fungi, they can enjoy a leash-free hike all the way to the falls. The terrain is primarily rolling hills, although there are a few quick steep climbs. The sound of the creek, the shade of the forest, and unique features keep you entertained the entire way. Just when you think the creek couldn't get any prettier, you arrive at the base of Big Laurel Falls. A deep swimming hole at the base makes this an ideal place to take a dip for both you and the dogs. And it's just big enough to play fetch. Tucked away in a peaceful little cove, this hike is easily one of my favorites. Bring a towel and a picnic and spend some time taking it all in.

The nearby Standing Indian Campground is named for Standing Indian Mountain. At 5,499 feet, it's the highest point in the Southern Nantahala Wilderness. Legend has it that an Indian scout was keeping watch atop the mountain after a small village child was snatched up and taken away in the talons of a great flying beast. In answer to the villagers' prayers, the Great Spirit sent down thunderbolts to destroy the monster. The lone sentinel was turned to stone where he stood, and to this day he keeps watch over the valleys below.

Big Laurel Falls Trail

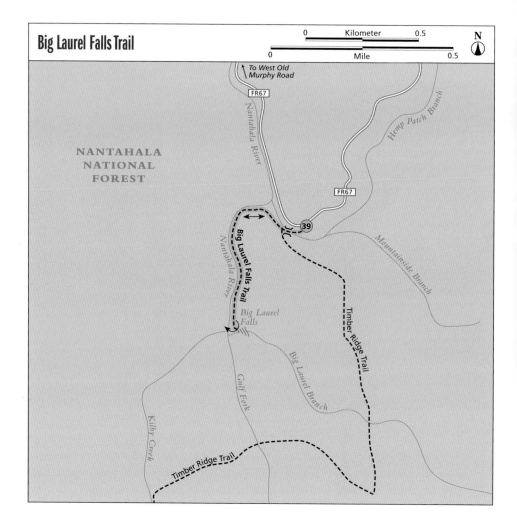

Miles and Directions

0.0 Hike southeast down the log steps.

0.05 Cross a footbridge and immediately come to a T. Left (east) is the Timber Ridge Trail. Go right (west) and follow the creek downstream.

0.6 Arrive at Big Laurel Falls (N35 01.095'/W83 30.388'). Backtrack to the trailhead.

1.2 Arrive back at the trailhead.

Resting up: Deerfield Inn, 40 Chatuge Ln., Hayesville; (828) 389-8272; www.deer field-inn.com; two dogs up to 20 pounds, pet fee per night.

Microtel Inn, 81 Allman Dr., Franklin; (828) 349-9000; two dogs up to 70 pounds, pet fee per dog per stay.

Camping: Clay County Park Campground, Myers Chapel Road, Hayesville; (828) 389-3532; open year-round.

True to her breed, Abbey Road loves the water and will spend all day fetching a stick in the swimming hole at Big Laurel Falls.

Standing Indian Campground; (828) 524-6441; www.fs.usda.gov/recarea/nfsnc/recreation/camping-cabins/recarea/?recid=48668&actid=29; open April 1–November 30; for reservations visit www.recreation.gov or call (877) 444-6777; no electric sites.

Fueling up: The Lazy Hiker, 188 W. Main St., Franklin; (828) 349-2337.

Motor Company Grill, 86 Main St., Franklin; (828) 534-0099.

HIGHLANDS TO CASHIERS

40 Cliffside Lake Loop Trail

Within Cliffside Lake Recreation Area there are hiking trails, a fishing "pier," a swimming beach, and of course the splendid lake itself. A trail connects the neighboring Van Hook Glade Campground to the recreation area, giving campers easy access and making this a great place to stay. The flat, easy trail loops around the lake, following the shoreline most of the way. Although dogs aren't allowed in the "people swimming area," there are ample opportunities for them to take a dip in the lake.

Start: At the northwest end of the parking lot
Distance: 0.8-mile loop
Hiking time: 25 minutes
Blaze color: None
Difficulty: Easy
Trailhead elevation: 3,454 feet
Highest point: 3,457 feet
Seasons: Year-round, sunrise to sunset
Trail surface: Gravel, hard-packed dirt
Other trail users: None
Canine compatibility: Leash required

Land status: Nantahala National Forest—Nantahala Ranger District
Fees and permits: Day-use fee, $
Map: *DeLorme: North Carolina Atlas & Gazetteer*, page 52, A1
Trail contact: Nantahala National Forest, Nantahala Ranger District; (828) 524-6441; www.fs.fed.us
Nearest towns: Highlands and Franklin
Trail tips: Restrooms, a water fountain, and trash cans are near the swimming area.

Finding the trailhead: *From the junction of US 64 and US 441 Bypass in Franklin*, drive east on US 64 for 12.1 miles. Turn left into the Cliffside Lake day-use area, and travel for 1.0 mile to the gate at the self-pay station. Pay the fee, and then go right at the fork. Travel 0.1 mile to the parking lot at the bottom of the hill.

From the junction of US 64 and NC 106 in Highlands, drive west on US 64 for 4.2 miles. Turn right into the Cliffside Lake day-use area and then follow the directions above. GPS: N35 04.735'/ W83 14.211'

Special Considerations: If you're camping at the Van Hook Glade Campground, you can hike to the Cliffside Lake Recreation Area via an access trail.

The Hike

The loop begins as soon as you enter the day-use area. To the right you'll see a gravel path where you'll finish the hike, and straight ahead leads toward the lake and past the public swimming area and restrooms. If you forgot your drinking water, you can fill up here. The swimming area is buoyed off from the rest of the lake and has a small sandy beach where visitors can soak up the sun. The area is popular with the locals, especially in summertime. A floating dock adds to the fun, but no pets are allowed in the swimming area. Not to worry: The trail closely follows the lakeshore, and there's plenty of places for the dogs to wade in. Beyond the restrooms, you cross a footbridge over Skitty Creek and then return to the edge of Cliffside Lake. As you follow the shoreline, you pass a few sets of steps that lead up and away from the water to a picnic area. Bypass them all, and you'll find yourself hiking through a picnic area that sits right next to the lake with tables, charcoal grills, and a water fountain. This is a great spot to let the dogs take a dip or play fetch. Beyond the picnic areas, the trail narrows and leads into the shade of the forest. You'll find the second half of the hike has some brush between you and the lake, but there are still a few good spots for the dogs to access the water. When you reach a fenced-off stone walkway that juts out into the lake, take a peek at the small dam that forms a beautiful little man-

A side trip to Dry Falls is worth a visit; you and Fido can even walk behind the falls.

made waterfall. Immediately after this "overlook," the Homesite Road Trail forks off to the left (south) and leads 1.5 miles to US 64. Stay right and continue past the base of the spillway. Continue hiking generally west, and you pass a small wooden dock that's used as a fishing pier. Beyond the pier the trail quickly brings you back to the trailhead.

If you're up for another hike while you're here, the Ranger Falls Trail is a moderate to strenuous 2.2-mile trek that leads you to Ranger Falls and back. This hike is good for dogs that have some extra energy, and they can splash around at the base of this lively waterfall. The falls stand at 40 feet tall, and the trail leads right across the base before making a small loop back out. It's found within the Cliffside Lake Recreation Area. From the gate, go left at the fork and drive 0.3 mile into the parking lot on your left. The trailhead is at the northeast corner of the parking area. N35 04.904'/W83 14.148'

Miles and Directions

0.0 A short paved path leads north toward the designated swimming area. Bypass the gravel trail on the right (the loop ends here). Immediately cross the footbridge and hike north toward the swimming area.

0.1 Hike along the shore past the swimming area and the restrooms.

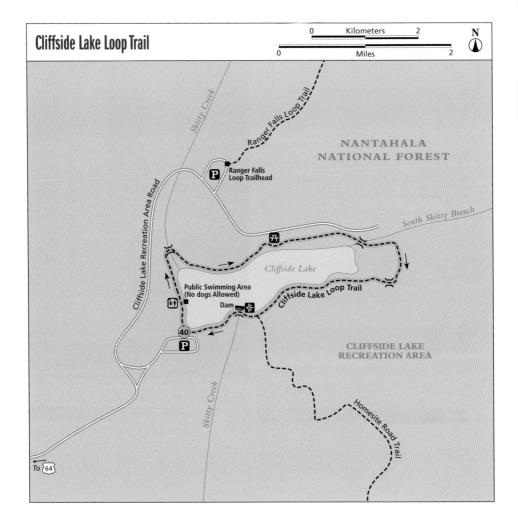

Cliffside Lake Loop Trail

0 Kilometers 2

0 Miles 2

N

Skitty Creek

Ranger Falls Loop Trail

NANTAHALA NATIONAL FOREST

Ranger Falls Loop Trailhead

Cliffside Lake Recreation Area Road

South Skitty Branch

Cliffside Lake

Public Swimming Area (No dogs Allowed)

Dam

Cliffside Lake Loop Trail

CLIFFSIDE LAKE RECREATION AREA

40

Skitty Creek

Homesite Road Trail

To 64

0.1 Cross a footbridge over Skitty Creek.

1.2 Bypass steps to the left (east) that lead up to a picnic area. Continue hiking south toward the lake.

0.21 Bypass more steps to the left and up. Continue hiking along the lakeshore.

0.22 Bypass more steps to the left and up. Continue hiking along the lakeshore.

0.3 Hike east across a picnic area.

0.45 Cross a footbridge, and the trail bends right (south).

0.5 Cross a footbridge and continue hiking west.

0.7 Arrive at a fenced-off stone walkway that juts out into the lake. Use this wall to overlook a small dam that forms a spillway (N35 04.763'/W83 14.115'). After the overlook, you immediately come to a fork. The left leads south on the Homesite Road Trail. Stay right and hike west past the spillway.

0.72 Cross a footbridge and continue hiking southwest along the lake.

0.8 Arrive back at the trailhead.

The dogs can swim in Cliffside Lake, just not in the designated swim area.

Resting up: Highlands House Bed and Breakfast, 101 Potter Ln., Highlands; (828) 787-1186; two dogs any size, no fee.

Highlands Inn Lodge, 96 Log Cabin Ln., Highlands; (828) 526-5899; two dogs up to 80 pounds, pet fee per dog per night.

Camping: Van Hook Glade Campground, just west of the Cliffside Lake Recreation Area on US 64; (828) 526-5912; www.fs.usda.gov/recarea/nfsnc/recreation/camping-cabins/recarea/?recid=48652&actid=29. Open April 1–October 31. For reservations visit www.recreation.gov or (877) 444-6777. No electric sites.

Fueling up: Bistro on Main, 270 Main St., Highlands; (828) 526-2590.

Cornucopia, 16 Cashiers School Rd., Cashiers; (828) 743-3750.

Wild Thyme Gourmet, 343 Main St., Highlands; (828) 526-4035.

41 Secret Falls Trail

You're in for a real treat when you arrive at the base of Secret Falls. The scenery is stunning, and the falls seem magical, sitting in their own peaceful cove. A swimming hole at the base is pristine and perfect for the whole family to take a dip. Or you can simply sit by the side and appreciate the force of the creek as it flows on by.

Start: At the northwest corner of the parking lot
Distance: 1.3-miles out and back
Hiking time: 1 hour, 30 minutes
Blaze color: Blue
Difficulty: Easy to moderate
Trailhead elevation: 2,579 feet
Highest point: 2,599 feet
Seasons: Year-round
Trail surface: Narrow, hard-packed dirt
Other trail users: None

Canine compatibility: Voice control
Land status: Nantahala National Forest—Nantahala Ranger District
Fees and permits: None
Map: *DeLorme: North Carolina Atlas & Gazetteer*, page 52 F1
Trail contact: (828) 524-6441; www.fs.fed.us
Nearest town: Highlands
Trail tips: Bring a hiking stick.

Finding the trailhead: *From the junction of US 64 (Main Street) and NC 28 South in Highlands*, drive east on Main Street and pass through the light at Fifth Street. After approximately 0.2 mile, Main Street becomes Horse Cove Road. Follow Horse Cove Road for 3.7 miles and turn right onto Walking Stick Road. Continue for 2.9 miles and turn right onto FR 4567. Travel for 0.2 mile to a small parking area on the left. GPS: N35 00.521'/W83 09.998'

The Hike

The falls are nestled away, not far from the quaint little mountain town of Highlands. Resting above 4,100 feet, the aptly named town is home to charming shops and classy restaurants, yet miles of hiking trails—and dozens of waterfalls—are within easy reach, Secret Falls included. This stoic waterfall was once a long-kept secret among locals and a privileged few outsiders. But in recent years the prized location of the falls has finally been outed. The hike begins on a narrow path that widens as you get farther along. By a quarter mile you begin downhill and rock hop a tributary where the dogs can take a water break. After passing through a rhododendron tunnel, you quickly cross another tributary, where a downed tree acts as a footbridge. Just past the half mile mark you come to a fork. Go left, following the blue-blazed trail south and downhill toward the sound of the falls. Passing through a primitive campsite, you can picture yourself camping

▶ **PUPPY PAWS AND GOLDEN YEARS: Visit the Chattooga River Trail (hike 42). It's an easy 0.5-mile hike that leads to a wonderful sandy beach and back. Or, visit Silver Run Falls (hike 43) near Cashiers. This one leads 0.2 mile (round-trip) to a stunning waterfall.**

Lilies grow wild throughout the state.

under the stars with the sound of the falls lulling you to sleep. The last leg of the hike leads you down some log steps and out to the base of the stupendous Secret Falls. The waterfall is tucked away in its own peaceful cove, with a magnificent swimming hole at the base. The whole family will enjoy taking a dip here, but use caution. Beyond the swimming hole, the creek continues downstream over another tall waterfall. Don't let the dogs stray to the brink of this second waterfall. The currents can be swift, and rocks slick, even for a four-legged fellow. Keep them near the base, and you can all safely enjoy the serene setting of Secret Falls.

Miles and Directions

0.0 Hike northwest on the narrow dirt path and hike past the gate.

0.4 Rock hop a small tributary.

0.45 Cross a second tributary.

0.5 Arrive at a fork where the trail you're on seems to go straight ahead (west), and a blue-blazed trail leads left (south) and downhill. Go left here.

0.6 Pass through a primitive campsite and hike west down the steps that lead to the falls.

0.65 Arrive at the base of Secret Falls (N35 00.281'/W83 10.310'). Backtrack to the trailhead.

1.3 Arrive back at the trailhead.

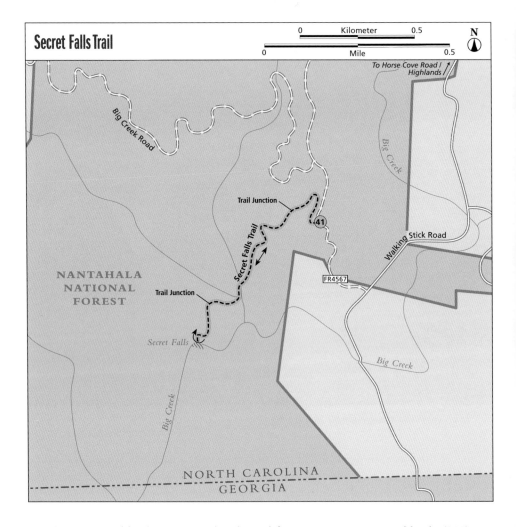

Resting up: Highlands House Bed and Breakfast, 101 Potter Ln., Highlands; (828) 787-1186; two dogs any size, no fee.

Highlands Inn Lodge, 96 Log Cabin Ln., Highlands; (828) 526-5899; two dogs up to 80 pounds, pet fee per dog per night.

Camping: Van Hook Glade Campground, just west of Cliffside Lake Recreation Area on US 64; (828) 526-5912; www.fs.usda.gov/recarea/nfsnc/recreation/camping-cabins/recarea/?recid=48652&actid=29. Open April 1–October 31. For reservations visit www.recreation.gov or call (877) 444-6777. No electric sites.

Fueling up: Bistro on Main, 270 Main St., Highlands; (828) 526-2590.

Cornucopia, 16 Cashiers School Rd., Cashiers; (828) 743-3750.

Wild Thyme Gourmet, 343 Main St., Highlands; (828) 526-4035.

42 Chattooga River Trail

Tucked away between the quaint mountain towns of Highlands and Cashiers you'll find the Chattooga River Trail. The trail follows the river for a quarter mile before leading you to an outstanding sandy beach on the river's edge. The water is calm enough to let the dogs swim, and the beach is big enough for them to run and play. Beyond the beach, the trail continues for another 2.75 miles, but follows the river from up above.

Start: From the parking area, walk downhill on the road and, before you cross the iron bridge over the river, you'll see the Chattooga River trailhead to the left (northwest side of the bridge).

Distance: 0.5-mile out and back

Hiking time: 20 minutes

Blaze color: None

Difficulty: Easy

Trailhead elevation: 2,432 feet

Highest point: 2,451 feet

Seasons: Year-round

Trail surface: Narrow, hard-packed dirt

Other trail users: None

Canine compatibility: Voice control; but keep them on a leash until you are a safe distance from the road.

Land status: Nantahala National Forest— Nantahala Ranger District

Fees and permits: None

Maps: *DeLorme: North Carolina Atlas & Gazetteer*, page 52, F2. National Geographic Trails Illustrated Map #785 Nantahala & Cullasaja Gorges, C12, Trail #432.

Trail contact: (828) 524-6441; www.fs.usda .gov/recarea/nfsnc/recreation/hiking/ recarea/?recid=48716&actid=50

Nearest towns: Highlands and Cashiers

Trail tips: Bring a towel and a picnic and enjoy a day at the "beach."

Finding the trailhead: *From the junction of US 64/Main Street and NC 28 in Highlands*, drive east on Main Street. Stay on Main Street and pass through the light at Fifth Street. After approximately 0.2 mile Main Street becomes Horse Cove Road (SR 1603). Follow Horse Cove Road for 4.5 miles (from the light at US 64 and SR 28) to a right onto the gravel Bull Pen Road. Follow Bull Pen Road for 3.0 miles to the pull-off-style parking area on the right. **Note:** When coming from the west (Highlands) Bull Pen Road becomes FR 1178 after 0.1 mile, and becomes paved after 2.0 miles. If you cross the bridge over the Chattooga River, you've gone too far.

From the junction of NC 107 and US 64 in Cashiers, drive south on NC 107 for 6.9 miles to a right onto Bull Pen Road (SR 1100). Travel 5.4 miles to the trailhead on the right. There is limited parking at the trailhead. If no parking is available, continue driving on Bull Pen Road for 0.1 mile to a pull out on the left. Park here and hike down the road to the trailhead. GPS: N35 00.962'/ W83 07.590'

The Hike

The Chattooga is the crown jewel of the Southern rivers. It's best known for forming the border between Georgia and South Carolina, but actually begins in North Carolina. The river cuts through the Ellicott Rock Wilderness, and the Chattooga River

The dogs enjoy a day at the beach along the wild and scenic Chattooga River.

Trail closely follows the banks of this rocky bottomed river for 3.0 miles from end to end. However, I recommend only hiking the first quarter mile to the beach when hiking with dogs. At the trailhead you'll see two trails. The right leads (northeast) down to the river's edge. Large, flat rocks rest right alongside the water, but the river is whipping by here, so please use caution, keeping the dogs on a tight leash! This is a nice side trip and a fabulous place for photography, or to simply enjoy the sights and sounds as the powerful river rushes by. You can also view a waterfall that flows beneath the iron bridge of Bull Pen Road by walking out onto the bridge, but there's no sidewalk, so use extreme caution!

To begin the hike, and to take the dogs to a safe place to swim, follow the trail to the left (north) at the trailhead. It leads into the forest and immediately brings you across a footbridge. The muddy path follows the river upstream and you bypass several small footpaths made by local fishers that lead to the river. As you continue upstream, the forest offers solitude. The birds chirping, the river passing by, and your own footsteps are all you hear. A quarter mile into the hike, you'll see a wide side path that leads to an open sandy beach right on the banks of the river. Here, the river is as passive as any other. The dogs can run free and splash around worry free. Bring a towel in case you decide to dip your own feet in the water. You may even meet other dogs here. This "beach" is popular with the locals, especially on weekends. Whether you spend minutes, or hours, you'll find it's a wonderful place to enjoy the outdoors, yet takes minimal effort to reach. You'll certainly put a smile on your puppies' faces, and their furry little tails will wag away. The trail continues for another 2.75 miles, but

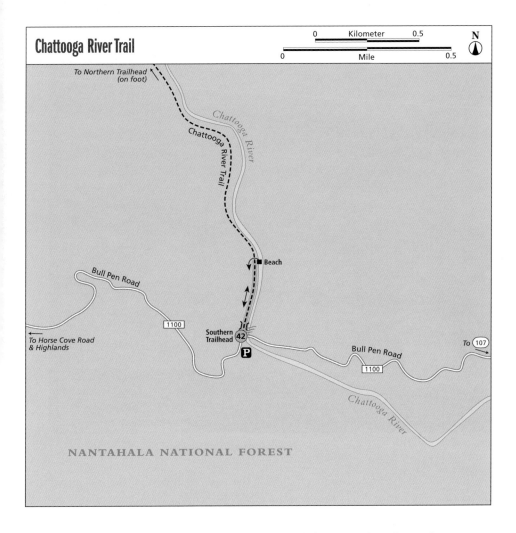

it climbs and follows the river from above it. Feel free to explore, but make sure you bring lots of drinking water for the dogs if you do.

Miles and Directions

0.0 Follow the left Chattooga River Trail 433 that heads north and away from the river.

150' Cross a footbridge and follow the muddy path upstream.

0.25 Take the side trail east to the sandy beach alongside the river (N35 01.125'/W83 07.533'). Backtrack to the trailhead.

0.5 Arrive back at the trailhead.

Options: Take the quick side trip to the river near the trailhead. It gives you fantastic views of a waterfall that flows beneath the iron bridge. Large flat boulders line the banks of the river, but keep the dogs on a tight leash while you're in this area. The river is raging over the falls here.

These charming black-eyed Susans grow like weeds along the roadway.

To lengthen the hike, continue following the trail north beyond the beach. But if you do, bring lots of drinking water, and please use caution with the dogs near the river. The current can be swift in places.

Resting up: Highlands House Bed and Breakfast, 101 Potter Ln., Highlands; (828) 787-1186; two dogs any size, no fee.

Highlands Inn Lodge, 96 Log Cabin Ln., Highlands; (828) 526-5899; two dogs up to 80 pounds, pet fee per dog per night.

Camping: Ralph Andrews Park Campground, Pine Creek Road, Glenville; (828) 743-3923; open April 15–October 31.

Van Hook Glade Campground, just west of the Cliffside Lake Recreation Area on the north side of US 64; (828) 526-5912; www.fs.usda.gov/recarea/nfsnc/recreation/camping-cabins/recarea/?recid=48652&actid=29; open April 1–October 31; for reservations visit www.recreation.gov or call (877) 444-6777; no electric sites.

Fueling up: Bistro on Main, 270 Main St., Highlands; (828) 526-2590.

Cornucopia, 16 Cashiers School Rd., Cashiers; (828) 743-3750.

Wild Thyme Gourmet, 343 Main St., Highlands; (828) 526-4035.

43 Silver Run Falls Trail

Representing beauty and grace, the crystal-clear water of Silver Run Creek prances over the rock face before forming a perfect pool at the base. The whole family will enjoy wading out into the creek, or sitting on the large stones perfectly placed along the water's edge—including your happy hounds. Bring a picnic, and a towel, you're probably going to want to stay a while.

Start: At the south end of the pull-off

Distance: 0.2-mile out and back

Hiking time: 10 minutes

Blaze color: None

Difficulty: Easy

Trailhead elevation: 3,075 feet

Highest point: 3,132 feet

Seasons: Year-round

Trail surface: Wide gravel path and narrow hard-packed dirt

Other trail users: None

Canine compatibility: Voice control

Land status: Nantahala National Forest– Nantahala Ranger District

Fees and permits: None

Maps: *DeLorme: North Carolina Atlas & Gazetteer*, page 52, F2. National Geographic Trails Illustrated Map #785 Nantahala & Cullasaja Gorges, D13, Trail #435.

Trail contact: (828) 524-6441; www.fs .usda.gov/recarea/nfsnc/recreation/hiking/ recarea/?recid=48722&actid=50

Nearest town: Cashiers

Trail tips: Bring your swimsuit and a towel, as a picture-perfect swimming hole lies at the base of the falls.

Finding the trailhead: *From the junction of NC 107 and US 64*, drive south on NC 107 for 4.0 miles to the pull-off on your left.

From the junction of NC 107 and the North Carolina/South Carolina state line, drive north on NC 107 for 4.1 miles to the pull-off on your right. GPS: N35 04.012'/W83 04.018'

The Hike

This short and easy-to-follow trail brings you back into the woods on a wide gravel path. The hike is shaded, and you instantly feel the cool air from the moving water. You can hear the falls and the birds singing the minute you step on the trail. As you stroll through the forest, you'll pass blossoming rhododendron, tall poplars, and colorful maple trees. The only downside of this hike is how populated it is, especially on the weekends. When you reach the falls, you'll see why so many people come to visit. The swimming hole at the base is fantastic, and large rocks give visitors several places to sit and take in the stunning scenery. The water is crystal clear, and Silver Run Falls is exquisite. Below the falls the creek flows into the mighty Whitewater River, best known for Whitewater Falls. At 411 feet, it's touted as the tallest waterfall east of the Mississippi River. This impressive waterfall is well worth a visit. It's located off of NC 281 South, 8.4 miles south of US 64 in Lake Toxaway. A wide paved path leads 0.25

Enjoy the journey as much as the destination.

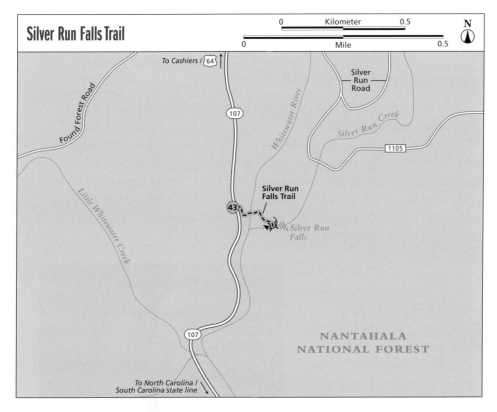

Silver Run Falls Trail

0   Kilometer   0.5
0   Mile   0.5

N

To Cashiers / 64

Found Forest Road

Whitewater River

107

Silver Run Road

Silver Run Creek

1105

Little Whitewater Creek

Silver Run Falls Trail

43

Silver Run Falls

107

NANTAHALA NATIONAL FOREST

To North Carolina / South Carolina state line

This little guy is trying to brave the chilly water of Silver Run Creek.

mile to the Whitewater Falls overlook. The dogs will enjoy stretching their legs, but they must remain on a leash, especially near the overlook.

Miles and Directions

0.0 Follow the gravel path as it bends left and leads east back into the woods.

0.1 Cross a footbridge.

0.1 Arrive at Silver Run Falls (N35-03.978'/W83-03.936'). Backtrack to the trailhead.

0.2 Arrive back at the trailhead.

Resting up: The Cabins at Seven Foxes, Seven Foxes Ln., Lake Toxaway; (828) 877-6333; www.sevenfoxes.com; pet fee per stay.

Highlands House Bed and Breakfast, 101 Potter Ln., Lake Toxaway, Highlands; (828) 787-1186; two dogs any size, no fee.

Highlands Inn Lodge, 96 Log Cabin Ln., Highlands; (828) 526-5899; two dogs up to 80 pounds, pet fee per dog per night.

Camping: Ralph Andrews Park Campground, Pine Creek Road, Glenville; (828) 743-3923; open April 15–October 31.

Van Hook Glade Campground, just west of the Cliffside Lake Recreation Area on US 64; (828) 526-5912; www.fs.usda.gov/recarea/nfsnc/recreation/camping-cabins/recarea/?recid=48652&actid=29; open April 1–October 31; for reservations visit www.recreation.gov or call (877) 444-6777; no electric sites.

Fueling up: Bistro on Main, 270 Main St., Highlands; (828) 526-2590.

Cornucopia, 16 Cashiers School Rd., Cashiers; (828) 743-3750.

Wild Thyme Gourmet, 343 Main St., Highlands; (828) 526-4035.

Bring a picnic and spend the day alongside the crystal-clear water of Silver Run Creek.

LAKE TOXAWAY

44 Schoolhouse Falls and Panthertown Valley Trail

You and your pups are in for a real treat! This fabulous hike first leads to a beautiful, free-falling waterfall. It then brings you to the "sandbar," where a spectacular sandy beach is found in the middle of the forest. The dogs love this hike! This is why it's among my favorites.

Start: At the end of the dirt road at the northeast corner (right of the trailhead information sign)
Distance: 3.1-miles out and back; Schoolhouse Falls, 2.0-miles out and back
Hiking time: 1 hour, 40 minutes; Schoolhouse Falls, 1 hour
Blaze color: Red
Difficulty: Easy to moderate
Trailhead elevation: 3,990 feet
Highest point: 3,996 feet
Seasons: Year-round
Trail surface: Gravel road, hard-packed dirt, and wide sandy road
Other trail users: Mountain bikers, equestrians, backpackers
Canine compatibility: Voice control
Land status: Nantahala National Forest—Nantahala Ranger District
Fees and permits: None

Maps: *DeLorme: North Carolina Atlas & Gazetteer*, page 52, D3. National Geographic Trails Illustrated Map #785 Nantahala & Cullasaja Gorges, F14, Trail #474.
Trail contact: Nantahala National Forest, Nantahala Ranger District; (828) 524-6441; www.fs.fed.us
Nearest town: Lake Toxaway
Trail tips: An intricate maze of well-trodden trails and narrow footpaths weave across Panthertown Valley. I *highly* recommend bringing a trail map along so you don't get turned around. "A Guide's Guide to Panthertown" by Burt Kornegay is a fantastic resource. It's a typical folding map, but focuses soley on Panthertown, and it's waterproof. You can buy it online or at local outfitters. You may need to dodge the occasional pile of horse manure. Bring lots of drinking water and a ball to toss around for your four-legged friends.

Finding the trailhead: *From the junction of NC 281 North and US 64 in Lake Toxaway*, drive north on NC 281 for 0.8 mile to a left onto Cold Mountain Road (across from fire station). Travel for 5.7 miles to where the road ends. Go left and travel for 0.1 mile to a right onto an unmarked dirt road. Follow this road for 0.2 mile to the end. GPS: N35 09.479'/W82 59.952'

The Hike

Panthertown (pronounced painter-town) was named in the early 1900s by the first settlers to the area. At that time, there were no trails in the valley. As a matter of fact, it was such a wild place they called it a town of painters, meaning "panthers." As you explore the valley, you may come across remnants of old homesteads, or a chimney

Play time on the sandbar in Panthertown Valley.

stack standing out in the forest. Even Schoolhouse Falls got its name because a small schoolhouse once stood near the brink of the falls.

The hike begins on a typical hard-packed dirt path through the forest. In less than 0.2 mile you cross a tributary and begin to follow a wide gravel "road" downhill. This part of the hike is quite mundane, but when you get down into the valley, creeks, waterfalls, and amazing views are available at every turn. You could easily spend an entire day exploring the valley and still not see it all. As the gravel road makes a hard switchback to the left (south), you'll see a narrow footpath goes straight ahead (north). Follow the footpath, and it quickly leads to a fork. Stay left, and the path puts you back on the gravel road just farther down. This footpath simply acts as a shortcut.

Continue downhill and bypass the Devil's Elbow Trail. You cross a sturdy bridge over Greenland Creek and immediately come to a T. The dogs can splash around in the shallow creek, but the waterfall is only 0.2 mile away. At this T, the left begins the Little Green Trail and leads south to Schoolhouse Falls. The right is the continuation of the Panthertown Valley Trail, which heads north toward the sandbar. Go left for now, and you easily see how this trail got its name. The lush terrain is lined with greenery and completely shaded. As the trail brings you over a long boardwalk, you can hear the sound of the falls beckoning you. As the Little Green Trail heads right (west) and uphill, follow a spur trail straight ahead (south), and it leads directly to the base of Schoolhouse Falls. Schoolhouse is spectacular! The falls are small, but free fall over a smooth rock ledge. A large swimming hole between you and the falls adds to the scenery. If your dogs love the water, they can chase a stick well out into the creek,

These happy hounds had a full day of fun in the forest.

while you enjoy watching them have such fun. If your pooch prefers dry land, you've got the best of both worlds. The spacious sandy area along the edge of the swimming hole is big enough for the dogs to run around. Flat rocks scattered around make a perfect perch for you to take it all in.

When the dogs have had their fill of fun, backtrack to the T, and now head the opposite direction (north). The trail is wide and nicely shaded no matter what time of day. As you delve deeper into Panthertown Valley, you cross another well-built bridge, and again come to a T immediately after the crossing. Go left, and continue following the Panthertown Valley Trail west. Just 0.1 mile upstream from the bridge, as the trail opens up to the sunlight and sky, you'll see a set of steps on the left that lead down to the spectacular sandbar. A beautiful little cascade near the sandbar adds to the scenery, and the area is big enough for the dogs to run free and frolic, play, wrestle, romp, swim, fetch, and simply have an amazing time on the cool sand and in the creek beside it. Bring a camera, and a towel, as you may want to hop in the water yourself, either here or at Schoolhouse Falls.

Miles and Directions

0.0 Follow the narrow, rooty dirt path northwest and downhill.

0.15 Cross a footbridge and immediately come to a T on the gravel road. Go left (west) and follow the gravel road downhill.

0.2 Hike under some power lines.

0.3 Continue hiking northwest past a gate.

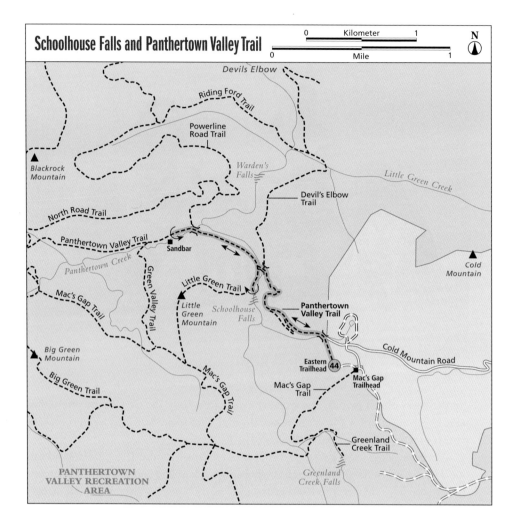

0.4 As the gravel road makes a U-turn to the left (south), you'll see a narrow footpath that leads straight ahead (north). Follow this footpath as a shortcut through the woods.

0.48 Come to a fork where a dirt path leads right (north–northeast) and another left (west). Go left (west) and hike downhill.

0.5 Arrive back on the gravel road. Go right (northwest), continue hiking downhill.

0.8 Come to a fork. The right (northeast) is the Devil's Elbow Trail #448. Bypass this, continuing straight ahead (northwest) on the Panthertown Valley Trail #474.

0.85 Cross a footbridge over Greenland Creek and immediately come to a T. The right is the continuation of the Panthertown Valley Trail and leads north to the sandbar. To reach Schoolhouse Falls, go left, and follow the Little Green Trail #485 south.

0.95 As you hike toward the falls, you cross a long boardwalk.

1.0 As the Little Green Trail heads up and to the right (southwest), follow the spur trail straight ahead (southeast), down a few steps, and to the base of Schoolhouse Falls. Backtrack to the T.

1.25 Arrive back at the T. Hike in the opposite direction (north), making your way toward the sandbar.

1.65 Cross a footbridge over the creek and again you immediately come to a T. The right (east) is the Powerline Road Trail #451. Go left and continue following the Panthertown Valley Trail west.

1.75 Arrive at the glorious "sandbar." After spending ample time playing with the dogs, backtrack to the trailhead.

3.1 Arrive back at the trailhead.

Option: To lengthen the hike, continue past the sandbar and keep hiking through the Panthertown Valley, but bring a map and compass. Many trails crisscross through the valley, so it's easy to get lost.

Resting up: The Cabins at Seven Foxes, Seven Foxes Lane, Lake Toxaway; (828) 877-6333; www.sevenfoxes.com; pet fee per stay.

Camping: Backcountry camping onsite.

Ralph Andrews Park Campground, Pine Creek Road, Glenville; (828) 743-3923; open April 15–October 31.

Sunburst Campground, off of NC 215 about 13.0 miles north of Balsam Grove; (828) 648-7841;www.fs.usda.gov/recarea/nfsnc/recreation/camping-cabins/recarea/?recid =48160&actid=29; open early April–late October; no electric sites.

Fueling up: Cornucopia, 16 Cashiers School Road, Cashiers; (828) 743-3750.

Micas Restaurant and Pub, 4000 US 64, Sapphire; (828) 743-5740; www.micas -restaurant.com.

Schoolhouse Falls is a must-see if you're anywhere near Panthertown Valley.

ROSMAN TO WAYNESVILLE

45 Courthouse Falls Trail

Leading to one of the most spectacular waterfalls in the region, Courthouse Falls is simply intoxicating. Breathtaking scenery lures you in as the water flows over a rugged rocky cliff before forming a pristine swimming hole of crisp green mountain fresh water at the base. The dogs will enjoy wading around in this powerful, yet tranquil, creek and climbing on the rocks that line the banks. Bring a towel; you may find it hard to resist the temptation to take a dip yourself.

Start: Northwest of the bridge; trailhead shared with the Summey Cove Trail
Distance: 0.8-mile out and back
Hiking time: 25 minutes
Blaze color: Orange
Difficulty: Easy to moderate
Trailhead elevation: 3,458 feet
Highest point: 3,467 feet
Seasons: Year-round
Trail surface: Hard-packed dirt; some rooty, rocky, and muddy sections
Other trail users: None

Canine compatibility: Voice control
Land status: Pisgah National Forest—Pisgah Ranger District
Fees and permits: None
Map: *DeLorme: North Carolina Atlas & Gazetteer,* page 52, C3
Trail contact: (828) 877-3265; www.fs.fed.us
Nearest towns: Balsam Grove, Rosman, and Waynesville
Trail tips: Bring a towel so you can take a dip in the inviting pool at the base of Courthouse Falls.

Finding the trailhead: *From the junction of NC 215 and US 64,* drive north on NC 215 for 10.3 miles to a right onto FR 140. Travel 3.0 miles to a pull-off on the right just after crossing the bridge.
From the junction of NC 215 and the Blue Ridge Parkway, drive south on NC 215 for 6.5 miles to a left onto FR 140 and follow directions above. GPS: N35 16.442'/W82 53.536'

The Hike

From the trailhead, the path is shared by both the Courthouse Falls Trail and the Summey Cove Trail. As you begin hiking, you immediately follow Courthouse Creek downstream. Although the creek is right next to the trail, there's no need to let the dogs in the water here. The hike is only 0.4 mile, and the best swimming hole you can ever imagine awaits at the base of the falls. The sound of the creek keeps you entertained the entire way, and as you make your way deeper into the forest, you'll catch a glimpse of the falls on your left. After hiking 0.3 mile, as the Summey Cove Trail begins to make a deep bend to the right (west), you'll see several orange blazes littering a tree. At this tree, a narrow spur trail makes a hard hairpin turn over your left shoulder northeast toward the falls. This is where the Courthouse Falls and Summey Cove Trails part ways.

Courthouse Falls forms a perfect, lush, green cove.

Follow the spur trail downhill, and the falls come into view in the distance. The closer you get, the more magnificent the waterfall becomes, tantalizing you as you draw near. When the trail ends, a steep staircase leads down to the creek at the base of Courthouse Falls. Crystal-clear greenish-hued water and large downed trees add to the scenery of this 45-foot falls. The waterfall flows over rocky cliffs, forming a

These siblings love splashing around in the creek.

perfect little private cove. The water is deep enough for you to swim out and behind the falls, yet the creek downstream is shallow enough for the dogs to comfortably walk around or lay down and cool off. Courthouse Creek got its name because it flows down from the Devil's Courthouse. The "courthouse" is a geological feature that you can hike to the top of. On a clear day you can see four states from the top: North Carolina, South Carolina, Georgia, and Tennessee. Cherokee folklore has it that Judaculla, a giant slant-eyed, seven-fingered devil, kept court in the courthouse. He could leap from mountain to mountain and cast thunderbolts down from the sky. Within the chambers of the courthouse, he would pass final judgment on the dead before they could move on to the spirit world. To this day many consider the waters of Courthouse Creek to be sacred. To view and hike to the top of Devil's Courthouse, visit the overlook between mileposts 422 and 423 on the Blue Ridge Parkway.

Miles and Directions

- **0.0** Hike southwest following Courthouse Creek downstream.
- **0.3** As the wide Summey Cove Trail begins to make a deep bend to the right (west), you'll see several orange blazes on the trees to the left. This is where the Courthouse Falls Trail heads left (northeast) down to the creek.
- **0.4** Arrive at the magnificent Courthouse Falls (N35 16.294'/W82 53.657'). Backtrack to the trailhead.
- **0.8** Arrive back at the trailhead.

Option: Extend the hike by continuing west on the Summey Cove Trail.

Resting up: Grandview Lodge, 466 Lickstone Rd., Waynesville; (828) 456-5212; www.grandviewlodge.com; two dogs any size, pet fee per dog per stay.

Holiday Inn Express, 1570 Asheville Hwy., Brevard; (828) 862-8900; www.hiexbrevard .com; two dogs any size, pet fee per dog per night.

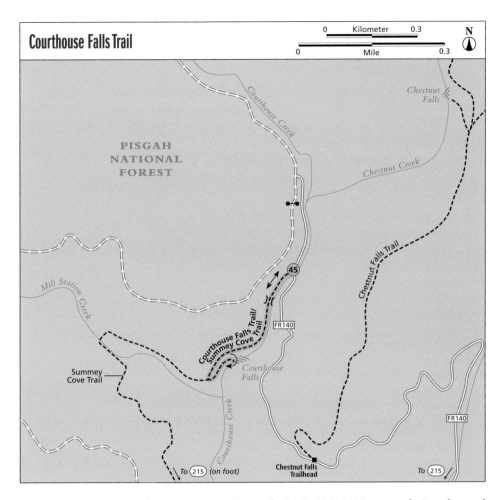

0   Kilometer   0.3

0   Mile   0.3

N

PISGAH
NATIONAL
FOREST

Courthouse Creek

Chestnut
Falls

Chestnut Creek

Chestnut Falls Trail

45

FR 140

Mill Station Creek

Courthouse Falls Trail/
Summey Cove Trail

Summey
Cove Trail

Courthouse
Falls

Courthouse Creek

FR 140

To 215 (on foot)

Chestnut Falls
Trailhead

To 215

The Inn at Brevard, 215 Main St., Brevard; (828) 884-2105; www.theinnatbrevard .com; two dogs up to 40 pounds, no fee.

Camping: Davidson River Campground, 1000 Pisgah Hwy., Pisgah Forest; (828) 877-3265 or (828) 862-5960; www.fs.usda.gov/recarea/nfsnc/recreation/camping-cabins/recarea/?recid=48130&actid=29; open year-round; for reservations visit www .recreation.gov or call (877) 444-6777.

Sunburst Campground, off NC 215 about 13.0 miles north of Balsam Grove; (828) 648-7841;www.fs.usda.gov/recarea/nfsnc/recreation/camping-cabins/recarea/?recid =48160&actid=29; open early April–late October; no electric sites.

Fueling up: Haywood Smokehouse, 79 Elysinia Ave., Waynesville; (828) 456-7275.

Hobnob Restaurant, 192 W. Main St., Brevard; (828) 966-4662.

Micas Restaurant and Pub, 4000 US 64, Sapphire; (828) 743-5740; www.micas-restaurant.com.

The Square Root, 33 Times Arcade Alley, Brevard; (828) 884-6171; www.squareroot restaurant.com.

46 Dill Falls Trail

Dill Falls is easy to reach, and the creek near the base of the falls is shallow enough for the dogs to tip-toe around in. A narrow path along the banks is fun for them to explore, while you do your best to get pictures of them near the falls. Standing at 50 feet, the waterfall is quite unique. This two-tiered beauty free falls from the top, and then when the water splashes down on the rocks below, it continues to form a cascading waterfall that rolls over the rocks to form the creek below it.

Start: From the parking area, you'll see a dirt road-like trail on the right that heads northwest and up, and one on the left that heads southwest and down. The trail on the left is the Dill Falls Trail.

Distance: 0.4-mile out and back

Hiking time: 15 minutes

Blaze color: No blazes

Difficulty: Easy to moderate

Trailhead elevation: 4,142 feet

Highest point: 4,142 feet

Seasons: Year-round

Trail surface: Hard-packed dirt

Other trail users: None

Canine compatibility: Voice control

Land status: Nantahala National Forest– Nantahala Ranger District

Fees and permits: None

Map: *DeLorme: North Carolina Atlas & Gazetteer,* page 52, C3

Trail contact: (828) 524-6441; www.fs.fed.us

Nearest towns: Balsam Grove, Rosman, and Waynesville

Finding the trailhead: *From the junction of NC 215 and US 64 near Rosman,* drive north on NC 215 for 14.2 miles to FR 4663, an unmarked gravel road. Turn left and travel for 0.5 mile to where a road forks off to the right. Continue straight ahead (north–northeast) at the fork and travel for another 1.3 miles to a second fork in the road where FR 4663B goes down and to the left. Follow FR 4663B for 0.6 mile to the end of the road.

From the junction of NC 215 and the Blue Ridge Parkway near milepost 425, drive south on NC 215 for 2.6 miles to a right onto FR 4663, an unmarked gravel road, and then follow the directions above. GPS: N35 16.962'/W82 56.467'

The Hike

The wide clay path leads you on a steady descent the entire way to the creek. No blazes are needed, because you're practically hiking in a small gully. You can't really go astray as the trail nearby makes a straight line, leading you directly to Tanasee Creek. When you reach the creek, as you look upstream, you realize you've arrived at the base of Dill Falls. This multi-tiered waterfall has lots of character. The top of the falls makes a free fall, diving down to the rocks below. The lower portion of the falls then forms a cascade, flowing swiftly over those same rocks. The dogs enjoy wading out into the water with you, and there are some large rocks in the creek where you can sit and enjoy the view. Tanasee Creek flows from the bald bearing its name. Tanasee Bald stands at a noble

This juvenile elk was spotted off the Blue Ridge Parkway.

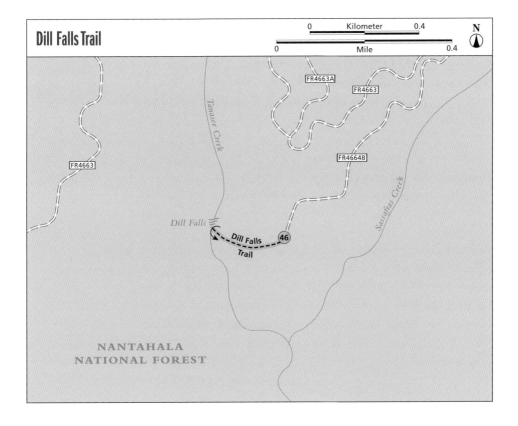

Mikey loves cooling off in a clear mountain creek.

5,565 feet and is part of the Great Balsam Mountains. Legend has it that Judaculla (English for the Cherokee word Tsul' Kalu), a giant slant-eyed, seven-fingered devil, lived atop the bald, frolicking along the ridge that also bears the Tanasee name.

Miles and Directions

0.0 Hike downhill and generally west on the wide clay path.

0.2 Arrive at the creek just downstream from Dill Falls (N35 16.971'/W82 56.612'). Backtrack to the trailhead.

0.4 Arrive back at the trailhead.

Resting up: Grandview Lodge, 466 Lickstone Rd., Waynesville; (828) 456-5212; www.grandviewlodge.com; two dogs any size, pet fee per dog per stay.

Holiday Inn Express, 1570 Asheville Hwy., Brevard; (828) 862-8900; www.hiexbrevard .com; two dogs any size, pet fee per dog per night.

The Inn at Brevard, 215 Main St., Brevard; (828) 884-2105; www.theinnatbrevard .com; two dogs up to 40 pounds, no fee.

Camping: Davidson River Campground, 1000 Pisgah Hwy., Pisgah Forest; (828) 877-3265 or (828) 862-5960; www.fs.usda.gov/recarea/nfsnc/recreation/camping-cabins/recarea/?recid=48130&actid=29; open year-round; for reservations visit www .recreation.gov or call (877) 444-6777.

Sunburst Campground, off NC 215 about 13.0 miles north of Balsam Grove; (828) 648-7841; www.fs.usda.gov/recarea/nfsnc/recreation/camping-cabins/recarea/?recid =48160&actid=29-; open early April–late October; no electric sites.

Fueling up: Haywood Smokehouse, 79 Elysinia Ave., Waynesville; (828) 456-7275.

Hobnob Restaurant, 192 W. Main St., Brevard; (828) 966-4662.

Micas Restaurant and Pub 4000 US 64, Sapphire; (828) 743-5740; www.micas-restaurant.com.

The Square Root, 33 Times Arcade Alley, Brevard; (828) 884-6171; www.squareroot restaurant.com.

47 Flat Laurel Creek Trail

The Flat Laurel Creek Trail leads you into the Shining Rock Wilderness, which boasts an impressive five peaks above 6,000 feet. The views are stunning, and Flat Laurel Creek is brimming with character. While the dogs wade out into the water, you'll sit alongside it, taking in the sights of the immense Sam Knob. The rock-faced mountain dwarfs the tall pine trees soaring above the waterway. Rock cairns left by campers pique your curiosity, as the crystal-clear water passes over a shallow rocky creek bed.

Start: At the northeast corner of the parking lot

Distance: 4.2-miles out and back

Hiking time: 2 hours

Blaze color: None (although there is one orange blaze three quarters of the way to the trail's end)

Difficulty: Easy to moderate

Trailhead elevation: 5,023 feet

Highest point: 5,400 feet

Seasons: Year-round

Trail surface: Hard-packed dirt with rocky sections

Other trail users: Mountain bikers, equestrian

Canine compatibility: Voice control, but keep them on a leash until you get past the first rock hop, as NC 215 is right next to the parking lot.

Land status: Pisgah National Forest–Pisgah Ranger District

Fees and permits: None

Maps: *DeLorme: North Carolina Atlas & Gazetteer*, page 52, C4. National Geographic Trails Illustrated Map #780 Pisgah Ranger District, F3, Trail #346.

Trail contact: Pisgah National Forest, Pisgah Ranger District; (828) 877-3265; www.fs.fed.us

Nearest towns: Brevard and Waynesville

Trail tips: This is a fairly dry trail, so bring lots of drinking water. There's often a breeze and a mix of sun and shade.

Finding the trailhead: *From the junction of NC 215 and the Blue Ridge Parkway near milepost 425*, drive north on NC 215 for 0.8 mile to a sharp, narrow right turn into the parking area for Flat Laurel Creek, marked by a small tent-camping sign reading "BR 1."

From the junction of NC 215 and US 276 near Waynesville, drive south on NC 215 for 16.7 miles to a sharp, narrow left turn into the parking area for Flat Laurel Creek, marked by a small tent-camping sign reading "BR 1." GPS: N35 18.486'/W82 54.527'

The Hike

From the trailhead, hike straight back (east), and you immediately pass through a small, primitive campsite. Beyond the campsite, you quickly need to rock hop a tributary. Because there aren't that many watering holes on this hike, take advantage of the cool mountain water and let the dogs enjoy their time here before continuing on into the wilderness. The trail begins to climb on an easy grade and leads you to a pretty, little waterfall. The water seems slight compared to the rock face it flows over, but the dogs enjoy cooling off in the shallow pool at the base. At the half-mile mark, a cement bridge passes over the top of Wildcat Falls. The falls flow over a rugged rock face and

The veiws along the Flat Laurel Creek Trail are stellar.

then directly under the bridge, so the dogs can't get any water here. This trail can be sunny, depending on when you hike, so make sure you bring plenty of water along. The only signs of civilization are the occasional sounds of a car on NC 215 or an airplane overhead. Other than those intrusions, nothing but the sweet sound of silence, the jingle of your dogs' tags, and your own footsteps on the firm ground beneath your feet. You'll rock hop a tiny tributary with crystal-clear water. It looks as though the spring comes up out of the ground right next to the trail. It doesn't get any fresher than that. As you continue to slowly climb, bypass the spur trail on your left that heads up to a small primitive camping area. Beyond the spur trail, the path opens up a bit, giving you spectacular views of the Shining Rock Wilderness. It's here that you realize how high you've climbed, even though it feels as though you've just been out for an easy stroll. The trail swings you around Little Sam Knob and brings you alongside Flat Laurel Creek. The hike is dry for most of the way, but as you near the creek, you can feel the air getting cooler. Several side paths lead down to the creek. Bypass them all, and you'll notice the sound of the water getting stronger as you begin to see the falls through the brush. Continue hiking southeast past the falls, and you come to a wooded primitive campsite on the left with a large stone fire ring in the middle. Just beyond that campsite is an opening that leads out to the creek. This is a perfect place to let the dogs play freely in the water. It's a safe distance upstream from the brink of the falls and sits at the foot of Sam Knob, a large rock-faced mountain. Two creeks converge here, and they are brimming with character. Hefty pine trees stand tall and proud above the rocky creek and large stones give you a fantastic spot to sit and enjoy

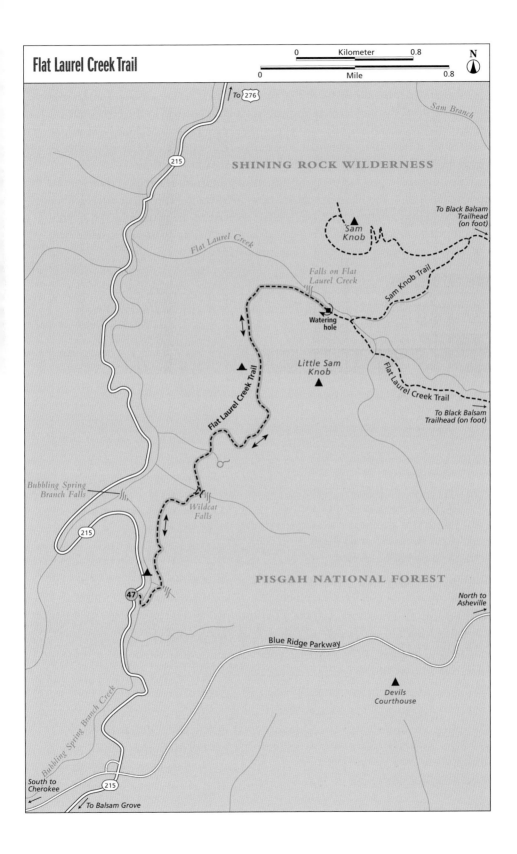

Flat Laurel Creek Trail

0   Kilometer   0.8

0   Mile   0.8

N

To 276

215

SHINING ROCK WILDERNESS

Sam Branch

Sam Knob

To Black Balsam Trailhead (on foot)

Flat Laurel Creek

Falls on Flat Laurel Creek

Sam Knob Trail

Watering hole

Little Sam Knob

Flat Laurel Creek Trail

Flat Laurel Creek Trail

To Black Balsam Trailhead (on foot)

Bubbling Spring Branch Falls

215

Wildcat Falls

PISGAH NATIONAL FOREST

North to Asheville

47

Blue Ridge Parkway

Devils Courthouse

Bubbling Spring Branch Creek

South to Cherokee

215

To Balsam Grove

the scenery. It's a beautiful place for you to have a picnic, while the dogs wet their feet and wag away. And the best part: You're likely to have this one to yourself.

After the dogs have their fill of fun, put them back on the leash and make your way back toward the trailhead. As you do, take a little side trip to the creek near the brink of the falls. Again large flat rocks give you a place to appreciate the breathtaking views of the surrounding wilderness. The random pile of rock cairns left by contemplative campers, the diversity of the flora, and the views of the valley below all come together to form a spectacular setting. When you return to the trail, you can let the dogs off the leash if you like. But remember to put them back on when you reach the first rock hop near the trailhead. NC 215 is too close to the parking lot. This trail is open to hikers, mountain bikers, and equestrians, but the many times I've hiked here, I've never seen anyone other than the occasional hiker.

Miles and Directions

0.0 Hike east past a primitive campsite; the trail then bends right (south) and leads you to Bubbling Spring Branch Creek.

0.05 Rock hop the creek and hike east southeast as you head into the Shining Rock Wilderness Area.

0.2 Pass a small waterfall (N35 18.521'/W82 54.439').

0.7 Cross a cement bridge at Wildcat Falls (N35 18.840'/W82 54.267'). Continue hiking north-northwest.

1.4 Bypass a narrow spur trail that leads off to the left and up to a primitive campsite. Continue hiking north on the Flat Laurel Creek Trail.

2.0 Pass by the brink of Falls on Flat Laurel Creek (N35 19.486'/W82 53.841'). Continue hiking upstream and southeast. You'll pass a wooded primitive campsite on the left.

2.1 Just beyond the primitive campsite you'll see an opening that leads to an amazing watering hole on the creek (N35 19.427'/W82 53.743'). Large stones make a perfect place for you to sit and enjoy the stunning scenery while the dogs dip their paws in Flat Laurel Creek. Backtrack to the trailhead.

4.2 Arrive back at the trailhead.

Option: To lengthen the hike, keep hiking past the watering hole at 2.1 miles, and the trail continues for another 1.6 miles to the Black Balsam trailhead.

Resting up: Grandview Lodge, 466 Lickstone Rd., Waynesville; (828) 456-5212; www.grandviewlodge.com; two dogs any size, pet fee per dog per stay.

Holiday Inn Express, 1570 Asheville Hwy., Brevard; (828) 862-8900; www.hiex brevard.com; two dogs any size, pet fee per dog per night.

The Inn at Brevard, 215 Main St., Brevard; (828) 884-2105; www.theinnatbrevard .com; two dogs up to 40 pounds, no fee.

Camping: Davidson River Campground, 1000 Pisgah Hwy., Pisgah Forest; (828) 877-3265 or (828) 862-5960; www.fs.usda.gov/recarea/nfsnc/recreation/camping -cabins/recarea/?recid=48130&actid=29; open year-round; for reservations visit www.recreation.gov or call (877) 444-6777.

Kate enjoys traipsing through the water while her mama rock hops the creek.

Sunburst Campground, off of NC 215 about 13.0 miles north of Balsam Grove; (828) 648-7841;www.fs.usda.gov/recarea/nfsnc/recreation/camping-cabins/recarea/?recid =48160&actid=29; open early April–late October; no electric sites.

Fueling up: Haywood Smokehouse, 79 Elysinia Ave., Waynesville; (828) 456-7275.

Panacea Coffee House, 66 Commerce St., Waynesville; (828) 456-6200.

The Square Root, 33 Times Arcade Alley, Brevard; (828) 884-6171; www.squareroot restaurant.com.

WAYNESVILLE TO BREVARD

48 Graveyard Fields Loop Trail and Upper Falls Trail

While the water flow isn't that exceptional, the views of the valley below and the surrounding mountains are outstanding. The trail leads you steeply down a paved path, and then cuts generally west through the heart of the Graveyard Fields. This is a trail for all seasons. In spring and summer there's an abundance of wildflowers. Autumn brings the colorful changing of the leaves, and in winter snow dusted over the valley glistens in the sun.

Start: At the northeast end of the parking lot near the restrooms
Distance: 3.0-mile loop
Hiking time: 1 hour, 30 minutes
Blaze color: Blue
Difficulty: Easy to moderate
Trailhead elevation: 5,129 feet
Highest point: 5,293 feet
Seasons: Year-round
Trail surface: Paved path, hard-packed dirt with rocky sections, several short boardwalks
Other trail users: None
Canine compatibility: Voice control, but keep the dogs on a leash until you reach the first fork at 0.15 mile. The trail is usually congested for the first few tenths of a mile, and the

overlook/parking lot is extremely busy throughout the year.
Land status: Pisgah National Forest—Pisgah Ranger District
Fees and permits: None
Maps: *DeLorme: North Carolina Atlas & Gazetteer*, page 52, C4. National Geographic Trails Illustrated Map #780 Pisgah Ranger District, F3 and F4, Trail #358A, 358C.
Trail contact: Pisgah National Forest, Pisgah Ranger District; (828) 877-3265; www.fs.fed.us
Nearest towns: Brevard and Waynesville
Trail tips: Tree cover is sparse, so make sure you bring plenty of drinking water for you and your four-legged friends. Sunscreen is also a good idea.

Finding the trailhead: *From the junction of the Blue Ridge Parkway (BRP) and US 276*, drive south on the BRP for 6.9 miles to a marked overlook on the right.
From the junction of the BRP and NC 215, drive north on the BRP for 6.3 miles to a marked overlook on the left.
Note: The overlook is between mileposts 418 and 419 on the BRP. GPS: N35 19.225'/W82 50.816'

The Hike

Head down the stone steps and follow the paved path downhill through a forest of mountain laurel that forms a lovely tunnel around you. When you reach Yellowstone Prong, a footbridge leads you across. You can take the dogs upstream along the flat stone banks of the creek, and they'll enjoy a quick dip. Beyond the footbridge, the boardwalk brings you to a fork. The right leads 0.15-mile to Second Falls. This is a

Tiger lilies grow on tall bushes along the Graveyard Fields Loop Trail.

nice side trip and the falls are stupendous, but the path is heavily populated. Go left at the fork and follow the boardwalk west toward the heart of the Graveyard Fields. If you're curious where the graveyard is, you're hiking in it.

During the logging boom of the early 1900s, this area was clear-cut, leaving nothing but hundreds of moss-covered stumps resembling gravestones. A devastating fire in 1925 and another in 1940 destroyed any remaining growth and rendered the soil sterile, leaving it barren for years to come. Today the underbrush is making a good comeback. You'll find an abundance of wildflowers in season, and in autumn the "fields" put on quite a colorful show. As you continue hiking deeper into the Graveyard Fields, you'll notice many narrow game trails running off the well-trodden path. Ignore them all, and bypass the yellow-blazed Graveyard Ridge Connector Trail, which leads to the right (north) up to the Graveyard Ridge. This portion of the hike isn't very shady, so bring lots of water. Although there's usually a nice breeze, sunscreen is a good idea too. At times you'll hear voices of other hikers, but you won't see them because the underbrush is thick and just a bit taller than you are. As you hike generally west, you'll catch an occasional glimpse of Yellowstone Prong. At 0.6 mile, you'll reach a fork where the left leg leads south to a bridge over the creek, and the right continues northwest.

After visiting the falls, when you return to this fork, you'll be crossing that bridge and taking an alternate route back to the trailhead. For now, continue straight ahead and the trail leads you across a few tributaries. The dogs enjoy dipping their paws in the water at these crossings while you keep your feet dry. As the trail becomes a rocky path, it begins to climb. After a quarter mile, the rocky path leads you out to the stone sides that surround the Upper Falls. While the water flow isn't that impressive, you can literally walk upon the rocky sides of the falls, and the views are phenomenal. Looking out over the valley you just hiked across, you get a different perspective and appreciation of the nature around you. After enjoying the spectacular scenery, return to the fork. Before crossing the bridge you could let the dogs run and play in and around the creek. It's a fantastic place for them to get some energy out before finishing the loop. Beyond the bridge, the trail narrows and leads you through a forest of rhododendron and mountain laurel. These flowering plants form a tunnel around you giving you plenty of shade for the remainder of the hike. The easy-to-follow path slowly climbs before leading you back up to the northwest end of the parking lot.

Miles and Directions

0.0   Hike steeply down the stone steps and then follow the paved path north.

0.15   Cross a footbridge over Yellowstone Prong. After crossing the footbridge, you can let the dogs take a quick dip, but make sure you take them upstream. Downstream is too close to the brink of Second Falls. Continue following the boardwalk northeast.

0.2   Come to a fork in the boardwalk. The right leads east 0.15 mile to Second Falls (N35 19.340'/W82 50.783'). This is a great side trip, but it's usually crowded, so keep the dogs on a leash if you head that way. If you don't want to deal with people, go left and follow the boardwalk west as you make your way toward Upper Falls.

0.4   Come to a fork where a spur trail heads left (south). Bypass this, and go right (north). You immediately come to another fork where the yellow-blazed Graveyard Ridge Connector Trail heads right (north). Stay left and continue hiking northwest on the Graveyard Fields Loop Trail.

0.6   Come to another fork. The left leads south to a bridge over Yellowstone Prong. After visiting the Upper Falls, you'll be going that way. For now, continue straight ahead as you make your way northwest toward the falls.

0.8   Cross a small footbridge over a tributary. Continue hiking northwest.

1.4   Come to a fork at some boulders. The left leads south–southwest to the lower portion of the falls. The right continues up the rocks to the upper part of the falls. I recommend seeing both, but the long range views are definitely better from the upper portion.

1.5   Arrive at the upper portion of Upper Falls (N35 19.086'/W82 51.987'). Backtrack to the fork that leads to the footbridge over Yellowstone Prong.

2.4   Arrive at the fork. Either way you go is 0.6 mile back to the trailhead. I recommend going right and crossing the footbridge. This route is shady, less populated, and diversifies the terrain.

2.45   Cross the footbridge over Yellowstone Prong. Continue hiking southwest.

3.0   Arrive back near the trailhead, at the northwest end of the parking lot (N35 19.202'/W82 50.852').

Bandit's ready to delve into the Graveyard Fields.

Graveyard Fields Loop Trail and Upper Falls Trail

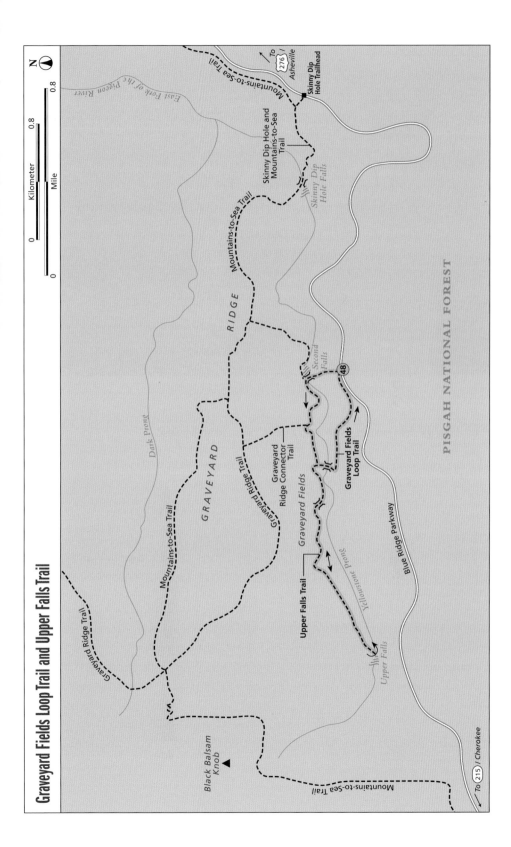

Black Balsam Knob

Graveyard Ridge Trail

Mountains-to-Sea Trail

Dark Prong

GRAVEYARD RIDGE

East Fork of the Pigeon River

Mountains-to-Sea Trail

Skinny Dip Hole and Mountains-to-Sea Trail

Skinny Dip Hole Falls

To 276 / Asheville

Skinny Dip Hole Trailhead

Second Falls

Graveyard Ridge Trail

Graveyard Ridge Connector Trail

Graveyard Fields

Upper Falls Trail

Yellowstone Prong

Upper Falls

48

Graveyard Fields Loop Trail

Blue Ridge Parkway

PISGAH NATIONAL FOREST

To 215 / Cherokee

Mountains-to-Sea Trail

N

Kilometer
0   0.8   0.8

Mile
0   0.8

Stay a while on the rocky face of Upper Falls in the Graveyard Fields.

Resting up: Grandview Lodge, 466 Lickstone Rd., Waynesville; (828) 456-5212; www.grandviewlodge.com; two dogs any size, pet fee per dog per stay.

Holiday Inn Express, 1570 Asheville Hwy., Brevard; (828) 862-8900; www.hiex brevard.com; two dogs any size, pet fee per dog per night.

The Inn at Brevard, 215 Main St., Brevard; (828) 884-2105; www.theinnatbrevard .com; two dogs up to 40 pounds, no fee.

Camping: Davidson River Campground, 1000 Pisgah Hwy., Pisgah Forest; (828) 877-3265 or (828) 862-5960; www.fs.usda.gov/recarea/nfsnc/recreation/camping-cabins/recarea/?recid=48130&actid=29; open year-round; for reservations visit www .recreation.gov or call (877) 444-6777.

Sunburst Campground, off of NC 215 about 13.0 miles north of Balsam Grove; (828) 648-7841;www.fs.usda.gov/recarea/nfsnc/recreation/camping-cabins/recarea/?recid =48160&actid=29; open early April–late October; no electric sites.

Fueling up: Haywood Smokehouse, 79 Elysinia Ave., Waynesville; (828) 456-7275.

MARCO Trattoria, 204 W. Main St., Brevard; (828) 883-4841; www.marcotrattoria .com.

Panacea Coffee House, 66 Commerce St., Waynesville; (828) 456-6200.

The Square Root, 33 Times Arcade Alley, Brevard; (828) 884-6171; www.squareroot restaurant.com.

49 Skinny Dip Hole Trail

Among my favorite hikes, the trail to Skinny Dip Hole Falls not only leads to a spectacular multi-faceted waterfall, but you also have the pleasure of hiking on one of the most famous trails in the state, the Mountains-to-Sea Trail. The dogs enjoy a cool, shady hike, and when you reach the falls, there's something for everyone. Inviting pools of crystal-clear water, large rocks to lay upon, and the soothing sound of the falls. Bring a towel, a picnic, and a good book. You may want to stay a while.

Start: From the Looking Glass Rock Overlook on the east side of the Blue Ridge Parkway, hike across the street to the west side of the road. The Skinny Dip Hole trailhead is right next to milepost 417 with a sign reading "To Mountains-to-Sea Trail."
Distance: 1.0-mile out and back
Hiking time: 30 minutes
Blaze colors: Blue and white
Difficulty: Easy to moderate
Trailhead elevation: 4,501 feet
Highest point: 4,528 feet
Seasons: Year-round
Trail surface: Hard-packed dirt with rooty and rocky sections
Other trail users: None

Canine compatibility: Voice control, but please keep them on the leash until you reach the T at 0.1 mile.
Land status: Pisgah National Forest–Pisgah Ranger District
Fees and permits: None
Maps: *DeLorme: North Carolina Atlas & Gazetteer*, page 52, C4. National Geographic Trails Illustrated Map #780 Pisgah Ranger District, F4, Trail #440.
Trail contact: Pisgah National Forest, Pisgah Ranger District; (828) 877-3265; www.fs.fed.us
Nearest towns: Asheville, Brevard, and Waynesville
Trail tips: A hiking stick helps navigate the rooty and rocky sections of the trail.

Finding the trailhead: *From the junction of the Blue Ridge Parkway (BRP) and US 276*, drive south on the BRP for 5.1 miles to the overlook on your left.
From the junction of the BRP and NC 215, drive north on the BRP for 8.1 miles to the overlook on your right.
Note: The overlook is located at milepost 417 on the BRP. GPS: N35 19.335'/W82 49.682'
Special Considerations: To reach the trailhead, you must cross the BRP from the overlook. Keep the dogs on a leash until you reach the first T at 0.1 mile. On the way back out to the trailhead, again, when you reach this T, be sure to put the dogs back on the leash before heading toward the road and trailhead.

The Hike

Follow the path northwest, straight back into the woods, and you quickly arrive at a T junction at the Mountains-to-Sea Trail. Just before the T, take note of the amazing "trail tree" on the east side of the trail. This fascinating tree was bent over many years ago to point which way the trail goes. Today two tree trunks have grown up from the

A distinctive trail tree points the way.

bent portion of the tree, forming what looks like the head of a dragon, with the twin limbs acting as horns reaching toward the sky. From the T, if you went right, you could literally hike all the way to Jockey's Ridge State Park and the Atlantic Ocean. But for today's hike, go left instead, and follow the Mountains-to-Sea Trail west, away from the parkway, and into the Pisgah National Forest. The trail leads you downhill on a rooty, rocky path before you climb a bit. You can see that volunteers have been diligently working on this trail, carefully laying perfectly placed stones and logs as steps. These natural staircases help prevent erosion and also make it easier and safer for you and your furry friends to hike upon.

As the trail flattens out, the sound of the water grows stronger. After crossing a tiny footbridge, you arrive at a set of wooden steps that brings you down to another footbridge across the creek near the base of Skinny Dip Hole Falls. A cool, refreshing pool at the base of the falls lures you into its inviting arms. Upstream from the footbridge, locals often leap from the boulders beside the falls into the chilly waters at the base. But for the dogs, it's best to head downstream before crossing the footbridge. This way, you can sit on the large flat rocks near the water, and the dogs can either lay with you or wade out into the creek. The water is stunning! Crystal-clear, crisp, clean water weaves between large rocks forming several perfect pools. If your pups are timid, they can walk on the rocks and wade out if they work up the courage. For the water lovers in the family, there's a pool deep enough for them to do a little doggy paddle in. Sandy patches on the banks offer a place for the dogs to dig around and explore. No matter what they fancy, they'll have fun here.

You're likely to see piles of rock cairns that people have built from the smooth stones that make up the creek bed. The Mountains-to-Sea Trail is well-known throughout the state. The trail is nearly 1,000 miles long and literally makes its way from the mountains to the sea. It starts at Clingmans Dome in the Great Smoky Mountains and travels all the way to the Atlantic Ocean at Jockey's Ridge on North Carolina's Outer Banks. The modern-day trail was started in 1973 but is said to follow the original path taken by Native Americans hundreds of years ago.

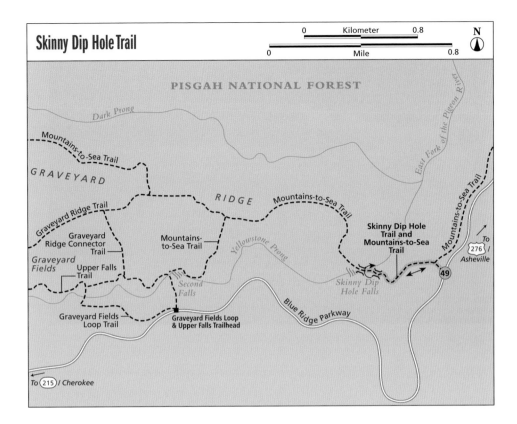

Skinny Dip Hole Trail

0   Kilometer   0.8

0   Mile   0.8

N

PISGAH NATIONAL FOREST

Dark Prong

Mountains-to-Sea Trail

GRAVEYARD

Graveyard Ridge Trail

RIDGE

Mountains-to-Sea Trail

East Fork of the Pigeon River

Mountains-to-Sea Trail

Graveyard Ridge Connector Trail

Mountains-to-Sea Trail

Yellowstone Prong

Skinny Dip Hole Trail and Mountains-to-Sea Trail

Mountains-to-Sea Trail

To 276 / Asheville

49

Graveyard Fields

Upper Falls Trail

Second Falls

Skinny Dip Hole Falls

Graveyard Fields Loop Trail

Graveyard Fields Loop & Upper Falls Trailhead

Blue Ridge Parkway

To 215 / Cherokee

Miles and Directions

0.0   Hike northwest into the forest.

0.1   Take notice of the trail tree on the right (east) side of the trail, just before the trail heads up the log steps (N35 19.375'/W82 49.726'). It's unlike any tree you've seen before.

0.1   Climb up the log steps and come to a T, where the Mountains-to-Sea Trail leads right (east) and left (west). Go left, following the famous white blazed trail the remainder of the way.

0.3   Climb up some stone and log steps. Continue hiking northwest.

0.35 Bypass a spur trail on the right that leads north steeply down to a primitive campsite. Continue hiking west toward the falls.

0.4   Cross a tiny footbridge and continue hiking west.

0.5   Arrive at a footbridge that leads across the base of Skinny Dip Hole Falls (N35-19.352'/ W82-50.018'). Before crossing the footbridge, hike down the rocks to the right, and they lead to the creek where you and the dogs can safely wade out into the crystal-clear water. Backtrack to the trailhead.

0.9   *Alert:* When you reach the T on the Mountains-to-Sea Trail, near the trail tree, put the dogs back on the leash before heading back to the trailhead.

1.0   Arrive back at the trailhead.

Large rocks and logs add to the scenery alongside Skinny Dip Hole.

Option: To lengthen the hike, continue across the footbridge at the base of the falls and follow the Mountains-to-Sea Trail. It leads for many miles; hike as far as you like, keeping your dog's stamina in mind.

Resting up: Grandview Lodge, 466 Lickstone Rd., Waynesville; (828) 456-5212; www.grandviewlodge.com; two dogs any size, pet fee per dog per stay.

Holiday Inn Express, 1570 Asheville Hwy., Brevard; (828) 862-8900; www.hiexbrevard .com; two dogs any size, pet fee per dog per night.

The Inn at Brevard, 215 Main St., Brevard; (828) 884-2105; www.theinnatbrevard .com; two dogs up to 40 pounds, no fee.

Camping: Davidson River Campground, 1000 Pisgah Hwy., Pisgah Forest; (828) 877-3265 or (828) 862-5960; www.fs.usda.gov/recarea/nfsnc/recreation/camping-cabins/recarea/?recid=48130&actid=29; open year-round; for reservations visit www .recreation.gov or call (877) 444-6777.

Sunburst Campground, off of NC 215 about 13.0 miles north of Balsam Grove; (828) 648-7841; www.fs.usda.gov/recarea/nfsnc/recreation/camping-cabins/recarea/?recid =48160&actid=29; open early April–late October; no electric sites.

Fueling up: Haywood Smokehouse, 79 Elysinia Ave., Waynesville; (828) 456-7275.

MARCO Trattoria, 204 W. Main St., Brevard; (828) 883-4841; www.marcotrattoria .com.

Panacea Coffee House, 66 Commerce St., Waynesville; (828) 456-6200.

The Square Root, 33 Times Arcade Alley, Brevard; (828) 884-6171; www.squareroot restaurant.com.

BREVARD

50   Pink Beds Loop Trail

Surprising diversity welcomes you on this long loop trail. Most of the hike is shaded by forest, while ferns and wildflowers form the underbrush. The lower leg of the loop is flat, and damp, making several water crossings. It even brings you through a boggy area where you may be lucky enough to spy a great blue heron patiently wading in the water. The upper leg of the loop is drier and leads you past several open fields. These meadows are vast and big enough for the dogs to chase a ball or a stick.

Start: At the northeast end of the parking lot

Distance: 5.2-mile loop trail

Hiking time: 2 hours, 35 minutes

Blaze color: Orange

Difficulty: Easy

Trailhead elevation: 3,339 feet

Highest point: 3,340 feet

Seasons: Year-round

Trail surface: Gravel road, sandy, hard-packed dirt, muddy sections

Other trail users: Mountain bikers seasonally from October 15–April 15

Canine compatibility: Voice control

Land status: Pisgah National Forest–Pisgah Ranger District

Fees and permits: None

Maps: DeLorme: North Carolina Atlas & Gazetteer, page 53, B5. National Geographic Trails Illustrated Map #780 Pisgah Ranger District, H7, Trail #118.

Trail contact: Pisgah National Forest, Pisgah Ranger District; (828) 877-3265; www.fs.fed.us

Nearest towns: Brevard and Asheville

Trail tips: During the summer months the trail can be buggy. Also, there have been reports of bees near the southern portion of the Barnett Branch Trail where it meets the Pink Beds Loop Trail. If you have a known bee allergy, use extreme caution. It's also wise to carry an EpiPen with you at all times.

Finding the trailhead: *From the junction of US 276 north and US 64 in Brevard*, drive north on US 276 for 11.5 miles to a right onto FR 160 into the parking area for the Pink Beds. *From the junction of US 276 and the Blue Ridge Parkway near milepost 412*, drive south on US 276 for 3.3 miles to the parking area for the Pink Beds on the left. GPS: N35 21.211'/W82 46.724'

The Hike

If you're looking for a place to take a peaceful stroll, this is your trail. It's a long stroll, but there are options to shorten it if you want. The Barnett Branch Trail runs between the northern and southern legs of the loop, essentially cutting it in half. You could use this as a shortcut. Another option is to hike a portion of the loop as an out and back. The trail begins by leading you past the picnic area and crosses a footbridge over the creek. Not far from the footbridge, you come to a fork where the loop begins. The southern and northern legs are very different from each other. The right leg, or

Mikey makes one of many creek crossings on the Pink Beds Loop Trail.

southern half of the loop, is primarily flat and follows the South Fork of the Mills River. As the trail weaves through the forest, it crosses several footbridges over the river and tributaries. Take advantage of these crossings, and let the dogs have their playtime in the water when you can. Although the trail follows the river, it's not always accessible. You'll find the northern leg of the loop much drier, and it takes you over rolling hills. The last mile of this northern leg leads you from one open field to the next. The grass is short in these meadows, so it's a great place to play fetch with your dogs, as there's plenty of room to run. Be sure, however, to bring water for the dogs and you; this part of the hike doesn't have the creek crossings of the lower leg. With the exception of the open meadows, maple, oak, poplar, and pine trees shield you from the sun. You'll also find that mountain laurel and rhododendron line the path, especially on the damper lower leg. If you hike in the summer months, you may be treated to the showy pink blossoms of these fantastic flowering plants. This is when the Pink Beds live up to their name. A variety of ferns and wildflowers mixed into the underbrush adds to the scenery.

You can bring the dogs on the grounds of the Cradle of Forestry, just not inside the buildings.

As you look at a topographical map, you can't help but notice that the Pink Beds is an oddly placed patch of relatively flat land in the middle of the rugged mountainous terrain of the Pisgah National Forest. Driving along US 276, it's clear to see how steep the terrain is, so to see this "bed" of flat land resting right in the middle of it is a pure marvel of nature. Just south of the Pink Beds on US 276, you'll find the Cradle of Forestry. The "cradle" is a National Historic Site and pays tribute to those who formed the humble beginnings of the National Forest Service. It was George W. Vanderbilt who, in the late 1800s, had the vision and foresight to protect areas such as Pisgah. He commissioned the help of foresters from all over the globe, who began America's first forestry school. Today you can stroll around the grounds of the Cradle of Forestry and see replicas of the buildings where students learned how to effectively manage the forest. Dogs are allowed on the trails and grounds, but only small dogs that can be carried in your arms are allowed inside the buildings. For more information visit www.cradleofforestry.com.

Miles and Directions

0.0 Begin by going around the gate and hiking east into the forest on a gravel "road." You immediately come to a fork. The right leads to the picnic area. Go left and follow the trail northeast.

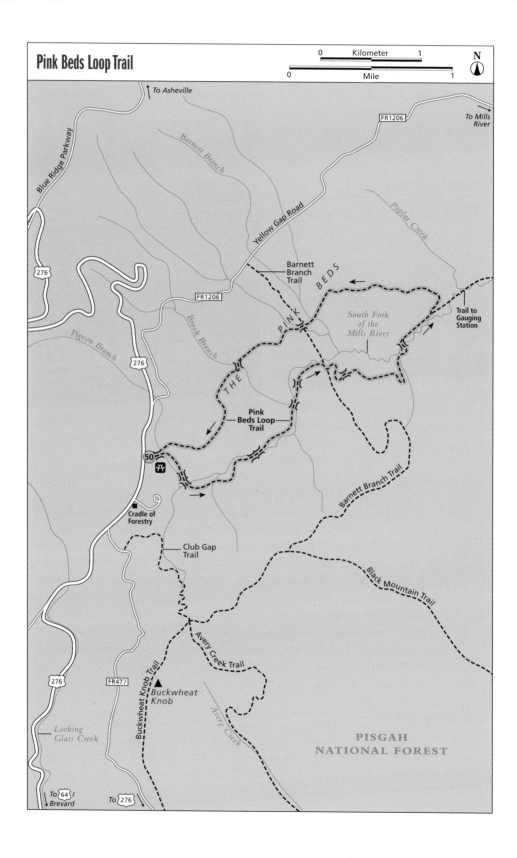

Pink Beds Loop Trail

0 Kilometer 1
0 Mile 1

N

To Asheville

FR1206

To Mills River

Blue Ridge Parkway

Barnett Branch

Yellow Gap Road

Poplar Creek

276

FR1206

Barnett Branch Trail

THE PINK BEDS

South Fork of the Mills River

Trail to Gauging Station

Pigeon Branch

Brook Branch

276

Pink Beds Loop Trail

Barnett Branch Trail

50

Cradle of Forestry

Black Mountain Trail

Club Gap Trail

276

FR477

Buckwheat Knob Trail

Avery Creek Trail

Buckwheat Knob

PISGAH NATIONAL FOREST

Looking Glass Creek

Avery Creek

276

To 64 / Brevard

To 276

0.1 Cross a footbridge over a shallow, clear-running creek. This is a nice spot for the dogs to get their feet wet. Continue east on the wide gravel path.

0.11 Come to a fork. This is where the loop begins. A trail to the left leads north across a grassy field, and a trail to the right heads southeast into the woods. You can go either way, but the trail is described in counterclockwise fashion, so go right and follow the hard-packed dirt back into the forest.

0.25 Cross a footbridge over a deep section of the South Fork of the Mills River. Continue hiking south.

0.33 Cross a footbridge over a barely trickling waterway, and the trail bends left (east).

0.5 Hike over a long boardwalk, and the trail bends left again, this time leading you north.

0.85 Cross a tiny footbridge, and then a larger one. Between these two footbridges is a fantastic swimming hole for the dogs.

0.9 Cross an old broken down boardwalk as you hike east under the damp cover of the forest.

1.25 Cross a very cool log bridge. Just before you cross there is another great swimming hole, and the log bridge is a nice place to get some photos of the dogs crossing over it.

1.35 Cross a footbridge over a tiny tributary.

1.6 Arrive at a fork. This is where the Barnett Branch Trail heads north and basically acts as a shortcut between the southern and northern legs of the Pink Beds Loop. If you want to shortcut, follow this trail north alongside Barnett Branch, and when you get to the intersection with the Pink Beds Loop, go left (west) and follow it back to the trailhead. This route would cut 2.0 miles off the hike. To hike the full Pink Beds Loop Trail, go right (south).

1.65 Come to another fork with the Barnett Branch Trail. To the right the Barnett Branch Trail heads south. Bypass this and go left (east), staying on the loop trail.

1.8 Cross a footbridge.

2.35 Rock hop a tributary.

2.55 Cross a footbridge. This is another fabulous place for the dogs to play in the water. Continue hiking northwest.

2.75 Come to a fork next to a great swimming hole in the river. At this fork a marked trail leads straight ahead (east) to a gauging station. Go left here (north northwest) and continue hiking on the loop trail, as you begin to head back toward the trailhead.

3.6 Rock hop a tributary. Continue hiking southwest.

3.8 Rock hop across Barnett Branch. Continue hiking southwest.

3.85 Arrive at an intersection with the Barnett Branch Trail. If you took the shortcut from the southern leg of the loop, this is where you would come out. To the right is where the Barnett Branch trail continues north to FR 1206. Hike straight across this intersection and continue hiking west back toward the trailhead. You'll immediately cross a footbridge.

4.25 Hike through a large open field, continue hiking west.

4.35 You come to Brook Branch; go left (south), and the trail leads you to a footbridge over the water. Continue hiking generally west, and over the next 0.8 mile you'll hike through a series of meadows.

5.15 Arrive back at the fork where the loop began. Go right (west) toward the trailhead.

5.2 Arrive back at the trailhead.

The dogs take a break along the Pink Beds Loop Trail.

Option: If you wanted to shorten the hike, shortcut between the legs of the loop on the Barnett Branch Trail. This will cut 2.0 miles off the hike.

Resting up: Barkwells, 290 Lance Rd., Mills River; (828) 891-8288,; www.barkwells .com.

Four Points by Sheraton, 22 Woodfin St., Asheville; (828) 253-1851; two dogs any size, pet fee per stay.

Holiday Inn Express, 1570 Asheville Hwy., Brevard; (828) 862-8900; www.hiexbrevard .com; two dogs any size, pet fee per dog per night.

Camping: Davidson River Campground, 1000 Pisgah Hwy., Pisgah Forest; (828) 877-3265 or (828) 862-5960; www.fs.usda.gov/recarea/nfsnc/recreation/camping-cabins /recarea/?recid=48130&actid=29; open year-round; for reservations visit www .recreation.gov or call (877) 444-6777.

Lake Powhatan Campground, 375 Wesley Branch Rd., Asheville; (828) 257-4200; www.fs.usda.gov/recarea/nfsnc/recreation/camping-cabins/recarea/?recid=48172 &actid=29; open April 1–October 31.

Fueling up: Asheville Brewing Company, 77 Coxe Avenue, Asheville; (828) 255-4077.

Laughing Seed Café, 40 Wall Street, Asheville; (828) 252-3445.

MARCO Trattoria, 204 W. Main St., Brevard; (828) 883-4841; www.marcotrattoria .com.

The Square Root, 33 Times Arcade Alley, Brevard; (828) 884-6171; www.squareroot restaurant.com.

51 Moore Cove Falls Trail

This enjoyable hike passes through the lovely Moore Cove, and then leads you to the unique Moore Cove Falls. The waterfall flows over a massive cliff that juts out enough to form a "rock house" behind it. A cool, damp, open cavern is formed, and you can go behind the falls and sit a spell. On the way to the falls, you'll make a few creek crossings that are perfectly spaced for the dogs to enjoy the water as much as you do.

Start: At the south end of the parking area

Distance: 1.4-miles out and back

Hiking time: 45 minutes

Blaze color: Yellow

Difficulty: Moderate

Trailhead elevation: 2,423 feet

Highest point: 2,587 feet

Seasons: Year-round

Trail surface: Hard-packed dirt

Other trail users: None

Canine compatibility: Voice control, but keep dogs on a leash until you're a safe distance from US 276.

Land status: Pisgah National Forest–Pisgah Ranger District

Fees and permits: None

Maps: *DeLorme: North Carolina Atlas & Gazetteer*, page 53, C5. National Geographic Trails Illustrated Map #780 Pisgah Ranger District, F5, Trail #318.

Trail contact: Pisgah National Forest, Pisgah Ranger District; (828) 877-3265; www.fs.fed.us

Nearest town: Brevard

Trail tips: Keep the dogs on a leash until you cross the second footbridge. This way you don't have to worry about cars and traffic on US 276 where the trailhead is. Also, bring a camera! Moore Cove Falls is one of the few waterfalls that you can go behind. You'll probably want to take some photos at the falls.

Finding the trailhead: *From the junction of US 276 north and US 64 in Brevard*, drive north on US 276 for 6.6 miles to a large pull-off on the right (just before crossing the bridge).

From the junction of US 276 and the Blue Ridge Parkway near milepost 412, drive south on US 276 for 8.2 miles to a pull-off on the left (just after crossing the bridge). GPS: N35 18.292'/W82 46.465'

The Hike

The hike begins by immediately leading you across a footbridge over Looking Glass Creek. The shallow, rocky creek is crystal clear. If you want to let the dogs in the water here, keep them on the leash, this creek is right next to US 276. It's a good idea to wait; there are plenty of opportunities for the dogs to safely wet their paws farther along the hike. Beyond the bridge the trail begins to climb and moves away from the creek and roadway. You cross a trickling tributary, and then pass some impressively large rock formations. This is a good place to take the dogs off the leash. It's a safe distance from the road, and it's a good landmark to remember to leash them back up on the way back out. The smooth, wide trail steadily climbs as it winds through the lovely cove. At 0.3 mile the trail reaches its peak, and then brings you down to the creek that runs through

The 50-foot Moore Cove Falls flows over a large cliff that juts out, forming an open cavern behind the falls.

Moore Cove. The dogs enjoy the cool, crisp creek water while you cross on a footbridge. The trail leads you over rolling hills and again back to the brownish-hued creek. It then makes one final climb even steeper, before bringing you to the grand finale: Moore Cove Falls. This distinctive waterfall is stupendous! It's not that the flow is mighty and powerful; actually it's quite passive. What makes this one so special are the massive cliffs the water flows over. They jut out enough to form a "rock house," behind the falls. You can explore the cavern, or sit on the large rocks resting below the cliffs. Echoes of the falling water resonate from the rocky walls, adding to the experience. The dogs enjoy the water

Hikers sometimes build rock cairns for fun, while other times they're used as blazes.

as it splashes down from above, while they explore the cool, damp area behind it. The trail does see some sunshine in the late afternoon, but it's short enough, and the creek crossings are well spaced to keep the dogs from overheating.

Moore Cove was briefly owned by Adam Q. Moore in the late 1800s. Moore was a local justice of the peace and a US commissioner. He sold this land to George W. Vanderbilt in 1891 for a great price, making his contribution to the foundations of forestry in this country and the formation of the Pisgah National Forest.

Miles and Directions

0.0 The trail immediately crosses a footbridge over Looking Glass Creek. Resist the temptation to let the dogs play in the water here unless you keep them on a leash. With US 276 right next to the creek, I recommend waiting until you're deeper into Moore Cove. Beyond the bridge, the trail bends right (north) and begins to climb.

0.1 Cross a footbridge over a trickling tributary. If your dogs are obedient to voice commands, this is a good spot to let them off leash. Bypass any narrow side trails that lead off to the right and down to the creek.

0.4 Cross a footbridge over Moore Cove Creek. This is a great watering hole, where the dogs can play a bit in the creek and cove. Continue hiking northwest, and you'll cross a few small boardwalks.

0.55 Cross a footbridge and the trail makes a short, steep climb as you continue hiking northwest.

0.6 Cross a footbridge, and the trail climbs steeper than before as you hike northwest toward the falls.

0.7 Arrive at Moore Cove Falls (N35 18.701'/W82 46.659'). The water flows over a massive rock overhang to form the falls, giving you shelter and shade while you explore the open cavern behind the falls. Large rocks are ideal for sitting with a good book, or having a picnic, while the dogs play in the creek as it splashes down from above. Backtrack to the trailhead.

1.4 Arrive back at the trailhead.

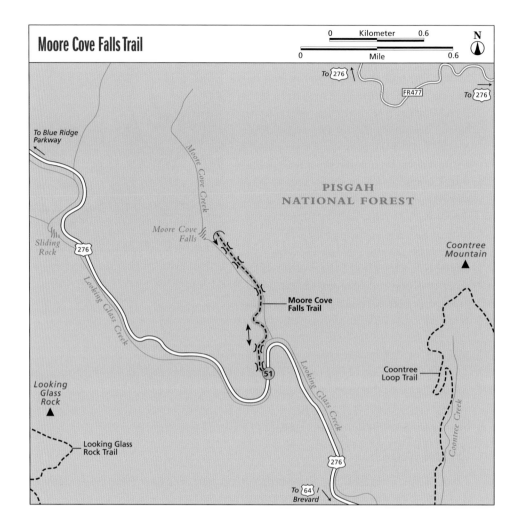

Moore Cove Falls Trail

0 Kilometer 0.6
0 Mile 0.6

N

To 276
FR477
To 276

To Blue Ridge Parkway

Moore Cove Creek

PISGAH
NATIONAL FOREST

Sliding Rock

Moore Cove Falls

276

Looking Glass Creek

Moore Cove Falls Trail

Coontree Mountain ▲

Looking Glass Rock ▲

51

Coontree Loop Trail

Looking Glass Creek

Looking Glass Rock Trail

Coontree Creek

276

To 64 / Brevard

Resting up: Holiday Inn Express, 1570 Asheville Hwy., Brevard; (828) 862-8900; www.hiexbrevard.com; two dogs any size, pet fee per dog per night.

The Inn at Brevard, 215 Main St., Brevard; (828) 884-2105; www.theinnatbrevard .com; two dogs up to 40 pounds, no fee.

Camping: Davidson River Campground, 1000 Pisgah Hwy., Pisgah Forest; (828) 877-3265 or (828) 862-5960; www.fs.usda.gov/recarea/nfsnc/recreation/camping -cabins/recarea/?recid=48130&actid=29. Open year-round. For reservations visit www.recreation.gov or call (877) 444-6777.

Fueling up: Hobnob Restaurant, 192 W. Main St., Brevard; (828) 966-4662.

MARCO Trattoria, 204 W. Main St., Brevard; (828) 883-4841; www.marcotrattoria .com.

The Square Root, 33 Times Arcade Alley, Brevard; (828) 884-6171; www.squareroot restaurant.com.

52 Cat Gap Loop Trail

Shaded the entire way, this pleasant hike leads you up to a splendid little waterfall, and then continues to climb as it circles around John Rock. Although you can't see John Rock from the trail, you can view it from the parking lot before you begin. The forest is fantastic, and you'll make several creek crossings at the beginning and end of the loop. The middle 2.0 miles of the hike have no natural water sources, so bring enough drinking water for you and the dogs—especially since this is the most strenuous section of the trail.

Start: At the southwest end of the parking lot. To the left as you face the fish hatchery, follow the paved FR 475C (Horse Cove Road) across the bridge. The Cat Gap Loop trailhead is immediately on your right (west).
Distance: 4.25-mile loop
Hiking time: 2 hours, 30 minutes
Blaze color: Orange
Difficulty: Moderate
Trailhead elevation: 2,320 feet
Highest point: 3,318 feet
Seasons: Year-round
Trail surface: Hard-packed dirt with rooty and rocky sections, muddy patches
Other trail users: Mountain bikers seasonally from October 15–April 15

Canine compatibility: Voice control
Land status: Pisgah National Forest–Pisgah Ranger District
Fees and permits: None
Maps: *North Carolina Atlas & Gazetteer*, page 53, C5. National Geographic Trails Illustrated Map #780 Pisgah Ranger District, G6, Trail #120.
Trail contact: Pisgah National Forest, Pisgah Ranger District; (828) 877-3265; www.fs.fed.us
Nearest town: Brevard
Trail tips: Skip the upper portion of the loop. It's overgrown, strenuous, and you don't get any better views than you do from the bypass. Bring lots of drinking water for you and the dogs.

Finding the trailhead: *From the junction of US 276 North and US 64 in Brevard*, drive north on US 276 for 5.2 miles and turn left onto FR 475 at the "Pisgah Fish Hatchery" sign. Travel for 1.4 miles to a left onto FR 475C into the parking area for the Pisgah Center for Wildlife Education and Fish Hatchery.
   From the junction of US 276 and the Blue Ridge Parkway near milepost 412, drive south on US 276 for 9.6 miles. Turn right onto FR 475 at the "Pisgah Fish Hatchery" sign and then follow the directions above. GPS: N35 17.007'/W82 47.522'

The Hike

This enjoyable hike makes a complete circle around John Rock. Look up from the parking lot, and you'll get a peek of the smooth, stone-faced mountain. You can also enjoy a stroll around the fish hatchery. The hatchery releases over 500,000 trout each year into the local streams. You can hike the loop either way, but I prefer counter-clockwise, so begin at the southwest end of the parking lot and immediately cross a

Beau is happy in and out of the creek.

bridge over the creek. The dogs can take a dip in the swiftly moving water, and then you'll immediately see the trailhead for the Cat Gap Loop Trail on the right. The trail slowly climbs alongside a fence line. When you leave the fence, you make a few water crossings and then cross a gravel service road. Beyond the road, the trail gently climbs and leads you to Cedar Rock Creek Falls. A primitive campsite at the base of the falls gives the dogs a flat area to run around.

Meanwhile the pool at the base of this two-tiered waterfall is terrific. It's small, but deep enough for the dogs to take a quick lap around. Downed trees and large rocks give you a place to sit and enjoy the view while the dogs have their playtime. Beyond the falls, the trail continues to climb and quickly leads to a fork. Go left and cross the first of several log bridge crossings. If the dogs are timid of the large logs, the water is shallow enough that they can traipse right across. You pass through some nicely formed tunnels of rhododendron and mountain laurel. After the third log bridge crossing, the trail climbs steeper than before as you hike on the most strenuous section of the loop. Even your four-legged friends begin to huff and puff, so bring enough water for you both. A few switchbacks ease the ascension, and at 1.8 miles you come to a fork. The Cat Gap Loop Trail heads right (southwest) and uphill, and the bypass trail continues straight ahead (southeast). If you opt to follow the loop trail, it's narrow, overgrown, and less traveled. It brings you up to Cat Gap, where you can access the Art Leob Trail. Honestly, although the loop trail climbs high above the bypass, it doesn't give you any better views except in wintertime. So the rewards aren't really worth the effort. I recommend you take the bypass trail instead. It gently climbs and follows a contour around the mountain.

After 0.65 mile you come to an intersection. This is where the loop trail comes back down, and also where the yellow-blazed John Rock Trail begins to the left. The John Rock Trail heads up and over John Rock, and the views are amazing. You can even see Looking Glass Rock from there, but the drop-offs from the top are deadly. I *urge* you to save that hike for another day when the dogs aren't with you, for their safety and your peace of mind. The loop trail now begins a steady, rocky descent. You pass the other end of the John Rock Trail, and then cross FR 475C. Beyond the forest road, you cross the creek a few times before the loop ends at the northeast end of the parking lot. John Rock stands at 3,320 feet and has earned the designation of one of North Carolina's Natural Heritage Areas. The strenuous hike to the top is worth a return trip, without the dogs in tow.

Miles and Directions

0.0 Follow FR 475C (Horse Cove Road) south around the gate and over the bridge. Immediately come to the Cat Gap Loop trailhead on your right. Follow this trail west, and it slowly climbs following a chain-link fence.

0.2 Rock hop a muddy tributary.

0.3 Cross a footbridge over Cedar Rock Creek, and then cross a gravel service road. Continue hiking south and uphill.

0.8 You'll see an obvious side trail that leads down to a primitive campsite. Follow this trail southeast, and you'll find yourself at the base of the delightful Cedar Rock Creek Falls (N35 16.662'/W82 47.998'). The campsite at the base is big enough for the dogs to run and play. While you enjoy the peaceful, steady sound of the falls, the dogs have fun climbing on the rocks and downed trees. Continue hiking south and uphill.

0.85 At the top of the hill, you come to a fork. The blue-blazed Butter Gap Trail continues straight ahead (southwest), and the Cat Gap Loop Trail heads left (southeast) and crosses a log bridge over the creek. Go left, cross the bridge, and the trail immediately bends right (southwest).

1.0 Cross another log bridge, and the trail leads you through a large primitive campsite. Continue hiking generally south.

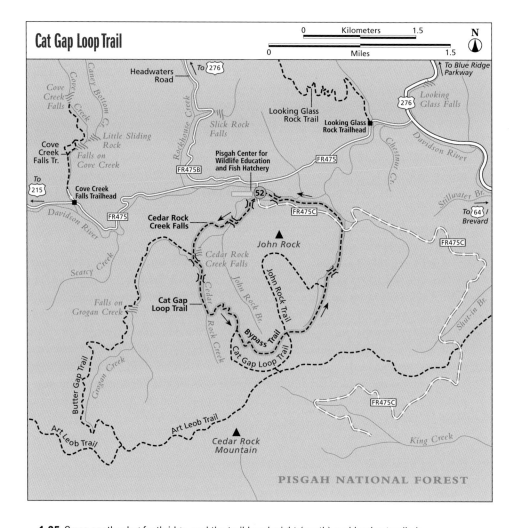

Cat Gap Loop Trail

0   Kilometers   1.5

0   Miles   1.5

N

1.25 Cross another log footbridge, and the trail bends right (south) and begins to climb.

1.8 As the trail finally flattens, you come to a fork. This is where the yellow-blazed bypass trail leads straight ahead (southeast), and the Cat Gap Loop Trail heads right (southwest) and climbs steeply up to Cat Gap and the Art Leob Trail. These trails parallel each other, with the loop trail being 0.4 mile longer than the bypass. The loop trail is overgrown and strenuous and doesn't give you any better views than the bypass trail, except in the wintertime. I recommend bearing left at the fork and following the bypass trail for 0.65 mile.

2.45 Come to an intersection where the bypass trail ends. On the right (south), the Cat Gap Loop Trail comes back down from Cat Gap. To the left (north) is the yellow-blazed John Rock Trail, which goes up and over John Rock and comes down farther along the trail you're on. Continue straight ahead (east) on the Cat Gap Loop Trail as you begin to make your way downhill and back toward the trailhead on the rocky path.

3.0 Pass by the John Rock Trail where it comes out from the west on the other side of the stone mountain. Continue hiking north and downhill on the orange-blazed Cat Gap Loop Trail.

3.1 Cross a log bridge.

3.3 The trail leads you straight across FR 475C. Continue north and downhill.

3.35 Rock hop across a creek. This is a fantastic place for the dogs to enjoy the cool refreshing water of a mountain stream.

4.15 Cross a footbridge and then immediately cross a narrow footpath as you hike north toward the river.

4.2 The trail brings you out alongside the Davidson River; head left and follow the river upstream.

4.25 Arrive back near the trailhead at the northeast end of the parking lot.

You can view John Rock from the parking lot before hiking the Cat Gap Loop Trail.

Options: Shorten the hike by turning around at Cedar Rock Creek Falls and making this a 1.6 miles out and back hike. Extend the hike by hiking the upper portion of the loop at 1.8 miles instead of taking the bypass.

Resting up: Holiday Inn Express, 1570 Asheville Hwy., Brevard; (828) 862-8900; www.hiexbrevard.com; two dogs any size, pet fee per dog per night.

The Inn at Brevard, 215 Main St., Brevard; (828) 884-2105; www.theinnatbrevard .com; two dogs up to 40 pounds, no fee.

Camping: Davidson River Campground, 1000 Pisgah Hwy., Pisgah Forest; (828) 877-3265 or (828) 862-5960; www.fs.usda.gov/recarea/nfsnc/recreation/camping -cabins/recarea/?recid=48130&actid=29. Open year-round. For reservations visit www.recreation.gov or call (877) 444-6777.

Fueling up: Hobnob Restaurant, 192 W. Main St., Brevard; (828) 966-4662.

MARCO Trattoria, 204 W. Main St., Brevard; (828) 883-4841; www.marcotrattoria .com.

The Square Root, 33 Times Arcade Alley, Brevard; (828) 884-6171; www.squareroot restaurant.com.

53 Cove Creek Falls Trail

Although this hike begins on a rather mundane gravel forest road, be patient. It leads to three fantastic waterfalls, each with its own unique characteristics. After visiting the first two falls, you'll leave the gravel road and enjoy a fantastic hike through the forest, leading you to the base of Cove Creek Falls.

Start: Hike around the gate following FR 809 north toward the Cove Creek Group Camp.
Distance: 2.3-miles out and back
Hiking time: 1 hour
Blaze color: Blue
Difficulty: Easy to moderate
Trailhead elevation: 2,542 feet
Highest point: 2,771 feet
Seasons: Year-round
Trail surface: Gravel road; hard-packed dirt
Other trail users: Mountain bikers on a small portion of the trail
Canine compatibility: Voice control
Land status: Pisgah National Forest—Pisgah Ranger District

Fees and permits: None
Maps: *DeLorme: North Carolina Atlas & Gazetteer*, page 52, C4 and 53, C5. National Geographic Trails Illustrated Map #780 Pisgah Ranger District, F4, Trail #361.
Trail contact: Pisgah National Forest, Pisgah Ranger District; (828) 877-3265; www.fs.fed. us
Nearest towns: Brevard and Balsam Grove
Trail tips: Watch out for mountain bikers flying down the mountainside on the Caney Bottom Trail. Keep the dogs on a leash while on the Caney Bottom Trail between the group camp and the fork with the Cove Creek Trail at 0.9 mile.

Finding the trailhead: *From the junction of US 276 north and US 64 in Brevard,* drive north on US 276 for 5.2 miles. Turn left onto FR 475 at the "Pisgah Fish Hatchery" sign and travel for 3.1 miles to a small parking area on the left, across from the Cove Creek Group Camp.

From the junction of US 276 and the Blue Ridge Parkway near milepost 412, drive south on US 276 for 9.6 miles. Turn right onto FR 475 at the "Pisgah Fish Hatchery" sign and follow directions above. GPS: N35 16.994'/W82 49.025'

Special Considerations: If the group camp is occupied, please be respectful of campers' space and leash the dogs.

The Hike

As you hike up the gravel forest road, the "trail" seems quite mundane and doesn't offer much hope. I assure you, it's worth it. Follow FR 809 uphill, and as the road leads across Cove Creek, there's a footbridge to the right, so you can keep your feet dry. After hiking on the road for a quarter mile, it leads past the first waterfall, Falls on Cove Creek. A few steep and muddy paths lead down to the falls, but I recommend viewing it from the road. Patience pays. The forest road soon leads you past the Caney Bottom Trail on your left (north). When you finish the hike, this is where you'll come out, but bypass it for now and follow the gravel road into the group camp and across the grassy field.

There's something for every pooch at the base of Cove Creek Falls.

At the far side of the grassy field, before the road heads back into the forest, you'll see a low split-rail fence to your right. Hop this fence (the dogs should have no problem going over or under), and you'll find yourself standing at the foot of Little Sliding Rock. An inviting pool of crystal-clear fresh mountain water sits at the base of the falls. This pit stop is exactly halfway to Cove Creek Falls, making it ideal. After enjoying a refreshing water break, return to the gravel road and hike straight across it, up the grassy hill past the restrooms, and into the forest. You'll arrive at a T on the Caney Bottom Trail. Go right (east), and the blue-blazed trail gently climbs. When you reach a fork, go right again (north), and you can let the dogs off the leash as you hike downhill to a primitive campsite near the creek. Follow the creek upstream for nearly 0.2 mile, and you'll find yourself humbled when you arrive at the base of Cove Creek Falls. Standing an impressive 65 feet tall, the water flows over the multi-faceted stone face. Large downed trees add to the scenery, and the creek is shallow enough for the dogs to wade around near the base to cool off.

▶ **PUPPY PAWS AND GOLDEN YEARS: The** parking area sits right next to the Davidson River. A narrow footpath leads south back to the river, where you can view another waterfall known as Whalebone. Dogs of all ages can enjoy wading in the river either up or downstream from the falls.

While returning to the trailhead, when you reach the T where you came up from Little Sliding Rock, stay on the Caney Bottom Trail. The trail swings around the group camp and then leads to the gravel road. Backtrack from there.

You can visit these big draft horses, among others, at the Pisgah Riding Stables off of FR 477.

Running through the heart of the Pisgah National Forest, the Caney Bottom Trail is open to mountain bikers so keep the dogs on a leash from Little Sliding Rock to the fork at 0.9 mile. This is a popular downhill route for mountain bikers, and it's possible they may come flying down the mountain here. Pisgah is a mecca for any outdoor enthusiast. Try your hand at fly-fishing, climb the face of Looking Glass Rock, or tube down the Davidson River; it's all within easy reach. Miles and miles of trails are open year-round for hiking, mountain biking, and equestrian use.

Miles and Directions

0.0   Hike north on the gravel FR 809 toward Cove Creek Group Camp.

0.1   A side trail crosses a footbridge over Cove Creek. Continue hiking north on the gravel road.

0.3   Arrive at Falls on Cove Creek (N35 17.225'/W82 49.043'). Enjoy the view from the road. Continue hiking north on FR 809.

0.45 Bypass the Caney Bottom Trail on your left (northwest). This is where you'll come out on your way back to the trailhead. Continue hiking northeast on the gravel road as it passes through the group camp.

0.6   Before the gravel road heads back into the woods, go right (east) and climb over the split-rail fence. This puts you at the creek near the base of Little Sliding Rock (N35 17.347'/W82 48.977'). This is easily the best swimming hole on this hike for you and the dogs. Backtrack to the gravel road and hike directly across it. You are now heading north uphill and past the restrooms at the east end of the grassy field.

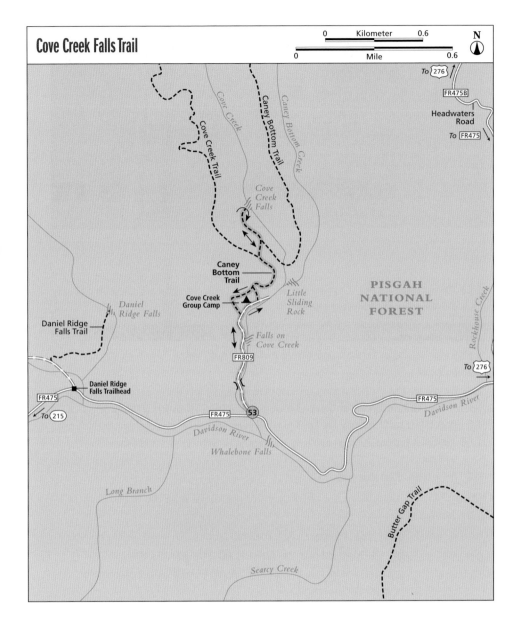

0   Kilometer   0.6

0   Mile   0.6

N

0.7   Arrive at a T in the forest. This is the Caney Bottom Trail. To the left swings west around group camp and back to the gravel road. Go right (east) and follow the blue-blazed trail as it gently climbs.

0.9   Come to a fork. The left is the yellow-blazed Cove Creek Trail. Go right (north) and downhill on the Caney Bottom Trail.

0.95 Bypass the Caney Bottom Trail off to the right (southeast) and arrive at a large primitive campsite. Hike left (west), and at the end of the campsite a narrow path leads to the creek. Follow the creek upstream and northwest on a narrow dirt path.

The lush, damp ground of Pisgah National Forest makes it prime habitat for a large variety of wildflowers.

1.00 The trail seems to end at some rocks near the creek. Hike over the rocks and you'll pick up the trail again. Continue hiking upstream.

1.15 Arrive at a fork; you can see the falls in the distance. Go right (northeast) and follow the trail toward the creek.

1.2 Arrive at the base of Cove Creek Falls (N35 17.629'/W82 49.051'). Backtrack to the trailhead.

1.7 Bypass the trail where you came up from Little Sliding Rock at 0.7 mile. Continue straight ahead (west) on the Caney Bottom Trail as it skirts around the group camp.

1.8 Rock hop a small tributary. The trail bends left (south).

1.85 The Caney Bottom Trail ends and puts you back on FR 809. Go right and backtrack to the trailhead.

2.3 Arrive back at the trailhead.

Option: Shorten the hike to 1.2 miles by visiting Little Sliding Rock and backtracking to the trailhead.

Resting up: Holiday Inn Express, 1570 Asheville Hwy., Brevard; (828) 862-8900; www.hiexbrevard.com; two dogs any size, pet fee per dog per night.

The Inn at Brevard, 215 Main St., Brevard; (828) 884-2105; www.theinnatbrevard .com; two dogs up to 40 pounds, no fee.

Camping: Davidson River Campground, 1000 Pisgah Hwy., Pisgah Forest; (828) 877-3265 or (828) 862-5960; www.fs.usda.gov/recarea/nfsnc/recreation/camping -cabins/recarea/?recid=48130&actid=29. Open year-round. For reservations visit www.recreation.gov or call (877) 444-6777.

Fueling up: Hobnob Restaurant, 192 W. Main St., Brevard; (828) 966-4662.

MARCO Trattoria, 204 W. Main St., Brevard; (828) 883-4841; www.marcotrattoria .com.

The Square Root, 33 Times Arcade Alley, Brevard; (828) 884-6171; www.squareroot restaurant.com.

54 Sunwall Trail

Pisgah National Forest is famous for miles of trails, many waterfalls, and Looking Glass Rock. This trail leads you directly to the base of the famed rock, giving you a fresh and new perspective of the natural wonder you've often viewed from afar. As you stand at the foot of the rock, you can literally lay your hands on the smooth stone while looking straight up what's known as "the nose" of the rock. Enjoy this rare opportunity, which is typically only taken by local climbers and the protected peregrine falcons who nest on the eyrie.

Start: From the trailhead information sign, walk southwest on FR 475B for about 75 feet. The Sunwall trailhead has a sign reading "To Nose."
Distance: 1.0-mile out and back
Hiking time: 30 minutes
Blaze color: Yellow
Difficulty: Moderate
Trailhead elevation: 3,101 feet
Highest point: 3,471 feet
Seasons: Year-round
Trail surface: Hard-packed dirt with some rooty sections and log overs
Other trail users: None
Canine compatibility: Voice control

Land status: Pisgah National Forest–Pisgah Ranger District
Fees and permits: None
Maps: *DeLorme: North Carolina Atlas & Gazetteer*, page 53, C5. National Geographic Trails Illustrated Map #780 Pisgah Ranger District, G6, Trail #601.
Trail contact: Pisgah National Forest, Pisgah Ranger District; (828) 877-3265; www.fs.fed.us
Nearest town: Brevard
Trail tips: Bring a hiking stick and a camera. There's no water along the trail, so bring enough for you and your happy hounds.

Finding the trailhead: *From the junction of US 276 north and US 64 in Brevard*, drive north on US 276 for 5.2 miles. Turn left onto FR 475 at the "Pisgah Fish Hatchery" sign and travel 1.3 miles to a right onto FR 475B (Headwaters Road). Travel 2.9 miles to the small parking area on your right.
From the junction of US 276 and the Blue Ridge Parkway near milepost 412, drive south on US 276 for 4.7 miles to a right onto FR 475B (Headwaters Road). Travel for 3.6 miles to the small parking area on your left. GPS: N35 18.605'/W82 48.005'

The Hike

One of the most notable natural formations in the area is the world-famous Looking Glass Rock. Whether you view it from the Blue Ridge Parkway, from atop John Rock, or on a postcard, the smooth stone face of Looking Glass Rock is unmistakable. There's a creek, a popular waterfall, and even a local outfitter's shop bearing its name. You can hike to the top of the sheer-faced rock, but few get the up-close and personal experience that you're about to have. The Sunwall Trail leads directly to the foot of this mammoth monolith. You enjoy the rare experience of actually putting

Looking Glass Rock is easily the most notable landmark in the area.

your hands upon the smooth stone wall as you look straight up "the nose" of Looking Glass Rock. It's truly jaw dropping to stand there and feel that rock and look up and know the power and strength and sheer size of it from the many times you've viewed it from afar. It's downright humbling. You may even have it to yourself. Usually the only people who visit the rock are local outfitters taking groups to climb and rappel on the rock. If you see vans at the trailhead, expect to see people literally on the rock.

From the trailhead, you're blessed with nothing but quiet solitude as the yellow-blazed trail makes a straight shot due south into the woods. Mountain laurel lines the pathway, forming an incomplete tunnel as the trail makes a steady climb. Right about the time you start to breathe heavy, the trail flattens out, giving you a breather before you have to start climbing again. Because there are no creeks or tributaries, make sure you bring enough drinking water for you and your canine companions. The path is shaded the entire way by tall trees, and their roots act as steps, helping you climb. Surprisingly, as you enjoy this peaceful hike, you can't even see Looking Glass Rock—yet. At 0.4 mile you come to a T at a large flat rock. It looks like a footpath heads right (southwest) and that the left goes nowhere. But actually, you want to go left (east), and the trail leads you around a tree with double yellow blazes on it. Climb up the rocks here for about 15 feet, and then you pick up the trail again at the top.

▶ **PUPPY PAWS AND GOLDEN YEARS:** Dogs of all ages enjoy the 0.1-mile hike to the base of Slick Rock Falls. The waterfall is also located off FR 475B, 1.8 miles south of the Sunwall trailhead.

The rocks aren't steep, and dogs seem to have an easier time with the short climb than their owners do. Beyond the rocks the trail continues uphill for another 0.1 mile. Along the way, roots and rocks act as a natural staircase as the climb gets steeper. It's while you're making the final push uphill that you realize you're standing at the base of the legendary Looking Glass Rock. A narrow, rocky footpath leads in both directions along the base of the rock. Explore at will, and get out your camera! You're going to want to keep these memories for years to come.

Miles and Directions

0.0 Follow the yellow-blazed trail up a few steps as it heads south into the woods. The trail gently climbs the entire way.

0.4 Come to a T at a large flat rock, where it looks like a footpath heads right (southwest) and the left leads nowhere. Go left (east) and around a tree with two yellow blazes on it. You then need to climb up the rocks about 15 feet, and you'll pick up the trail again at the top of the rocks. Continue hiking east toward Looking Glass Rock.

0.5 Arrive at the "nose" of Looking Glass Rock (N35 18.314'/W82 47.742'). Backtrack to the trailhead.

1.0 Arrive back at the trailhead.

Local outfitters take people on guided trips to climb and rappel over "the nose" of Looking Glass Rock.

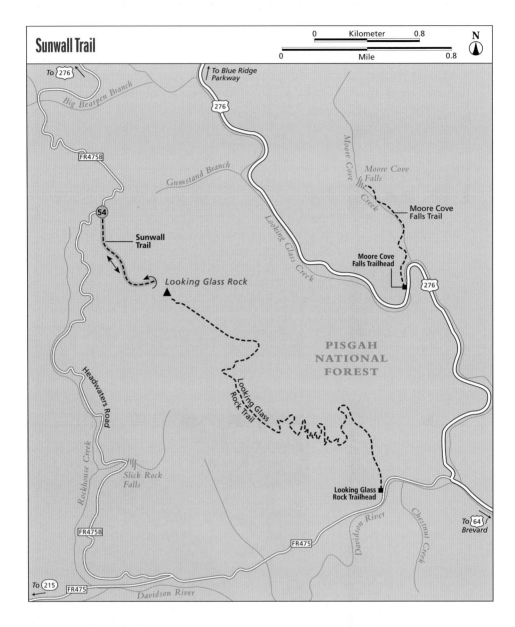

0   Kilometer   0.8

0   Mile   0.8

N

To 276

To Blue Ridge Parkway

Big Bearpen Branch

276

FR475B

Gumstand Branch

54

Sunwall Trail

Moore Cove Creek

Moore Cove Falls

Moore Cove Falls Trail

Looking Glass Rock

Moore Cove Falls Trailhead

276

Looking Glass Creek

PISGAH NATIONAL FOREST

Headwaters Road

Looking Glass Rock Trail

Rockhouse Creek

Slick Rock Falls

Looking Glass Rock Trailhead

To 64 Brevard

Davidson River

Chestnut Creek

FR475B

FR475

To 215 FR475

Davidson River

Resting up: Holiday Inn Express, 1570 Asheville Hwy., Brevard; (828) 862-8900; www.hiexbrevard.com; two dogs any size, pet fee per dog per night.

The Inn at Brevard, 215 Main St., Brevard; (828) 884-2105; www.theinnatbrevard .com; two dogs up to 40 pounds, no fee.

Camping: Davidson River Campground, 1000 Pisgah Hwy., Pisgah Forest; (828) 877-3265 or (828) 862-5960; www.fs.usda.gov/recarea/nfsnc/recreation/camping -cabins/recarea/?recid=48130&actid=29. Open year-round. For reservations visit www.recreation.gov or call (877) 444-6777.

You can view Looking Glass Falls from the roadside, or let the dogs dip their paws at the base.

Fueling up: Hobnob Restaurant, 192 W. Main St., Brevard; (828) 966-4662.

MARCO Trattoria, 204 W. Main St., Brevard; (828) 883-4841; www.marcotrattoria
.com.

The Square Root, 33 Times Arcade Alley, Brevard; (828) 884-6171; www.squareroot
restaurant.com.

55 Andy Cove Nature Trail

All in all this is a lovely stroll through Andy Cove, and over the short distance of this hike, you're treated to quite a few unique man-made and natural features. The loop begins by climbing and leads you across an elevated boardwalk and suspension bridge. The trail then heads down into Andy Cove and follows a tiny clear-running creek. The dogs enjoy playing in the water, while a variety of birds serenade you. Toward the end of the hike, the Exercise Trail merges onto the loop trail, where it remains for the final 0.1 mile.

Start: At the northeast corner of the parking lot directly across from the entrance to the Pisgah National Forest Ranger Station

Distance: 0.6-mile loop

Hiking time: 20 minutes

Blaze color: None

Difficulty: Easy to moderate

Trailhead elevation: 2,138 feet

Highest point: 2,243 feet

Seasons: Year-round

Trail surface: Hard-packed dirt, wooden boardwalk

Other trail users: None

Canine compatibility: Leash required

Land status: Pisgah National Forest–Pisgah Ranger District

Fees and permits: None

Maps: *DeLorme: North Carolina Atlas & Gazetteer*, page 53, C5. National Geographic Trails Illustrated Map #780 Pisgah Ranger District, G6, Trail #288.

Trail contact: (828) 877-3265; www.fs.fed.us

Nearest town: Brevard

Trail tips: Bring a few dog treats along in case you need to coax your pooches across the suspension bridge.

Finding the trailhead: *From the junction of US 276 and US 64 in Brevard*, drive north on US 276 for 1.3 miles to a right into the parking lot for the Pisgah National Forest Ranger Station.
From the junction of US 276 and the Blue Ridge Parkway, drive south on US 276 for 13.3 miles to a left into the parking lot for the Pisgah National Forest Ranger Station. GPS: N35 17.113'/ W82 43.597'

The Hike

This entertaining nature trail forms a small loop that leads through Andy Cove. You can hike the loop either way, but it's described counterclockwise. The hike begins directly across from the entrance to the ranger station, and the trail quickly leads up some steps. Beyond the steps you cross a boardwalk that seems to be clutching onto the mountainside. You cross a footbridge with no water beneath it, but be patient: You'll reach the creek in 0.2 mile. After the footbridge you come to one of the highlights of the hike, a suspension bridge. The bridge is sturdy, despite some movement, and crosses a

▶ **PUPPY PAWS AND GOLDEN YEARS:** If you're pups are unable to climb, hike this trail clockwise and follow it to the creek. Return by the same route.

little ravine. Most dogs should be fine here, although some may need a little coaxing.

After crossing the bridge, the trail becomes hard-packed dirt and follows a tiny creek. A variety of birds make this cove their home, so no matter what time of day you hike, you're likely to hear them singing, chirping, and tweeting away. Although the beginning of the hike has you climbing a bit, the rest of the way is a peaceful stroll. For such a short hike, there's a nice variety of scenery. Between a pair of footbridges, you pass an outdoor lectern with a small seating area. On occasion the forest service hosts educational programs here in the cove.

As you continue hiking, you can't help but notice the unique trail tree that's been carved out by Mother Nature and is bent over to point the way. Some steps lead you up, and then back down, into the cove before crossing the creek again, giving the

This little guy will sleep anywhere.

dogs one last chance to splash around. At 0.55 mile the Exercise Trail merges onto the Andy Cove Nature Trail. Continue east, and in less than 0.1 mile the loop trail ends back at the parking lot. The Pisgah National Forest Ranger Station is a fantastic resource for visitors to the area. They're a wealth of knowledge. No matter what you're looking for in the forest, they can help you find it. The ranger station also has educational exhibits and a gift shop where you can buy books, maps, or a commemorative T-shirt to remember your trip. It's open Monday–Friday 8:00 a.m.–4:30 p.m.; peak season hours (mid April–early November) Monday–Friday 9:00 a.m.–5:00 p.m. Only service dogs are allowed inside.

Miles and Directions

0.0 Hike north into the woods, climb up the steps to cross a boardwalk.

0.15 Cross a footbridge with no water below it.

0.2 Cross a suspension bridge (N35 17.213'/W82 43.700').

0.3 Cross a footbridge, and the trail makes a switchback west.

0.35 Cross another footbridge over a small creek. Past the creek take note of the unique trail tree.

0.38 Pass an outdoor amphitheater.

0.4 Cross a footbridge, climb some steps, and then quickly come back down into Andy Cove.

0.47 Cross a final footbridge over the creek. Continue hiking south.

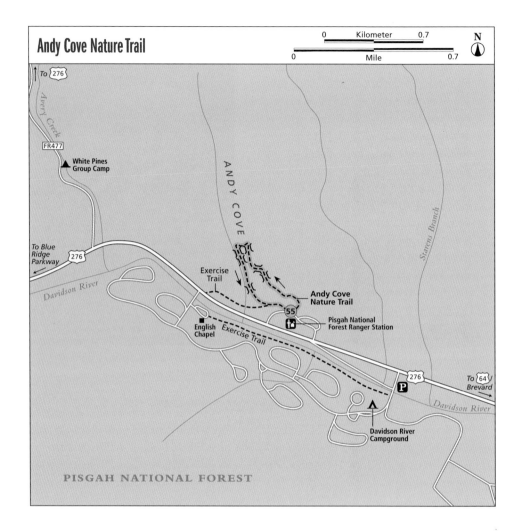

0.55 The Exercise Trail merges onto the Andy Cove Nature Trail from the right (southwest). Continue hiking straight ahead (east).

0.6 Arrive back near the trailhead.

Resting up: Holiday Inn Express, 1570 Asheville Hwy., Brevard; (828) 862-8900; www.hiexbrevard.com; two dogs any size, pet fee per dog per night.

The Inn at Brevard, 215 Main St., Brevard; (828) 884-2105; www.theinnatbrevard .com: two dogs up to 40 pounds, no fee.

Camping: Davidson River Campground, 1000 Pisgah Hwy., Pisgah Forest; (828) 877-3265 or (828) 862-5960; www.fs.usda.gov/recarea/nfsnc/recreation/camping -cabins/recarea/?recid=48130&actid=29. Open year-round; for reservations visit www.recreation.gov or call (877) 444-6777.

Fueling up: Hobnob Restaurant, 192 W. Main St., Brevard; (828) 966-4662.

Out for an afternoon stroll on Andy Cove Nature Trail.

MARCO Trattoria, 204 W. Main St., Brevard; (828) 883-4841; www.marcotrattoria
.com.

The Square Root, 33 Times Arcade Alley, Brevard; (828) 884-6171; www.squareroot
restaurant.com.

MILLS RIVER TO ASHEVILLE

56 Carolina Mountain Trail

Within the fabulous North Carolina Arboretum, this hike leads through a diverse forest over easy rolling hills. Signs along the way not only identify the flora, they actually explain how nature works. Toward the end of the hike, you'll reach a few places where the dogs can romp around and splash in the creek. There's even a bench and a cascade so you can enjoy the water as much as the dogs.

Start: The trailhead is southwest of the Education Center. Follow the gravel path around the building to the right. The marked Carolina Mountain trailhead is immediately on the right.

Distance: 1.9-miles out and back

Hiking time: 1 hour

Blaze color: Green

Difficulty: Easy to moderate

Trailhead elevation: 2,266 feet

Highest point: 2,266 feet

Seasons: January 5–March 31, 8:00 a.m.–7:00 p.m.; April 1–October 31, 8:00 a.m.–9:00 p.m.; closed November and December

Trail surface: Mulch and gravel path

Other trail users: None

Canine compatibility: Leash required; no dogs allowed in the buildings

Land status: North Carolina Arboretum

Fees and permits: $$; parking is free on Tuesday

Map: *DeLorme: North Carolina Atlas & Gazetteer,* page 53, A6

Trail contact: North Carolina Arboretum, 100 Frederick Law Olmsted Way, Asheville; (828) 665-2492; www.ncarboretum.org/

Nearest town: Asheville

Trail tips: Trail maps are available at the visitor's center.

Finding the trailhead: *From the junction of NC 191 and I-26 in Asheville (exit 33),* drive south on NC 191 for 2.1 miles to a right at the sign for "Blue Ridge Parkway and the NC Arboretum." Travel for 0.2 mile to the entrance to the NC Arboretum (NCA) on the right. Pay at the gate, and continue driving another 0.8 mile to the parking lot near the Education Center.

From the junction of NC 191 and NC 280 in Asheville, drive north on NC 191 for 7.3 miles to a left at the sign for the "Blue Ridge Parkway and the NC Arboretum," and then follow the directions above.

From the Blue Ridge Parkway, exit near milepost 393 at the sign for "NC Arboretum, Highway 191, and Interstate 26." As you exit the parkway, the entrance to the NCA is on the left before reaching the traffic light at NC 191. Pay the fee at the gate, and then follow the directions above.

Note: Most GPS units don't lead to the main gate of the NCA, so closely follow the directions above. GPS: N35 29.781'/W82 36.593'

The Hike

The mulch path brings you down some stone steps and leads you around a single switchback as you begin this peaceful stroll through the forest. You cross a paved road

Explore the many gardens at the North Carolina Arboretum.

and return to the comfort of the forest. Interpretive signs don't just identify the trees, they educate you on the ways of nature and how it interacts with the trees. Some of the relationships are harmful, while others are symbiotic. A diverse forest of cherry, oak, maple, holly, poplar, and pine shade the trail.

You cross a tiny tributary, where the dogs enjoy their first taste of fresh water, and at 0.5 mile you come to a marked T. The right leads to the greenhouse, but dogs are not allowed. Also, tours of the greenhouse are by appointment only. However, if you need water, there's a soda machine there that sells water. Go left (south) at the T, and the easy-to-follow path leads you over a dried-up tributary. As the trail parallels Bent Creek Road from above, you begin to hear the sounds of moving water. At 0.8 mile you cross the gravel road and immediately head back into the forest. Within 0.1 mile the trail now leads across two footbridges, both of which are fantastic for the pooches to play in the water. Twisted trunks of a mountain laurel thicket form a tunnel around the trail, and after the second footbridge a bench rests perfectly placed alongside Wolf Branch. Sit a spell while the dogs play in the pools of the creek near the base of a delightful cascade. Beyond the bench the trail comes to an end at a gravel road that leads to Bent Creek Road. When you've finished the hike, enjoy a stroll throughout the grounds of the arboretum. There's over a dozen gardens just waiting for you to explore. Please be respectful: Keep the pups on a leash and pick up after them.

▶ **PUPPY PAWS AND GOLDEN YEARS: The Snow's Cut Trail (hike 1) is found within the same state park. It's short and easy and leads from the picnic area to a fantastic sandy beach along Snow's Cut.**

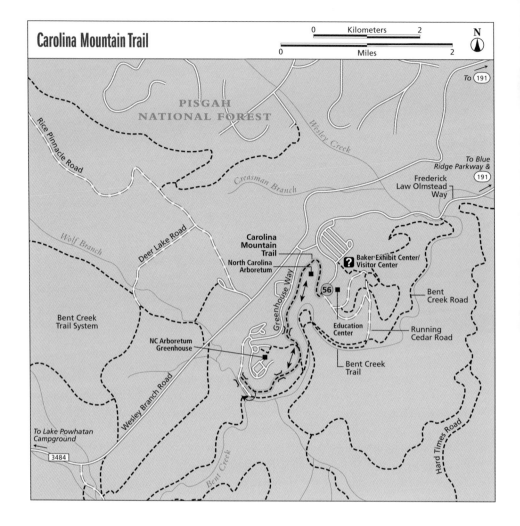

Map labels:

Carolina Mountain Trail

0 Kilometers 2
N

0 Miles 2

PISGAH NATIONAL FOREST

To 191

Rice Pinnacle Road

Wesley Creek

Creasman Branch

To Blue Ridge Parkway & 191

Frederick Law Olmstead Way

Wolf Branch

Deer Lake Road

Carolina Mountain Trail

North Carolina Arboretum

Baker Exhibit Center/ Visitor Center

Greenhouse Way

56

Bent Creek Road

Bent Creek Trail System

NC Arboretum Greenhouse

Education Center

Running Cedar Road

Bent Creek Trail

Wesley Branch Road

To Lake Powhatan Campground

3484

Bent Creek

Hard Times Road

Miles and Directions

0.0 Pick up the Carolina Mountain Trail off of the gravel path on the right (west) side of the Education Center. Hike down the stone steps and west into the woods.

0.15 Cross a paved road, continue hiking northwest.

0.25 Bypass a spur trail that leads northwest up to the road. Continue hiking straight ahead (southwest).

0.45 Cross a footbridge over a tiny tributary. The dogs enjoy the fresh water.

0.5 Come to a T. The right leads 0.1 mile to the greenhouse, but no dogs are allowed. However, they do have a soda machine that sells water, if you need some. Go left, continue hiking south.

0.7 Cross a footbridge over a dry tributary. Continue hiking west.

0.8 Hike across Wolf Branch Road and then down some steps.

0.85 Cross a footbridge.

0.9 Cross a footbridge, and the trail bends left (east). Arrive at a bench alongside Wolf Branch. A small cascade here is perfect for the dogs to take a water break.

0.95 The trail ends at a gravel forest road. Backtrack to the trailhead.

1.9 Arrive back at the trailhead.

Option: You could make a loop out of the hike, following the Bent Creek Trail, but that route weaves on and off Bent Creek Road and then leads up Running Cedar Road to return to the arboretum.

Resting up: Four Points by Sheraton, 22 Woodfin St., Asheville; (828) 253-1851; two dogs any size, pet fee per stay.

Hotel Indigo, 151 Haywood St., Asheville; (828) 239-0239; two dogs up to 80 pounds, pet fee per stay.

White Gate Inn & Cottage, 173 E. Chestnut St., Asheville; (828) 253-2553 or (800) 485-3045; www.whitegate.net; innkeeper@whitegate.net.

Camping: Lake Powhatan Campground, 375 Wesley Branch Rd., Asheville; (828) 257-4200; www.fs.usda.gov/recarea/nfsnc/recreation/camping-cabins/recarea/?recid =48172&actid=29; open April 1–October 31.

Fueling up: Asheville Brewing Company, 77 Coxe Ave., Asheville; (828) 255-4077.

Laughing Seed Café, 40 Wall St., Asheville; (828) 252-3445.

Posana Café, 1 Biltmore Ave., Asheville; (828) 505-3969.

Keep the dogs on a leash where posted, so they don't disturb the natives.

57 South Mills River Trail

This hike begins as a rutted-up rocky path, but once you cross a suspension bridge over the river, it smooths out and leads you nearly due west alongside the river for most of the way. Take advantage of the watering holes near the beginning, middle, and end of the hike. The South Fork of the Mills River is crystal clear. You'll enjoy dangling your own feet in it as much as your dogs do.

Start: At the northwest corner of the parking lot

Distance: 6.0-miles out and back

Hiking time: 3 hours

Blaze color: White

Difficulty: Easy to moderate

Trailhead elevation: 2,580 feet

Highest point: 2,590 feet

Seasons: Year-round

Trail surface: Hard-packed dirt, with some rocky sections at the beginning of the trail (first 0.4 mile); muddy during times of heavy rain

Other trail users: Mountain bikers and equestrian

Canine compatibility: Voice control

Land status: Pisgah National Forest—Pisgah Ranger District

Fees and permits: None

Maps: *DeLorme: North Carolina Atlas & Gazetteer,* page 52, B6. National Geographic Trails Illustrated Map #780 Pisgah Ranger District, E7, Trail #133.

Trail contact: Pisgah National Forest, Pisgah Ranger District; (828) 877-3265; www.fs.fed.us

Nearest towns: Mills River, Brevard, and Asheville

Trail tips: This trail is great for trail running with your dogs.

Finding the trailhead: *From the junction of NC 280 and US 276 in Brevard,* drive north on NC 280 for 5.0 miles to a left onto Turkey Pen Road. Travel for 1.2 miles to the trailhead at the end of the road.

From the junction of NC 280 and NC 191 in Mills River, drive south on NC 280 for 6.2 miles to a right onto Turkey Pen Road and follow the directions above. GPS: N35 20.580'/W82 39.572'

The Hike

Several trails begin at the "Turkey Pen Trailhead," so make sure you have the right one. The hike begins by leading you down a rutty, rocky path. But when you reach the river, it smooths out. Coax the dogs across the suspension bridge, and you come to the first fantastic watering hole. A primitive campsite next to the river gives the dogs room to run, and a smooth slope lets them easily get in, and out, of the water. Beyond the campsite the wide path begins its long trek generally west. You bypass the Mullinax Trail, and as you meander through the forest, you hike through an area full of tall hemlock trees. Mountain laurels, rhododendrons, wild blackberries, and ferns fill in the underbrush. Just before the 2.0-mile mark, you come to one of my favorite spots to stop and enjoy the river. Large flat rocks out in the river give you a resting place where the dogs can easily wade into the water. About 0.1 mile past this swimming hole, you'll

Even the robot has a puppy.

bypass the Poundingmill Trail. Continue hiking west, enjoying the peaceful solitude of the forest. Many trails weave through the woods here, so you have lots of route options if you want to extend the hike. Nearly a mile from the Poundingmill Trail, you'll see a second suspension bridge over the river to the left (south). This is where the South Mills River Trail continues on for several more miles. Bypass the bridge and continue straight ahead (northwest). The trail dead-ends at the river. This is where equestrians wade across the river, since they can't cross the suspension bridges. While the hike ends here, the dogs will find this is a highlight. The shallow, rocky-bottomed river is crystal clear and ideal for the dogs to wade out into the water and cool themselves off after a lovely 3.0-mile hike through the forest. When they're done taking a refreshing dip, backtrack to the trailhead, stopping at the watering holes on the return trip.

The town of Mills River is home to Barkwells, a vacation rental that doubles as a fantastic retreat for you and your furry family. You and your best friends can run, swim, play, and stay onsite. The property has more than 8 acres of fenced-in meadows and a pond, so your dogs can enjoy a leash-free vacation experience. They're centrally located near Asheville and Brevard, so you could explore many hikes in the area without having to travel too far. Contact information is listed under "Resting up."

Miles and Directions

0.0   Hike north and downhill on the rocky path.

0.4   Come to a fork, go left (south) and cross the suspension bridge over the South Fork of the Mills River.

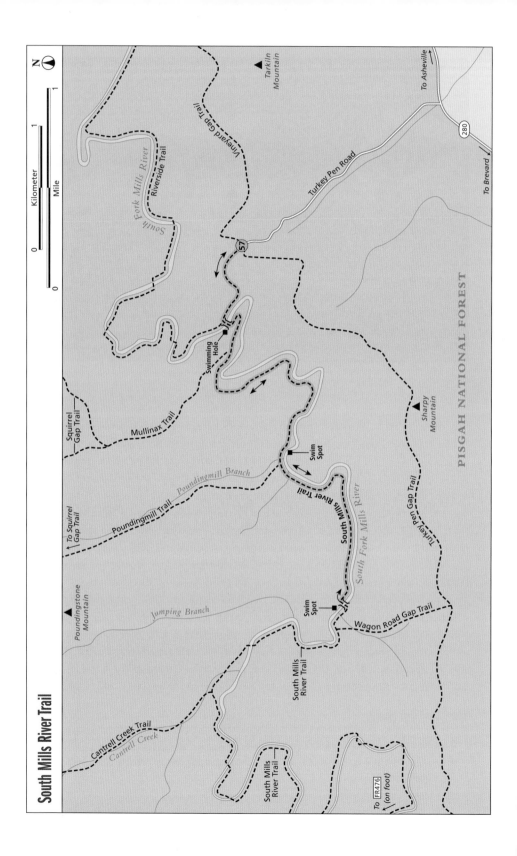

South Mills River Trail

N

Kilometer
0   1

Mile
0   1

Tarkiln Mountain

South Fork Mills River

Riverside Trail

Vineyard Gap Trail

Squirrel Gap Trail

Mullinax Trail

To Squirrel Gap Trail

Poundingmill Trail   Poundingmill Branch

Poundingstone Mountain

Jumping Branch

Swimming Hole

57

Turkey Pen Road

To Asheville

280

To Brevard

Sharpy Mountain

Swim Spot

South Mills River Trail

South Fork Mills River

Turkey Pen Gap Trail

PISGAH NATIONAL FOREST

Swim Spot

Wagon Road Gap Trail

Cantrell Creek Trail

Cantrell Creek

South Mills River Trail

South Mills River Trail

To FR476 (on foot)

0.45 After crossing the bridge, the trail leads you to a T. Before reaching the T, on your right is a primitive campsite next to the river. This is one of the best places for the dogs to play in the water. They can get some energy out running around the campsite too.

0.5 Return to the trail and follow it to the T. The right leads to a river crossing. Go left (southeast).

0.7 Come to a fork. To the right (west) is the yellow-blazed Mullinax Trail, which leads uphill. Stay left (southwest) and follow the wide white-blazed South Mills River Trail downhill.

0.9 Bypass a narrow overgrown trail on the left that leads south–southeast over your left shoulder down to the river.

1.95 Before reaching the Poundingmill Trail, stop at a fabulous swimming hole in the river. Continue hiking west.

2.0 Bypass the orange-blazed Poundingmill Trail, which forks off to the right (north). Continue hiking straight ahead (west).

2.95 Bypass the trail to the left that crosses a suspension bridge over the river. This is where the South Mills River Trail continues for several miles more. Continue hiking straight ahead (west).

3.0 The trail ends at the river. Take advantage of this marvelous watering hole. The river is crystal clear and shallow enough for the dogs to wade out into. Backtrack to the trailhead.

6.0 Arrive back at the trailhead.

Options: Shorten the hike by turning around at any point and returning to the trailhead. Lengthen the hike by exploring the Mullinax or Poundingmill Trails, or by crossing the second suspension bridge and continuing to follow on the S. Mills River Trail.

Resting up: Barkwells, 290 Lance Rd., Mills River; (828) 891-8288; www.barkwells.com.

Comfort Inn Asheville Airport, 15 Rockwood Rd., Fletcher; (828) 687-9199; two dogs any size, pet fee per night.

Holiday Inn Express, 1570 Asheville Hwy., Brevard; (828) 862-8900; www.hiexbrevard.com; two dogs any size, pet fee per dog per night.

Quality Inn & Suites Biltmore South, 1 Skyline Inn Dr., Arden; (828) 684-6688; two dogs any size, pet fee per pet per night.

One of several swimming spots along the South Mills River Trail.

Ellie Pearl stays fit mountain biking with her dad along the South Mills River Trail.

Camping: Davidson River Campground, 1000 Pisgah Hwy., Pisgah Forest; (828) 877-3265 or (828) 862-5960; www.fs.usda.gov/recarea/nfsnc/recreation/camping-cabins/recarea/?recid=48130&actid=29; open year-round; for reservations visit www.recreation.gov or call (877) 444-6777.

Lake Powhatan Campground, 375 Wesley Branch Rd., Asheville; (828) 257-4200; www.fs.usda.gov/recarea/nfsnc/recreation/camping-cabins/recarea/?recid=48172&actid=29; open April 1–October 31.

Fueling up: Asheville Brewing Company, 77 Coxe Ave., Asheville; (828) 255-4077.

Laughing Seed Café, 40 Wall St., Asheville; (828) 252-3445.

Posana Café, 1 Biltmore Ave., Asheville; (828) 505-3969.

The Square Root, 33 Times Arcade Alley, Brevard; (828) 884-6171; www.squareroot restaurant.com.

BREVARD TO HENDERSONVILLE

58 Hooker Falls Trail

This quick and easy hike follows Little River downstream the entire way. It first leads to an overlook alongside the falls, before continuing downhill around a switchback and out to the rocky beach across from the delightful Hooker Falls. This wide waterfall smoothly drops over a rock ledge the entire width of the river. The whole family will enjoy dipping their feet, or entire body, into the large inviting swimming hole at the base of the falls.

Start: At the southeast corner of the upper parking lot
Distance: 0.8-mile out and back
Hiking time: 40 minutes
Blaze color: No blazes
Difficulty: Easy
Trailhead elevation: 2,229 feet
Highest point: 2,251 feet
Seasons: Year-round
Trail surface: Wide gravel road
Other trail users: None

Canine compatibility: Leash required
Land status: DuPont State Forest
Fees and permits: None
Map: DeLorme: North Carolina Atlas & Gazetteer, page 53, D6
Trail contact: (828) 877-6527; www.dupont forest .com
Nearest town: Brevard
Trail tips: Bring a swimsuit! The swimming hole is far too inviting to pass up. A trail map is posted near the trailhead.

Finding the trailhead: From the junction of US 276 south and US 64 in Brevard, drive south on US 276 for 10.8 miles. Turn left onto Cascade Lake Road (SR 1536). Travel 2.4 miles to a right onto Staton Road (SR 1591). Travel 2.3 miles to a left into the parking area for the Hooker Falls Access Area.
From the junction of US 64 and US 276 north in Brevard, drive east on US 64 for 3.6 miles. Turn right onto Crab Creek Road (SR 1127). Travel 4.2 miles to a right onto DuPont Road (SR 1259). Travel 3.0 miles to a right into the parking area for the Hooker Falls Access Area. GPS: N35 12.153'/W82 37.175'

The Hike

The wide gravel path follows the fabulous Little River downstream and southwest nearly the entire way. Despite its width, the trail remains shaded the whole time. At 0.3 mile you pass a small area where you can overlook the falls near the brink. A split-rail fence is all that separates you from the steep, muddy banks of the river, so keep the pups on a leash. Plus, this trail is heavily populated with locals and out-of-towners alike—especially in summertime. Near this overlook you'll see an elevated seating area for those who don't want to, or can't, make it down the hill that leads to the base

White squirrels are native to the Brevard area.

of the falls. From the overlook the trail leads northwest and downhill for about 200 feet. At the bottom of the hill, it makes a hard U-turn to the left and leads southeast to the base of the delightful Hooker Falls. Although the falls are small, compared to its neighbors Triple and High Falls, this little beauty packs a punch. The waterfall is wide and spans the entire width of Little River. An inviting pool at the base mesmerizes you and lures you and your four-legged friends into the chilly mountain water. Rocks line the banks of the river, giving you a perfect place to perch. Bring a towel; you may want to stay awhile.

Kayakers frequent the rapids upstream from the falls. While downstream, the Little River passively flows into the tranquil Cascade Lake. You may see canoeists paddling around the base of the falls enjoying the calmer waters. If you have extra time, I highly recommend a visit to Triple and High Falls (hike 59) while you're here. The hike is longer and moderate, but it leads to two stunning waterfalls. The trail begins by crossing the bridge near the trailhead for Hooker Falls. The hike is 0.4 mile to Triple Falls and 1.0 mile to High Falls (one way), but worth every step. A large trail map is posted near the trailhead, and trail maps are available at the visitor's center.

Miles and Directions

0.0 Follow the gravel roadlike trail southwest and downstream along Little River.

0.3 Arrive at an overlook near the brink of the falls (N35 12.127'/W82 37.389'). An elevated seating area is available for those who don't want to hike downhill to the base of the falls. Continue hiking downhill and northwest.

0.35 At the bottom of the hill, the trail makes a hard bend to the left (southeast) toward the falls.

0.4 Arrive at Hooker Falls (N35-12.121'/W82-37.424'). Backtrack to the trailhead.

0.8 Arrive back at the trailhead.

Resting up: Holiday Inn Express, 1570 Asheville Hwy., Brevard; (828) 862–8900; www.hiexbrevard.com; two dogs any size, pet fee required per dog per night.

The Inn at Brevard, 215 Main St., Brevard; (828) 884–2105; www.theinnatbrevard .com; two dogs up to 40 pounds, no fee.

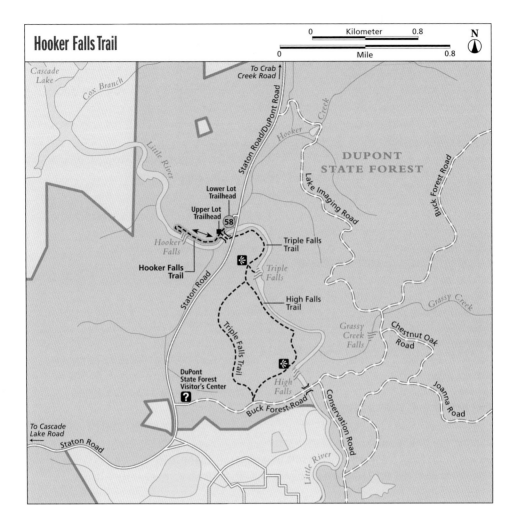

Camping: Cascade Lake Campground, 1679 Little River Campground Rd., Penrose; (828) 877-4475; www.cascadelakerecreationarea.com/index.html; open April 1–October 31.

Davidson River Campground, 1000 Pisgah Hwy., Pisgah Forest; (828) 877-3265 or (828) 862-5960;www.fs.usda.gov/recarea/nfsnc/recreation/camping-cabins/recarea/?recid=48130&actid=29; open year-round; for reservations visit www.recreation.gov or call (877) 444-6777.

Fueling up: Hobnob Restaurant, 192 W. Main St., Brevard; (828) 966-4662.

MARCO Trattoria, 204 W. Main St., Brevard; (828) 883-4841; www.marcotrattoria .com.

The Square Root, 33 Times Arcade Alley, Brevard; (828) 884-6171; www .squarerootrestaurant.com.

59 Triple and High Falls Trail

It's not often that one trail leads to two stupendous waterfalls. Well you're in luck! You'll get your first glimpse of the glorious Little River crossing a bridge over it near the trailhead. The Triple Falls Trail then follows the river upstream before leading you to an overlook with a stunning view of Triple Falls. Next a spur trail leads out to the middle of this fanciful waterfall. The main path then continues following the river upstream before leading to an overlook of the breathtaking High Falls.

Start: At the southeast corner of the upper parking lot. Begin by crossing the large foot-bridge over Little River.

Distance: 1.9-miles out and back; 0.8-mile out and back for Triple Falls only

Hiking time: 1 hour, 10 minutes; 30 minutes for Triple Falls only

Blaze color: None

Difficulty: Moderate

Trailhead elevation: 2,217 feet

Highest point: 2,470 feet

Seasons: Year-round

Trail surface: Wide gravel and sandy road

Other trail users: Mountain bikes, equestrians

Canine compatibility: Leash required

Land status: DuPont State Forest

Fees and permits: None

Map: DeLorme: North Carolina Atlas & Gazet-teer, page 53, D6

Trail contact: (828) 877-6527; www.dupont forest.com

Nearest town: Brevard

Trail tips: Bring a hiking stick and a camera! A large trail map is posted near the trailhead, or you can pick one up at the visitor's center.

Finding the trailhead: *From the junction of US 276 south and US 64 in Brevard*, drive south on US 276 for 10.8 miles. Turn left onto Cascade Lake Road (SR 1536). Travel for 2.4 miles to a right onto Staton Road (SR 1591). Travel for 2.3 miles to a left into the parking area for the Hooker Falls Access Area.

From the junction of US 64 and US 276 north in Brevard, drive east on US 64 for 3.6 miles. Turn right onto Crab Creek Road (SR 1127). Travel for 4.2 miles to a right onto DuPont Road (SR 1259). Travel for 3.0 miles to a right into the parking area signed for the Hooker Falls Access Area. GPS: N35 12.112'/W82 37.192'

The Hike

This wonderful hike begins and ends with stunning views of Little River. As you cross the sturdy bridge near the trailhead, look up, or downstream, to appreciate the beautiful river flowing below you. The trail then brings you underneath DuPont Road. From here it follows the river upstream for the next 0.2 mile. As the Triple Falls Trail bends right (south), you'll see a spur trail that leads to the river. This is a nice place to let the dogs access the water. Continue following the wide, roadlike trail as it climbs. The trail quickly leads you to an overlook, and as Triple Falls comes into view, you literally catch your breath at the beautiful scenery before you. As the name suggests, this astounding

Falling in three distinct sections, Triple Falls is stupendous.

waterfall drops in three distinct sections, in essence, three unique waterfalls come together to form the much bigger stupendous Triple Falls. Continue hiking uphill past the overlook, and you'll see a narrow footpath on the left that leads southeast toward the falls. This spur trail puts you right out onto the large flat ledges in the middle falls of Triple Falls. The fact that you can safely stand in the center of this phenomenal waterfall is exhilarating! You'll see people enjoying picnics, drawing in their sketchbooks, taking family photos, or reading a book. Others will be dangling their feet in the chilly water as they simply enjoy the scenery. You can too, but keep the dogs on a leash while you're exploring the stone banks of this magical place. Once you're satiated with the stunning scenery, backtrack to the main trail and continue hiking uphill. Stay left (southeast) at the first fork as you now begin to follow the High Falls Trail. Continue following the river upstream, and you'll

▶ **PUPPY PAWS AND GOLDEN YEARS: Take your puppy or senior dog on the Hooker Falls Trail (hike 58). This easy 0.4-mile trail (one way) follows Little River downstream to the base of the delightful Hooker Falls. You won't be disappointed!**

reach a second fork where the River Bend Trail goes straight ahead (east). Stay right (south) on the High Falls Trail, and you quickly arrive at an overlook similar to the one at Triple Falls. From the overlook you can see the entire 150 feet of this magnificent waterfall. A covered bridge crosses over the top of the falls, adding to the picturesque setting. There used to be a spur trail to the base, but it's been closed indefinitely.

At 150 feet, you can feel the power and might of High Falls from the overlook.

The DuPont State Forest is comprised of more than 10,000 acres. Many miles of trails are open to hiking, mountain biking, and equestrian use. As you explore this outdoor wonderland, you'll be certain to enjoy yourself, no matter what your mode of travel. If you have extra time, I highly recommend you visit Hooker Falls (hike 58)

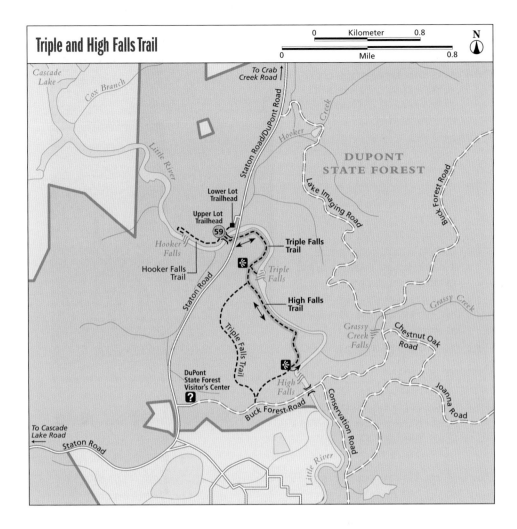

0   Kilometer   0.8   N

0   Mile   0.8

while you're here. It's a quick and easy hike, and the wide waterfall smoothly drops over a rock ledge. The entire family will enjoy dipping their feet, or entire body, in the large swimming hole at the base of the delightful Hooker Falls. From the bridge at the trailhead, do not cross. Instead follow the Little River downstream all the way to the falls (0.4 mile one way).

Miles and Directions

0.0 Hike east across the large footbridge over Little River.

0.05 Hike under the bridge for DuPont Road. Continue hiking east.

0.2 Bypass a spur trail that leads to the river. Continue following the Triple Falls Trail as it bends right (south) and climbs.

0.3 Arrive at an overlook for Triple Falls (N35 12.020'/W82 37.051'). Continue hiking uphill and southwest.

0.35 Follow the spur trail on your left (southeast) toward the falls.

0.4 Arrive at the large flat rocks near the middle waterfall of Triple Falls (N35 11.965'/W82 37.037'). Backtrack to the Triple Falls Trail.

0.45 Arrive back at the main trail. Go left (south), and continue to climb on your way toward High Falls.

0.5 Come to a fork. The Triple Falls Trail leads right (southwest). Go left (southeast) and follow the High Falls Trail alongside the river.

0.8 Come to a fork. Bypass the River Bend Trail straight ahead (east), and go right (south) on the High Falls Trail.

1.0 Arrive at an overlook of High Falls (N35 11.615'/W82 36.902'). Backtrack to the trailhead.

1.9 Arrive back at the trailhead.

Options: To shorten the hike, after visiting Triple Falls, return to the trailhead. Another option is to park at the visitor's center and hike in from Buck Forest Road. Trail maps are available at the visitor's center.

Visitors enjoy a side trip to the middle falls of Triple Falls.

Resting up: Holiday Inn Express, 1570 Asheville Hwy., Brevard; (828) 862-8900; www.hiexbrevard.com; two dogs any size, pet fee required per dog per night.

The Inn at Brevard, 215 Main St., Brevard; (828) 884-2105; www.theinnatbrevard .com; two dogs up to 40 pounds, no fee.

Camping: Cascade Lake Campground, 1679 Little River Campground Rd., Penrose; (828) 877-4475; www.cascadelakerecreationarea.com/index.html; open April 1–October 31.

Davidson River Campground, 1000 Pisgah Hwy., Pisgah Forest; (828) 877-3265 or (828) 862-5960; www.fs.usda.gov/recarea/nfsnc/recreation/camping-cabins/recarea/ ?recid=48130&actid=29; open year-round; for reservations visit www.recreation.gov or call (877) 444-6777.

Fueling up: Hobnob Restaurant, 192 W. Main St., Brevard; (828) 966-4662.

MARCO Trattoria, 204 W. Main St., Brevard; (828) 883-4841; www.marcotrattoria .com.

The Square Root, 33 Times Arcade Alley, Brevard; (828) 884-6171; www.squareroot restaurant.com.

SALUDA

60 Little Bradley Falls Trail

This enjoyable hike keeps you alongside Cove Creek for most of the way, before leading you to the grand finale: Little Bradley Falls. Although it only stands at 35 feet, this waterfall is absolutely stupendous! Clean-cut ledges give you a place to sit and enjoy the strength of the water, while the dogs run and splash around on the sandy beach near the fantastic catch pool at the base of the falls. Two thumbs up!

Start: The Little Bradley Falls Trail is the narrow red-blazed trail that heads uphill and southeast. (Do not take the trail that follows the creek upstream southwest.)

Distance: 1.8-miles out and back

Hiking time: 1 hour, 45 minutes

Blaze color: Red

Difficulty: Easy to moderate

Trailhead elevation: 2,028 feet

Highest point: 2,060 feet

Seasons: Year-round

Trail surface: Hard-packed dirt with several creek crossings

Other trail users: Open to foot traffic only

Canine compatibility: Voice control, but wait until you are far from the road before taking your dogs off the leash.

Land status: Pisgah National Forest—Pisgah Ranger District

Fees and permits: None

Map: *DeLorme: North Carolina Atlas & Gazetteer*, page 54, D1

Trail contact: Pisgah National Forest, Pisgah Ranger District; (828) 877-3265; www.fs.fed.us

Nearest town: Saluda

Trail tips: Bring a picnic, or a book, because you're going to want to stay awhile.

Finding the trailhead: *From I-26 in Saluda*, take exit 59 and drive north on SR 1142 (Holbert Cove Road) for 3.6 miles to a small pull-off on your right. GPS: N35 15.739'/W82 17.058'

The Hike

After climbing about 20 feet up the roots, the red-blazed trail follows the creek nearly the whole way. For the first 0.3 mile you are high above the creek, but as you bypass a side trail, and stay right at the fork, you soon find yourself back down at the level of the water.

Other than a few quick climbs, the trail is smooth sailing and an easy trek. You'll hear the occasional car passing by on Holbert Cove Road, but it's not intrusive enough to override the sounds of the creek. Trees shade you the entire way, and at 0.5 mile you rock hop across Cove Creek. You now closely follow it west and upstream the remainder of the way. About 0.2 mile from the creek crossing, you'll have to maneuver your way over a small boulder field where gray granite rocks have tumbled down the hill and cover the pathway. Beyond the stone obstacle continue hiking

Large flat rocks are perfect to perch upon when you visit Little Bradley Falls.

west, and you'll come to a fork where the trail splits around an old homestead. Go right (west) and you'll get a great view of the stone wall remnants where someone once lived alongside the beautiful, active waterway. You can picture this being your backyard.

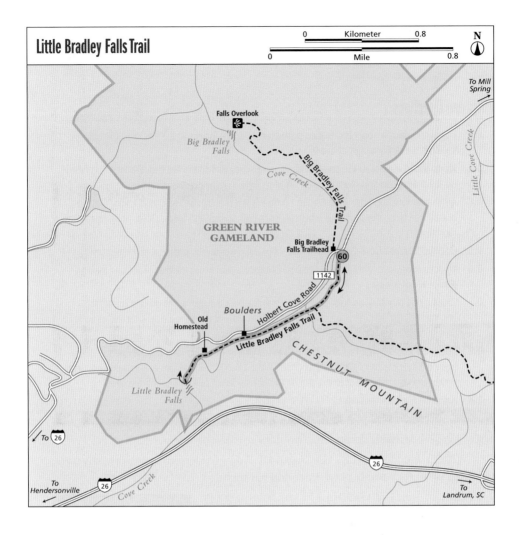

After letting your imagination run wild, continue hiking generally west. Rock hop a tributary, and you'll find yourself standing at the base of the magnificent Little Bradley Falls. Character oozes from this multitiered waterfall, and you'll find yourself drawn to its beauty. A sandy beach at the base makes it easy for the dogs, or you, to wade out and swim near the base of the falls. If you prefer to stay dry, large boulders with clean-cut ledges make a perfect platform for you to soak in the sun, or sit and enjoy a picnic or good book. The soothing sound of the water is perfection, as it swiftly flows over the rocky face of the falls. Although it's only 35 feet, there's something about the serenity of the catch pool, the strength of the water, and the way the sunlight dances off it, that makes you want to sit and stay awhile. Aside from locals, this waterfall doesn't see much traffic, so you may have this mighty yet peaceful waterfall to yourself. Both Little and Big Bradley Falls were named for an early settler who had a home and orchard in the area. If you hike to Big Bradley Falls, you'll pass right through the old orchard. But save that for another day, when you don't have the dogs with you. The only way to "safely" view Big Bradley Falls is from a cliff overlook, which is not so safe for the dogs.

Miles and Directions

0.0 Follow the narrow, rooty red-blazed path steeply uphill for about 20 feet, and the trail follows the creek from high above it.

0.1 When you're almost at the crest, bypass an obscure trail to the left (southeast). Continue on the main path and cross a small tributary.

0.3 Arrive at a fork, the path you've been on bends left (south). Go right, and follow the red-blazed trail west, downhill to a tributary. Rock hop across and follow Cove Creek upstream (southwest).

0.5 Rock hop across Cove Creek. Continue following it upstream and west southwest.

0.6 Work your way over and around the small boulders that cover the trail. Continue hiking generally southwest.

0.7 Cross a tiny tributary, and you'll come to a fork where the trail splits around an old homestead. Go right and you quickly get a good view of the home site. After letting your imagination run a bit, continue hiking west.

0.9 Rock hop a small tributary, and the trail leads you to the magnificent sandy beach at the base of Little Bradley Falls (N35 15.282'/W82 17.707'). Backtrack to the trailhead, and make sure you remember to put the dogs back on leash before nearing the road.

1.8 Arrive back at the trailhead.

Resting up: The Oaks Bed & Breakfast, 339 Greenville St., Saluda; (828) 749-2000; www.theoaksbedandbreakfast.com; two dogs any size, pet fee per stay.

Best Western Hendersonville, 105 Sugarloaf Rd., Hendersonville; (828) 692-0521; two dogs up to 80 pounds, pet fee per dog per night.

The Orchard Inn, 100 Orchard Inn Ln., Saluda; (828) 749-5471 or (800) 581-3800; www.orchardinn.com; limited pet accommodations (call ahead), dogs up to 40 pounds.

Camping: Orchard Lake Campground, 460 Orchard Lake Rd., Saluda; (828) 749-3901; www.orchardlake campground.com.

Red Gates RV Park and Camping, 259 Red Gates Ln., Hendersonville; (828) 685-8787; www.redgatesrv.com; tents welcome.

Fueling up: Flat Rock Wood Room, 1501 Greenville Hwy., Hendersonville; (828) 435-1391.

Green River BBQ, 133 Main St., Saluda; (828) 749-9892.

The Purple Onion, 16 Main St., Saluda; (828) 749-1179.

Creatures big and small enjoy exploring the forest.

Hike Index

Clean cut ledges and a pristine swimming hole at Little Bradley Falls makes it a favorite for both me and the dogs (hike 60).

About the Author

Waterfall hunter, nature enthusiast, tree hugger, and avid hiker, **Melissa Watson** is truly at her best when she's in the forest. Her passion for waterfalls, hiking, and nature in general stems back to her childhood, and she continues to fulfill that passion to this day. For more than twenty-five years Melissa has been exploring the forests of Georgia, North Carolina, South Carolina, and Florida. Hiking by day and camping by night, with her beloved companions Mikey and Bandit at her side every step of the way. She continues her quest for new trails new adventures, and new territory to explore.

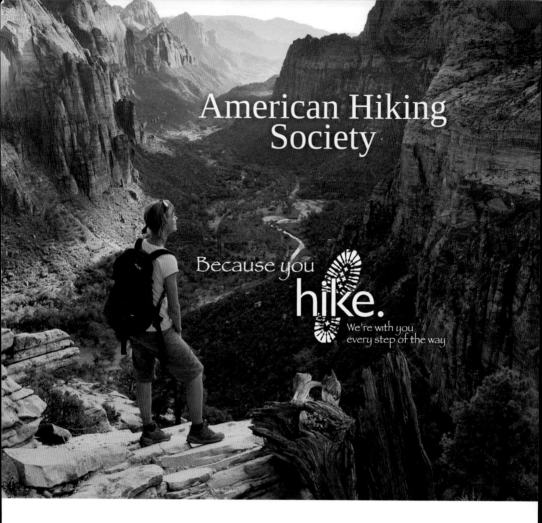

American Hiking Society

Because you **hike.**
We're with you every step of the way

As a national voice for hikers, **American Hiking Society** works every day:

- Building and maintaining hiking trails
- Educating and supporting hikers by providing information and resources
- Supporting hiking and trail organizations nationwide
- Speaking for hikers in the halls of Congress and with federal land managers

Whether you're a casual hiker or a seasoned backpacker, become a member of American Hiking Society and join the national hiking community! You'll enjoy great member benefits and help preserve the nation's hiking trails, so tomorrow's hike is even better than today's. We invite you to join us now!

American Hiking Society